*W*YATT *E*ARP
AND *C*OEUR *d'A*LENE *G*OLD!

*S*tampede *T*o Idaho *T*erritory

Jerry Dolph
and
Arthur Randall

EAGLE CITY PUBLICATIONS
Post Office Box 237
Post Falls, Idaho 83877-0237

Other non-fiction books by the authors:

FIRE IN THE HOLE: THE UNTOLD STORY OF HARDROCK MINERS ©: 1994, WSU Press, Jerry Dolph.

EAGLE CITY: PRIDE OF THE COEUR D'ALENES ©: 1994, Private Printing, Arthur Randall.

EADSVILLE A TOWN THAT WAS ©: 1986, Private Printing, Arthur Randall.

CASPER "OLD TOWN" AND FREMONT, ELKHORN AND MISSOURI VALLEY RAILROAD © 1991, Mountain States Lithographing Co., Casper, Wyoming, Arthur Randall.

A SHORT HISTORY AND POSTAL RECORD OF IDAHO TOWNS, © 1994, Private printing, Arthur Randall.

NOAH KELLOGG AND HIS ASS, © 1999, (forthcoming) Eagle City Publications, Jerry Dolph.

WYATT EARP

AND COEUR d'ALENE GOLD!

Stampede To Idaho Territory

Library of Congress Cataloging.
Dolph and Randall.
Wyatt Earp and Coeur d'Alene Gold: Stampede to Idaho Territory/Dolph and Randall.
Includes bibliographical references.
ISBN 0-9671058-0-3
1. Coeur d'Alene Mining District--Idaho--History. 2. Coeur d'Alene Mining District--Idaho--Anecdotes.

Printed in the United States of America

FIRST EDITION

To the pioneering men and women of the American West who blazed a trail
for the rest of us.
May you rest in peace with our Lord

OLD PROSPECTOR, KNOTT'S BERRY FARM AND GHOST
TOWN, Buena Park, Calif.

Table of Contents

City Directories

Additional Information

Illustrations

Page #

Front cover illustrations (front) Eagle City, 1897 [8-N84 University of Idaho Library, Moscow] with inlay of Wyatt Earp at age 36 [Craig Fouts, San Diego].

Back cover, Wyatt at age 80, one year before his death in 1929 [Arizona Historical Society #76,616]. Gold nugget found near the site of Eagle City, in 1997, by Steve Burris.

Author's Preface

Wyatt Earp and the gunfight at the ok corral, exciting words for my brother and me as we played cowboys and Indians in our youth, back on our parent's ranch near Casper, Wyoming. We'd sneak down gulches and ravines stalking each other out until the "big gunfight." Whimsical thoughts of men blazing away at each other with six shooters and falling dead into dusty streets flooded through our young minds. Ah, but that was so long ago.

Times changed and, as an adult, a husband and father, my thoughts were focused on my family's well-being. That's what brought me to north Idaho's Coeur d'Alene Mining District and its fabulous Silver Valley. It was also what kept me working thousands of feet down in the bowels of Mother Earth until I was disabled in an underground accident.

Then, unable to work anymore, I turned back to my first love…writing. Memories of the sixteen years I spent toiling in darkness rolled easily from my mind, producing my first book *FIRE IN THE HOLE, THE UNTOLD STORY OF HARDROCK MINERS*.

I wondered what project I would tackle next and those long forgotten whimsical thoughts of Wyatt Earp and my youth reemerged. Folks in the Coeur d'Alenes had always told me that Wyatt Earp was in the district back in the 1880s, so I made it my business to find out for sure. This is when I met retired geologist and fellow writer Arthur Randall. We agreed on our common interest and goals, deciding to work together on this book.

After reading everything we could find about the affairs of Wyatt Earp and his brothers and the beginnings of the Coeur d'Alene mining district, we came to the conclusion that very little has been known or written about the subject. Consequently, the largest portion of the material in this work is fresh and has been gleaned from many hours of research, much of which has been done on the Internet and through court records. We've also discovered previously unknown manuscripts, personal collections, and photographs from various historical archives throughout the west.

*   *   *

The 1882 discovery of gold in the Coeur d'Alene Mountains of north Idaho Territory began as only one more in a long list of gold rushes in the American West. But, as it turned out, the "stampede" of humanity that followed set into motion a chain of events that would ultimately change the mining industry in the

United States and, indeed, the world. It lured thousands of hopeful pioneers into Idaho territories' untamed wilderness.

On they came in a mad, frenzied rush, snow-shoeing for miles over air-thin mountain passes and hunkering down against bitterly cold, freezing temperatures. They trudged doggedly along through howling blasts of blinding, wind-driven ice crystals. Surrounded by the emptiness of tree-top-deep snow, dragging all of their worldly possessions along behind on crude, home-made sleds. Everyone was anxious to stake their own claims to this new bonanza.

But, to better understand the circumstances these intrepid pioneers faced, it is important to also understand the elements that molded the country they had stampeded into. It was that very same, seemingly endless, maze of snow-covered cliffs and peaks that had nearly snuffed out the lives of Lewis and Clark and their famed 1805 Freedom Corps expedition.

What fantastic geologic forces could have carved out the rugged Sawtooth, Bitterroot, and Coeur d'Alene Mountain Ranges? These catastrophic forces pushed Idaho's tallest peak, Mount Borah, over 14,000 feet into the sky, and yet left pristine mountain lakes, wind-blown desert regions, and the lowest point in Idaho only a few miles away. Indeed, why has such a wealth of gold and other precious gems, minerals, and metals been found throughout the "Gem State" over the years?

In search of answers, my old computer hummed to life scanning the Internet and began to spit out historical material like you wouldn't believe. It was true...Wyatt and his third wife, Josephine, and his brothers, James and Warren, were in the Coeur d'Alenes, as was the colorful Calamity Jane and many others.

This manuscript is unique in that it contains many "firsts." The first time names of over 1,500 pioneers who lived in the Coeur d'Alenes have been put to the pen. The first time many photographs, maps, and stories have been in print. Possibly, even more importantly, it offers an actual "look" into the beginnings of our planet, the State of Idaho, lives of the gold seekers of the 1880s, and into Wyatt and his brother's lives while they were in Idaho Territory.

Our research was made easier because of the many courtesies that people across the country have shown us while we were acquiring material for this book. Unfortunately, it is not possible to specifically and individually credit each of the hundreds of those who have contributed. Invaluable assistance has been given to us by historical societies from all of the western states, as well as many of those in the east. University librarians, historians, and newspapermen, along with private persons have helped in many ways. Special thanks are given to Richard Magnuson and Wendell Branard for generously contributing materials from their own historical collections.

This thoroughly researched and documented work is as historically accurate as we and our resources have been able to make it. Therefore much of the narrative has been taken directly from newspaper accounts of the day. In an effort to make the work more readable, in some cases we've recreated conversations and even thoughts, all the while following the historical record using common-sense thinking. Additionally, we have provided photographs of actual, or similar, events whenever possible to help illustrate this work,.

Come back with us now to a time of change, back to the very beginnings of our planet when it was an enormous ball of gasses and molten fire. Then we'll work our way quickly forward through time up to the discovery of gold in the Coeur d'Alene Mountains.

We'll then go back to the birth of the most famous gun-slinging sheriff of the Old West, Wyatt Earp. We'll follow the events that made him famous and led up to his fateful decision to head north to the new Golden Eldorado of the West-Idaho Territories, Eagle City.

Jerry Dolph
&
Arthur Randall
1999

Acknowledgements

Grateful acknowledgement is made to the following for their assistance in preparing and formatting this long overdue book.

Historical Societies: Oregon; Montana (M. H. S.); Idaho (I. H. S.); Kansas; Arizona (A. H. S.); Silverton, Colorado; Washington; California; Colorado; and Texas.

Universities: Idaho (U. I.), Montana (U. M.), Montana State, Washington State, University of Washington-Seattle, Eastern Washington State, Gonzaga University, and Montana Tech in Butte, Wyoming, Nevada, and Utah. Idaho Public TV. (Board of Education.)

Public libraries: Denver, Spokane; Thompson Falls; Fort Worth; El Paso; Salt Lake City; Seattle; New York; Dublin, Ireland; Butte; Davenport, Washington and Kellogg, Wallace, Hayden and Post Falls, Idaho.

Museums: Tombstone Courthouse, Cheney Cowles, Coeur d'Alene, and Wallace Mining District.

Private persons: Dave Alexander, Wendell Brainard, Allan Bird, Richard Magnuson, Ben T. Traywick, Pauline Battien, Glenn G. Boyer, Merle Wells, Bridget Smith, Chuck Parsons, Richard Selcer, Joan Draszt, Joe Dulle (White Elephant Saloon), Jacq Ashmore (Ireland), Canda Mitchell, Donna Randall Hagner, Kent Randall, Sharon Unruh, Bob Card, Joe Peak, Richard Dolph, Margaret Clancy, Candace Urton, Margaret Goodwin, John Goodwin, Leo Goodwin, Nancy Graese and Linda Erickson.

1

Geology, Man and Idaho Gold!

EE—dah-hoe was supposedly an Indian word meaning "Gem of the Mountains." However, it turned out to be nothing more than a word made up by unscrupulous 19th century Colorado land speculators. Since then, less than half of the state has been geologically mapped in detail, but it has been found that Idaho is indeed the Gem of the Mountains. Between 1863, when Abraham Lincoln signed a bill making Idaho a territory, and statehood in 1890, the territory had sixteen governors, four of whom never set foot in Idaho.

Idaho has the widest variety of wild game in the United States. It produces nearly 85 percent of the commercial trout sold in the country, more than anywhere else in the world, in Hagerman Valley near Twin Falls. The state's bird is the Mountain Bluebird, state's flower the Syringa, and the Idaho State tree is the Western White Pine. The largest Western White Pine in the world is near Elk River standing 219 feet high. Idaho's state horse—the Appaloosa—was the war-horse of the Nez Perce Indian Nation.

Landscape

When Idaho is viewed latitudinally, it lies halfway between the equator and the North Pole, and has numerous unique historical and geographical characteristics within her borders. Idaho has 13,000 miles of single-track trails and 18 million acres of wilderness. With eighty recognized mountain ranges, and forty percent of its 53 million acres covered by trees, Idaho is more mountainous and the most heavily forested of all the Rocky Mountain States. It is often touted as, "The Way America Used To Be."

Within Idaho's 83,000 square miles are 2,000 lakes. The highest point in the state is 12,662 feet above sea level at the summit of Mt. Borah in the Lost River Range of Custer County. The state's lowest point is 770 feet above sea level at the Snake River at Lewiston. The state's length is 479 miles and its width, at its widest point, is 305 miles.

Idaho offers 6,600-foot-deep, 70-mile long, Hell's Canyon which is North America's deepest river gorge. The Snake River runs through the gorge. Dubbed "The River of No Return" by explorers Lewis and Clark, the untamed Salmon River is the largest free-flowing river in the world.

The enormous spirals of Seven Devils rise majestically from Hells Canyon to over one and a half miles in height. Among the peaks hide thirty of Idaho's 300 alpine lakes. These peaks, just outside of Riggins, are normally snowcapped through July.

Shoshone Falls is the highest waterfall in the nation, higher even than Niagara. Bruneau Dunes some as high as 470 feet are the nation's tallest sand dunes, taller even than those of California's Death Valley. The 1,200-foot-deep Lake Pend Oreille is one of the largest fresh water lakes in the world.

Idaho's Sawtooth, Owyhee and Rocky Mountain Ranges offer more than 200 peaks of 8,000 feet or higher. It is estimated that if the dramatic elevations of her towering mountains and rolling plains were flattened out as a child might flatten a relief map made of soft clay, the lands of Idaho would be larger than the state of Texas.

Today Idaho is justly honored for the star garnet (state gemstone), jasper, smoky quartz, opal and a multitude of other gems. One of the largest diamonds, ever found in the United States weighing nearly 20 carats was discovered in Idaho near McCall.

With eighty varieties of precious and semi-precious stones, some of which can be found nowhere else in the world, Idaho has proven to be a bonanza for rockhounds over the years.

It is from the state's tortured geologic past that we find gems of such diversity. Beryl and garnet form at great depths, requiring intense heat and pressure. Agate, opal, and petrified wood form on the surface, the products of hot water and dissolved minerals deposited in cavities and veins.

Geology

Idaho's passage through time has left us with a great variety of must-see locations, having everything to do with understanding and enjoying not only basic geology, but the unique geology of Idaho. From our school days we may remember the three general rock types: igneous rock, which rises from deep within the earth; the more rounded sedimentary rock formed from particles of organic matter or other rocks; and metamorphic rock which is igneous or sedimentary rock that has been changed by intense heat or pressure.

Three Billion years ago

In the beginning all rock was igneous (from the Latin word for fire) and atoms migrated freely through the sphere of molten lava. Eventual cooling allowed elements like oxygen, silicon, aluminum and calcium to emerge and combine in chance encounters with the rarer elements. These form the 3,000 or so minerals that make up the earth's approximately 60-mile-thick outer mantle— the lithosphere. The lithosphere is broken into approximately twelve great plates, which are riding on a partially molten-core layer of rock called the asthenosphere.

In the Late Archean period, three billion years ago, North America, and what we now know as Idaho, were on the other side of the planet, riding on a sea of fire in one giant land mass named Gondwanaland. Then waves in the blazing ocean (plate tectonics) ripped the Americas away from Europe and Africa. From there the continents began drifting apart at about the same rate as your fingernails grow—one mile in 30,000 years.

There are many schools of thought concerning how water came to be on our planet. One is that the earth was formed from materials that came from the early sun. This material included the elements that make up water. Then, as the earth cooled and grew solid, water was trapped in rocks in the earth's crust and then water was gradually released filling the great ocean basins. Another theory is that over countless millions of years, the earth has been bombarded by water-rich comets from the icy far reaches of the solar system.

Idaho's earliest rocks are three billion years old—Late Archean in age—and consist of granites, schists, and gneisses.

1.5 Billion years ago

Some geologists believe that about 1.5 billion years ago a very deep basin was formed in Idaho during the Precambrian period. The belief is that an enormous meteorite impacted what has become northern Idaho and western Montana, creating a crater and forming the basin which was several hundred miles across and thousands of feet deep. Then 800 million years ago, a huge rift, or fault, broke off from Idaho, and Oregon and Washington drifted to the west while Idaho moved to the east .

225 Million years ago

Eons passed and 225 million years ago dinosaurs emerged. They lived on the earth during the three great periods of Mesozoic time, from 225 to 65 million years ago.

Plate Collision

100 Million years ago

The earth's crust folded, with the moving of the earth's plates, and was in a constant state of change. This left prehistoric Idaho a steaming sea shore at about equator level. Bits of this ancient sea bed are now found on top of the Lost River Range, a mile and a half above the valley floor.

Then came a collision between the Pacific and the North American plates. The Pacific plate dove twenty miles into the fiery sea, beneath the North American plate. That folded and buckled Idaho even more, creating forces great enough to shove Borah Peak over 12,000 feet into the sky, yet within thirty miles of Borah mountain is some of the state's lowest and flattest land.

Idaho's eastern border follows the highest ridges of this ancient uprising— the Rocky Mountains. Those same forces created California's San Andreas Fault, with the collision zone running up through western Idaho, north to south, along Interstate Highway 90 and US 95. On a scale of earthquake probability, Idaho ranks second only to California. In the state's recent past it has experienced earthquakes in 1884, 1905, 1916, 1944, and 1975. Even today, the Pacific plate continues to move toward and beneath the North American plate at a rate of about 2 ½ inches a year.

A 1959 quake centered in Montana, barely across the Idaho border, registered 7.5 on the Richter scale, bringing down entire mountainsides in the process. Many cars were passing through the canyon bottom at the time and their occupants were instantly entombed, where they remain to this day. That was the largest quake ever recorded in the lower 48. There was much property damage; water levels in underground wells changed in Idaho and other nearby states. The Clayton Silver Mine flooded and Yellowstone Park's Old Faithful became unfaithful. It raised Idaho's Borah Peak two feet while lowering the valley below it by five feet. On October 28, 1983, the largest earthquake recorded inside Idaho pushed the Richter scale to 7.3.

Volcanoes

72 Million years ago

Seventy-two million years ago, a huge granitic intrusion, called the Idaho batholith, was formed in central Idaho. Its boundaries were Butte, Montana on the east; Missoula, Montana on the north; Riggins, Idaho on the west; and Boise, Idaho on the south.

This phenomena can be best viewed near the town of Lenore on Idaho 12 on the Clearwater River. The batholith lay like a giant glowworm about 50 miles beneath the surface. Since it was still hot in the center, pressure caused melted minerals to ooze and shoot through cracks in the shell. Quartz cooled slower than the granite around it, leaving veins of gold, silver, lead, zinc, cobalt, copper, and all of the gemstones. Over eons of time, most of the overburden has been worn away.

Northern Idaho's Coeur d'Alene mining district owes its success to the batholith. From the beginning of underground lode mining in 1884, the district's mines have produced well over one billion ounces of silver, and vast quantities of other metals as well.

Comet impact causes extinction of the big lizards!

65 Million years ago

Within a very short time 65 million years ago, a thin layer of reddish colored iridium covered the entire earth. Taking into account that Iridium is not naturally occurring on our planet, and the fact that no dinosaur fossils have been found above the layer of iridium, scientists believe it was left by a cataclysmic event. The impact of a giant comet.

Some years ago, evidence of the largest impact crater ever found on the earth was discovered just off the Yucatan Peninsula. The massive, twenty mile deep, seven mile wide crater left by the comet's impact, and the amount of collateral damage done to the earth's crust, leads scientist to also believe that the awesome chunk of fiery inbound ice was at least a mile in diameter. The firestorm it must have created, scientist agree, would have been much more powerful than if all of the nuclear weapons on earth were detonated at the same time.

One theory is that the impact of this massive body on the earth caused the atmosphere to "explode," in a sense, raining down fire for thousands of miles in all directions. The ensuing cloud of dust and ash was so dense that it blotted out the sun, plunging our world into a perpetual darkness that lasted for a period of at least three months. The lack of sunlight caused all plant life to die and, with nothing to eat, the plant eaters died off as well. Then the huge carnivorous meat eaters such as the fabled tyrannosaurus-rex that lived off the plant eaters were next to slip into extinction.

Mere thousands of years ago

Idaho rides the North American land mass, but there is a thin spot in the hull. A stationary, exceptionally hot-mass of boiling hot rock created the weak spot beneath the state. That fire burst to the surface with a sixty mile long crack in the earth's crust at Craters of the Moon National Monument—best viewed eighteen miles west of Arco. The lunar-like landscape includes over thirty lava flows covering eighty three square miles. There are cinder cones, lava tubes and spatter cones which were all part of the Great Rift System that began erupting about 15,000 years ago and ceased only 2,000 years ago.

North of Shoshone, it left black blisters, breaking through in a huge volcano at Harriman's State Park, visible from satellites high above the earth. It is one of the largest volcanic circles on our world.

Snake River Aquifer

Lava found its way to the surface across a vast strip of southern Idaho; on our maps, it's the Snake River Plain. It continues today a hot spot that stationed itself in Idaho's path and has seen the southern half of the state pass over it. Today it finds the sun in Yellowstone National Park.

Since gaining statehood in 1890, Idaho, and the rest of the American continent, has continually moved eastward and the Pacific plate continues to dive beneath the North American plate. This phenomenon has caused the eruptions from the hot spot to move about twelve feet into Wyoming. Countless tons of lava flowing over the Snake River Plain has left a legacy crucial to Idaho's recent past and future. Within its dark labyrinth of bubbles and cracks is space for water storage. The "Snake River aquifer" takes in and releases eight million acre feet of water every year. There is enough water stored here to make the whole state a lake four feet deep. It's enough water to fill Lake Erie, and it keeps a constant water temperature of fifty two degrees. Early Idaho miners heated their homes with geothermal heat from Lava Hot Springs.

Glaciers

During the age of glaciation (Pleistocene) 100,000 years ago, huge glaciers began invading Idaho from the north. Then more recently, fifteen thousand years ago and ending ten thousand years ago, glaciers formed Priest and Pend Oreille Lakes.

You can still see scratches in the granite left by millions of tons of ice grinding past it at Slip Rock, not far from McCall. When the glaciers receded they dropped pieces of granite onto the rock powder they had ground from the batholith. Today McCall sits on the mud and rock dumped by the south pointing finger of a glacier. The first water in Payette Lake was ice water dripping from a dying glacier. Near the eastern edge of the batholith, other glaciers would make the Sawtooth Range as sharp as the teeth of any cross-cut saw. From the batholith, and all the actions working to break it down, soil would be formed.

The enormous "dunes" of soil in the Palouse were built up from glacial dust, volcanic ash, vegetation and dust blown in over millions of years of time. Idaho has eight of the world's ten soil types. This is best viewed near Potlatch.

Floods

Sixteen thousand years ago the second largest flood in recorded history was the Bonneville flood. The original Lake Bonneville covered 20,000 square miles in northern Utah and part of Nevada. It was similar in size to Lake Michigan. There were 2,000 miles of shoreline around water over a thousand feet deep. Then a lava flow blocked Bear River. The flow filled Lake Thatcher, then drained into Lake Bonneville. Then Red Rock Pass gave way and, in what must have been seconds, thousands of tons of soil and rock exploded northward into Idaho. Water roared down through the canyon, blowing away resistant rock and forming 1,000-foot wide, 212-foot-high, Shoshone Falls. The raging waters deposited boulders from ten to fifteen feet in diameter downstream. There are some reports of gravel about 400 feet, or perhaps a little higher, above the Snake River in Hell's Canyon which have been attributed to the Bonneville flood. Lake Bonneville was the predecessor of what is now the Great Salt Lake. The lake was so large that it deformed the crust by its sheer weight.

Alt and Hyndman, 1995

Glacial Lake Missoula shorelines at Missoula, Mont.

We can only imagine the sound and fury of the flood, but it's possible there were actually people there at the time who saw and heard the awful destruction. Tools, dated from about the same time period, have been found inside of the Wilson Butte Cave, near Eden, Idaho, which overlooks the Bonneville flood plain (canyon).

From 12,000 to 18,000 years ago an even larger flood, the largest ever recorded in world history, broke through a weakened ice sheet on the Clark Fork River. The surface of Lake Missoula was nearly 950 feet above the present city of Missoula and covered most of western Montana. This Inland Sea was held in place by glacial ice at Cabinet Gorge (on the Montana/Idaho border). Then the ice dam became unstable, through various means, and suddenly failed, releasing up to 600 cubic miles of water.

A two-thousand-foot-high wall of water, carrying with it blocks of ice and boulders the size of apartment buildings, roared into Idaho with earth shaking fury, rushing through what is now the Great Basin of Lake Pend Oreille and down the Little Spokane River past Newport. The enormous wall of water also came through Rathdrum Prairie, down through the present city of Spokane, and progressed on into the Columbia River.

So great was the water's force that its sheer weight deformed lands all the way into central Washington, permanently scarring the surface of the earth in these areas. The flood waters formed Lake Pend Oreille, the Rathdrum Prairie, the northward-flowing St. Joe River, and beautiful Lake Coeur d'Alene. Recent evidence has been found that the Missoula flood occurred many times over eons of time. There was nothing like it in history to which we can relate. At maximum flow, the volume of water was on the order of ten plus times the total flow of all of the rivers of the world![1]

Man's arrival upon the scene

Even though recent discoveries indicate that man may have existed on planet earth for a few million years, archeologists don't believe that "we" moved into Idaho until 15,000 to 16,000 years ago. Some of these hunter-gatherers came by way of Siberia, across the land bridge into the New World from northeast Asia. The North American and Asian continents have long since been separated by the Bearing Sea.

Idaho State Historical Society, 66-1.5

Wilson Butte Cave

Our earth was gripped in an ice age then, and glacial ice stretched down the mountains into the valleys of what would become western Canada. Between 20,000 and 18,000 years ago, glacial ice was at its maximum, covering most of what would become Montana. A second migration of early man came from Asia 12,000 years ago, after the mountainous glaciers had melted, creating great Bonneville and Missoula Lakes. Then 6,000 years ago came a third migration of brown-skinned Aleuts and Eskimos.

The first evidence of Idaho's earliest inhabitants was discovered by Ruth Gruhn and other Idaho archeologists in the Wilson Butte cave, which overlooks the Bonneville flood plain near Eden in south-central Idaho. Among the artifacts found at the long-used campsite were spear points dating back some 16,000 years. Along with the bits and pieces of hunting arrows and tools, bone fragments from the skeletons of mammoths, mastodons, great sloth, musk oxen, moose, bison, elk and carillon were found. As the ice age was ending, glaciers receded, the weather warmed, and many of the wandering nomadic peoples established themselves in Idaho. It is estimated that in total there were from six to ten thousand aborigines within the boundaries of the state.

Descending from these early people were the Salshian Indians who, in turn, branched off to form the much-later Kutenai, Nez Perce, Coeur d'Alene, Pend Orellie, Shoshone, Bannock and northern Prairie tribes. They lived off the land, taking only what they needed to survive from the bounty of their "mother" earth. Until, that is, the mid-1800s when reservation systems were invented by an intrusive United States Government.

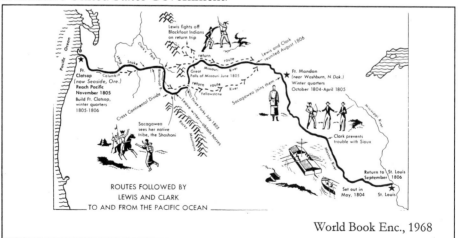

ROUTES FOLLOWED BY
LEWIS AND CLARK
TO AND FROM THE PACIFIC OCEAN

World Book Enc., 1968

With explorers like Lewis and Clark, David Thompson, and many others leading the way, hoards of white settlers and miners poured over trails into tribal lands. In most cases they were welcomed openly by their Indian counterparts.

But, when the red man saw some of the atrocities these strangers were perpetrating against them and their lands, they tried to fight back. These simple people were badly outnumbered by the invading masses and "out gunned" by sticks that shot fire from their ends. The term "The only good Indian is a dead Indian," was born and a near genocide of the "savages" ensued, reducing their numbers dramatically. Just to be fair about it, the US Government established treaties with the various Indian tribes, then broke them routinely whenever the situation warranted.

Finally it was decided that red men were in the way altogether, and reservation systems were invented, on which the "rebellious" Indians were placed. Then, shamefully, many of the white Indian agents responsible for running the reservations lined their own pockets by fleecing the starving Indians.

Explorers Lewis and Clark

1801

Thomas Jefferson had always been intrigued by the question of what wonders lay to the American West, even when he was a boy. So President Jefferson decided to send an expedition to find out. In preparation for this, he gave 26-year-old army officer, Meriwether Lewis, a position as his private secretary. Lewis would be the expedition's leader, and was well qualified since most of his service was on the, then, western frontier beyond the Alleghenies. He'd acquired ample experience with the wilderness and with the aborigines.

1803

January-Lewis was designated the expedition's commander, and he, in turn, invited Lt. William Clark to join him as the expedition's co-leader. Their party would be known as "The Corps of Discovery." Arguably this was the most important American expeditionary force ever assembled.

1804

May 21-The two army officers assembled a volunteer force of 27 unmarried soldiers, a half-Indian scout, and Lewis' black slave. They trained their men near St. Louis, Missouri, where they also gathered the necessary equipment and supplies. Finally ready, their "Corps of Discovery" set out for the West. They would soon loose one man (their only casualty) to sickness, and later face a myriad of life-threatening dangers. In the next several years they would cross American continent twice, discovering that it was much larger and more complex than anyone of European descent had anticipated.

1805

August 9-Meriwether Lewis and three of his companions stood atop 7,373 foot-high Lemhi Pass, at the summit of the Continental Divide. It was the first time the eyes of a white man had looked down on Idaho—the last of the lower 48 states to be explored. In their encounters with native Americans, Lewis noted in his journal that he estimated the Salshian's population to be 5,000 persons strong. (Lewiston, Idaho was named after Meriwether Lewis and Clarkston, Washington, which is just across the river from Lewiston, was named after William Clark.)

The expedition crossed over Lolo Pass into present day Idaho and from there went on to Lewiston. They continued their journey on to the Pacific Ocean and Oregon, where they built Fort Clatsop from logs, which was the first military fort in the Pacific Northwest. The Corps of Discovery spent a miserable winter, short of supplies, and waiting for the arrival of a promised ship of fresh stores. It never came.

1806

March 23-The Corps of Discovery spent the winter of 1805-6 in near starvation, loneliness and sickness. Finally, to the jubilation of their men, both Lewis and Clark decided that it was time to leave Fort Clatsop. They followed the Columbia River east, returning to Idaho.

May 5-On their return trip across the state, the furthest north they walked and rode was when they crossed the Clearwater River at a point thirteen miles above modern day Potlatch, Idaho. They eventually reported back to President Jefferson, bringing with them maps, sketches, and tales of the many great wonders they had seen. The Corps of Discovery was a catalyst for the further exploration and the eventual colonization of our great nation.[2]

Explorer David Thompson

1808

April 25-Two years after Lewis and Clark had crossed over Lolo pass on their way back to the east, one of the greatest geographers of all time, David Thompson, crossed into the United States from Canada. He was acting on behalf of a Northwest Company of Merchants.

May 7-Thompson and his associates camped near Bonner's Ferry, at Kootenai Falls, on the Kootenai River.

1809

September 9-They built Idaho's earliest fur trading post, a fort-like structure, on the eastern shore of Lake Pend d'Oreille near what would become Hope, Idaho. With tents and a lodge, he named the structure "Kullyspell" house, after the Kalispell Indians. It was the first white habitation in the state.

In his travels, Thompson skirted along the shore of Lake Pend Oreille and came to a place he noted as "A point of sand." The site was later to become the present-day city of Sandpoint. He then crossed Priest River and continued on to the south finding what he called "Pointed Heart's Lake." This beautiful lake was later named Lake Coeur d'Alene, in favor of the Coeur d'Alene Indian tribe.

Chuck Peterson painting
Kullyspell House

Thompson drew the first map of Idaho. It was his learned opinion that "The Kutenai and Coeur d'Alene are industrious people who pride themselves in their industry and their skill in doing anything, and are as neat in their persons as circumstances will allow."

In the four years he was in north Idaho, he explored routes that are still used today by transcontinental railways and highways. He also opened permanent communications with the east, formed friendly relationships with the Indians, and established the fur trade as a reputable business. Good fortune for his great expeditionary deeds escaped him, though, as he left Idaho and settled in Montreal where he eventually died in sickness and poverty.[3]

Fur Traders, Indians and Missionaries

1812

David Thompson would be followed by many other explorer-trappers with such familiar names as Andrew Henry, Wilson Price Hunt, Donald Mackenzie, William H. Ashley, Jedediah Smith, Francis Payette, B.L.E. Bonneville, Nathaniel Wyeth, and Peter Skene Ogden.

Living unto themselves, diseases were unknown to the Salishan Indians, but that would all change when the "dirty," fur-trading whites came along. Even though they were a healthy and vibrant people, they had no defense against silent killers like venereal diseases and smallpox.

1832

That terrible year, disease ravaged their nation, killing tribesmen by the hundreds. Only some 500 persons, one in ten, were left alive of the tribe's original number that Meriwether Lewis had estimated to be 5,000.

By the end of the 1830s, fur traders had all but vanished from Salishan lands and a new phase of development was beginning. Pioneering missionaries were arriving such as Marcus Whitman, and Henry H. Spalding and black robed Jesuits from St. Louis. These holy men brought with them the words of Christ to replace their tribal pagan Gods.

One of the Indian tribes that the black robes would be ministering to was the Coeur d'Alenes. But these people were difficult to deal with. So much so that Father Joseph Joset, one of the early Jesuit missionaries, couldn't even find an interpreter who could speak their language.

First Mission

1842

These simple people were much taken with the sincerity and holiness of the black robes. Emissaries of the Coeur d'Alene tribe traveled to St. Louis, Missouri, and at their pleadings, the black robes decided to build a mission on the bank of the St. Joe River (near present day St. Maries). The story of what happened to that mission is best told by US Forest Service marker at the site on Idaho Route 93:

> "Established on the St. Joe River near St. Maries, Dec. 4, 1842 eagerly sought by the Coeur d'Alene Indians, the black robed missionaries supervised the building of a log cabin, and in the spring began to teach the mysteries of plowing and planting. Soon two thirds of the tribe were baptized. But floods gave trouble here and in 1846 the mission was moved north to Cataldo."

Old Cataldo Mission

1847

An important figure in the development of this "newer" mission was Father Antonio Ravalli, who was born in Italy and was skilled in medicine and architecture. At Cataldo, he designed a large church building ninety feet long, forty feet wide, and thirty feet high, with a portico supported by six massive pillars. The Coeur d'Alene Indians, who were constructing the building, had no nails, so Father Ravalli and his native workers bored holes into the beams and boards and put wooden pegs through the holes to hold the pieces together. The walls were made of saplings and grass, and then smeared with mud.

Washington Territorial Governor Stevens Visits Old Mission

1853

March 17-Washington Territory was organized and Isaac Stevens, a graduate of West Point, was its first governor. He was given the commission of surveying the inland northwest for railroad routes and began that task at St. Louis with 240 soldiers. Once he and his force reached the Bitterroot Mountains in Western Montana, they followed a trail, long used by the Nez Perce and Coeur d'Alene Indians, through the valley of the South Fork of the Coeur d'Alene River.

Stevens' efforts eventually led Congress to set aside more funds, $30,000 for a survey and $230,000 for a road, for survey and exploration of the land between the great falls of the Missouri River and Fort Walla Walla.

On the way through what would become northern Idaho, Governor Stevens and his party visited the Sacred Heart (Cataldo) Mission and he described it and its five hundred inhabitants as follows:

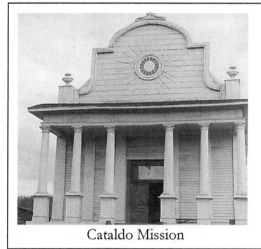

Cataldo Mission

"It is indeed extraordinary what the fathers have done at the Coeur d'Alene Mission…They have a splendid church nearly finished by the labor of the fathers, laymen, and Indians; a large barn, a horse-mill for flour, a small range of buildings for the accommodations of the priests and laymen, a store-room, a milk or dairy-room, a cook room and good arrangements for their pigs and cattle. They are putting up a new range of quarters and the Indians have some twelve comfortable log cabins…They have a large cultivated field of some two hundred acres and a prairie from two to three thousand acres. They own a hundred pigs, eight yokes of oxen, thirty cows and a liberal proportion of horses, mules and young animals."

Fall of 1857-Govonor Stevens went to Washington D. C. as the delegate of the Territory of Washington and, by personal contacts, supplemented the material of the reports he had made from the west. Thereafter, with an appropriation granted by Congress early in 1858, construction of the Mullan Military Road began under the supervision of Lieutenant John Mullan. Construction was to have begun in March, but little was accomplished at first on account of hostile Indians. [4]

Battle of Steptoe Butte

1858

May 16-The Indians resented Lieutenant (later Captain) Mullan's intrusion on their lands for the building of the military road. There were other tensions between the "whites" and the Coeur d'Alene, Palouse, Spokane, Nez Perce, and Yakima tribes that caused the battle at Rosalia, south of Spokane Falls, Washington Territory.

Colonel Edward Steptoe and his seven officers, 152 dragoon cavalry, and thirty civilian scouts were attacked by the various tribes. The battle lasted ten hours, and Colonel Steptoe was defeated. The troops retreated to the south, with Steptoe having lost seven of his men. An unknown number of Indians were killed in the melee.

Battle of Four Lakes

September 1-Soon after Col. Steptoe's defeat at Rosalia, preparations, under the command of Col. George Wright, were being made to punish the Indians. The battle began on September 1st, with 570 men of Wright's being involved. Seventeen Indians were killed at Four Lakes, just west of Spokane Falls. The Colonel did not lose a man.

Battle of Spokane Plains

September 5-The battle directed by Col. Wright took place ten miles west of Spokane. Five hundred Indians were engaged in the battle and many of them were killed. As before, thanks to the longer-ranged repeating rifles carried by the Army troops, there were no casualties in the colonel's group. [5]

Winter of 1858-59

Captain Mullan was also a guest of the Old Mission and called it "St. Bernard in the Coeur d'Alene Mountains." Father De Smet wintered there in 1858-1859.

Work on the road was delayed until 1859, but then it proceeded rapidly. At one time, 150 men were at work cutting a 25-foot swath through the Bitterroot and Coeur d'Alene Mountains, grading across open country, building hundreds of bridges and establishing many ferries. The road was completed in August, 1860. Almost immediately an army unit traveled its full length, an accomplishment that required fifty-seven days. Although the road was never important as a military route, it played a significant role for north Idaho and Montana during the historic Pierce gold rush that began in 1861 and was resumed with undiminished vigor in the 1880s. The road was 624 miles in length and cost $230,000.

Years after its completion, Captain Mullan reflected on this supreme achievement of his life:

> "Night after night I have laid out in the unbeaten forests, or in the pathless prairies with no bed but a few pine leaves (needles), with no pillow but my saddle, and in my imagination heard the whistle of the engine, the whir of the machinery, the paddle of the steamboat wheels as they plowed the waters of the sound. In my enthusiasm, I saw the country thickly populated, thousands pouring over the borders to make homes in this Far Western land."

Chief Joseph-Thunder of the Mountains

1877

June 17-An uneasy state affairs had existed between the Indian Nations and the whites for many years, with an occasional battle cropping up now and then. Finally Chief Joseph, under threat of imminent attack by the whites, because he did not take his people to the reservation, was forced to leave his tribal home in the Wallowas. His long-running battle tactics afterwards would earn him the respect of his many white enemies and he would go down in wartime annals as one of America's greatest generals. The agency doctor, who was called to the campfire where Joseph had toppled over in death, said: "He died of a broken heart."[6]

When new boundaries were proposed for the Coeur d'Alene reservation in 1877, the Sacred Heart Mission at Cataldo was found to lie outside the reservation, so in 1878 a new mission was begun in DeSmet, in Benewah County, where it still functions. Another group of people wanted to use Father De Smet's name for their town. But, since the name was already taken, they decided to use his named spelled backward: Temsed. Someone misspelled the name so the town is known as Tensed.

IDAHO GOLD!

More than a dozen years had passed since the California gold rush of 1848, and the search for new gold fields was expanded in every direction by anxious miners. Then E. D. Pierce, one of the California miners who made bean money by trading with the Nez Perce Indians, managed to prove that gold could be found in the Nez Perce country. A rush to Pierce's new mines in north central Idaho, was quickly followed by the much bigger excitement to the south at Florence.

In the summer of 1862 gold was also found in Montana (then part of Dakota) and southwestern Idaho (then part of Washington). But of the 1862 discoveries, the one in Boise Basin turned out to be the most important.[7]

1882

Other discoveries were made in following years, and then came the big one: Civil War veteran A. J. Prichard's discovery of gold in the rugged Coeur d'Alene Mountains of north Idaho Territory (Idaho). It began as only one more in a long list of gold rushes in the West, but as it turned out, the "stampede" that followed set into motion a chain of events that would ultimately change the mining industry in the United States and, indeed, the entire world. It lured thousands of hopeful pioneers into Idaho's untamed wilderness.

They came in a mad,

3-781-Hist. photo collection, University of Idaho Library Moscow

Andrew J. Prichard

frenzied rush, snow-shoeing for miles over air-thin mountain hunkering down against bitterly cold, freezing temperatures, trudging doggedly along through howling blasts of blinding, wind-driven snow. Dragging all of their worldly possessions behind them on crude, home-made toboggans. All were anxious to stake claims to this new bonanza.

Wyatt Earp, famous for his role in the shoot out at the Okay Corral several years earlier, his third wife, Josephine, and brothers, James and Warren joined those hearty souls. As did the famous lady of the West, Calamity Jane. Then there were those of lesser notoriety like poor old Snuffy Smith who turned up dead one day and was buried with a flour sack over his head.

The rawest of conditions in the gold camp forged the character in those who were there. By her selfless acts of charity and mercy, one local woman, Molly-B-Damn, was raised to the status of an Angel when she gave her own life protecting those of others against the dreaded camp disease of consumption (tuberculosis).

It is important to understand the mettle of these famous and not so famous characters of the western frontier. So come back with us now to the very beginning of Wyatt Earp's life, a lad who would grow to become famous as one of the West's deadliest lawmen and killers.

2

The Fightin' Earps

1848

March 19-wyatt berry Stapp Earp was born in Monmouth, Illinois. His father, Nicholas, named him after Wyatt Barry Stapp, a neighbor who, the year before had served as commander of Nicholas' regiment in the war with Mexico. Little Wyatt was the third child to be born to Nicholas and Virginia, who were themselves both born in Virginia.[1]

Wyatt had three older brothers, Newton, from his father's first marriage, Virgil and James. He had two younger brothers, as well: Morgan and Warren. He also had three sisters: Adelia, Martha, and Virginia Ann. Virginia Ann and Martha died young, but Adelia lived on to a ripe old age.

While fighting in the Mexican-American War, Captain Nicholas Earp was badly injured when a contrary army mule kicked him in the privates. He was mustered out of the army and received a land grant of 160 acres in Pella, Iowa. In 1850, when Wyatt was two years old, the Earps moved across the Mississippi River, to the little Dutch community of Pella, Iowa to claim the grant. Wyatt and his many brothers spent their childhood years there, spending most of their spare time working on the family farm. The Earps were to live in Pella off and on for sixteen years.

1860

Meanwhile, the nation had become embroiled in turmoil. In a highly politicized atmosphere, the Republicans won the presidential election. Their candidate, Abraham Lincoln of Illinois, was elected almost entirely by the votes of northerners. His name was not even on the ballot in most of the South. Many southerners believed they had lost their voice in governing the Union. They also believed that only by seceding from the United States could they preserve their way of life.

December-South Carolina became the first state to secede from the Union. The other states of the deep south soon followed, banding together to form the Confederate States of America.

Civil War declared in 1861

April 12-The newly formed army of the Confederacy bombarded Fort Sumter in Charleston harbor. The Civil War had begun.[1]

May 25-Nicholas and his sons objected to secession by the south. Compelled by those convictions, but more importantly just for the pure excitement of it all, twenty-year-old James and his older brother, Newton, ran away from home in Monmouth, Illinois to join the Union Army.

James signed up for a three-year tour of duty, enrolling as a private in Company F of the 17th Regiment of the Illinois Volunteer Infantry, commanded by Captain Josiah Moore. It is a fair assumption that Newton joined the same outfit. James' service records note that he was born in Ohio Country in the state of Kentucky in 1841, and was 5' 8" tall, had a fair complexion, blue eyes, light hair, and was a coach driver at time of enlistment. After the Confederates' attack on Fort Sumter, the 17th was mustered into the service of the United States at Peoria, Illinois.

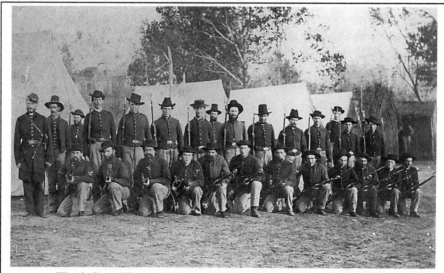

Illinois State Historic Library, Old State Capitol Bldg., Springfield, IL. 62701
Soldiers, 17th infantry

June 17-New recruit James Earp, and his fellow infantrymen, marched proudly out of Peoria for Alton, Illinois, a staging area used by the Union Army for the purpose of more fully completing, organizing and arming. (In other words, the Union's version of "boot camp.")

In the next few months, James and his fellow "ground pounders" would march and ride all over the state of Missouri and part of Kentucky in pursuit of the elusive Confederate General, Jeff Thompson and his men.

July-The 17th Regiment left Alton, marching to St. Charles, Warrenton, and St. Louis, Missouri. Then the troops traveled by train to Bird's Point, Missouri, where they pulled garrison duty for several weeks. From there they went on to Sulphur Springs Landing and, by way of Pilot Knob and Ironton, to Fredericktown, Missouri.

Commanders of the 17th had lost the Confederate's trail, so the regiment joined up with Union General B. M. Prentiss' command at Jackson, Missouri. Then this larger force left Jackson, proceeding into Kentucky to aid in the construction of Fort Holt. From there the regiment was ordered to Elliott's Mills where it remained only a short while before returning to Kentucky and Fort Holt again.

October 21-Union scouts spotted Confederate General Jeff Thompson's forces, and the 17th joined with other regiments in the chase. The two armies finally met to draw blood at Fredericktown, Missouri, which is about 75 miles south of St. Louis.

Soldiers on both sides fought bravely, but in the end the 17th had captured two Confederate 6-pound howitzers and 200 prisoners. In the confusion following the skirmish, the Confederates fled, leaving their dead and wounded strewn about the battlefield.

In the melee, James had been wounded severely according to the casualty sheet. His Certificate of Discharge notes, in part:

> "Received a musket ball at the battle of Fredricktown that passed from behind the shoulder through the joint coming out near the breast bone. Has done no duty since and never will recover the use of his arm. Disability one half."

James would spend seventeen months in military hospitals, one of which was at Ironton, Missouri twenty miles west of Fredricktown.[2] His commander, Captain Josiah Moore, would recommend his honorable discharge by writing:

> "During the last two months said soldier has been unfit for duty. A lameness of the left arm, left shoulder of the said Earp while in his line of duty at the Battle of Fredricktown, Mo. Oct. 21st-1861 renders him unfit to use a musket; has done no duty since receiving his wound hence I urge his discharge." Station: Providence, Louisiana."

Further, the Muster-out Roll dated June 4, 1864 notes in Remarks: (He was discharged at Memphis, Tennessee.)

> "Discharged for disability from wounds rec'd at Fredericktown Mo. Oct 22, 1861 by ord. Gen McPherson Mar. 22, '63. Final statements given. [3]

The two Earp boys hadn't been the only ones in the family to join the army. Their father's experience as a ·Captain in the war with Mexico earned him a position of honor in the second major war of his lifetime. He was appointed U.S. Provost Marshal of Marion County, Iowa, with the responsibility of training Union forces.

1862

Meanwhile, Wyatt's older brother, seventeen-year-old Virgil, had married an Iowa girl by the name of Ellen Rysdam, who was even younger than he was. She bore them a daughter whom they named Nellie Earp. Unfortunately, his bride's parents would never accept him into their family.

July 26-Then, in a spirit of dismay, when baby Nellie was but two weeks old, Virgil followed his brother's lead and enlisted as a private in Company C of the 83rd regiment of the Illinois Volunteer Infantry. He would remain in the infantry until after war's end in 1865.

Taking advantage of the situation, Ellen's parents had spread the notion that Virgil was killed in action and took their daughter and granddaughter west into Oregon Territory. Ellen later remarried, and many years afterwards Virgil's long-forgotten daughter, Nellie, then Mrs. Levi Law, read about him in a Portland, Oregon newspaper. She contacted her father and reestablished a relationship with him.

Virgil traveled to Portland from Prescott, Arizona and enjoyed a very pleasant visit with her and his two grandchildren at her home which was near that of Mrs. Ellen Eaton, his first wife, in north Portland. He remained for several days more before he started on the journey home. The years had taken away the pain of the meeting between former husband and wife, and the little visit was most happy for all.[4]

When Virgil died in 1905, his loving daughter had him buried beside her mother in Portland. Virgil and his first love were finally reunited. Meanwhile, Virgil's second wife, Allie, lived on until 1947, and followed him in death at age 99. She was buried at Mt. View Cemetery, San Bernardino, California.

Wanting to join his older brothers in the army, young Wyatt ran away from home to enlist. But, as luck would have it, he was discovered by his father and sent back home again.

1863

March 22-James was honorably discharged from the Union Army at the military hospital at Memphis, Tennessee. At the bottom of his discharge certificate it is noted:

"The soldier desires to be addressed at town Monmouth, County Warren, state Illinois."

Nicholas' hitch in the army ran out soon after James returned home, and by then he'd become troubled with the government's actions. While he was against the further spread of slavery, he fervently disagreed with President Lincoln's idea of freeing the slaves. After all, many of the Earp's relatives depended on their slaves to work their land.

Headin' Out West in '64

May-Nicholas decided it was high time for the family to head out west. So, in a flurry of excitement, the Earps loaded all of their worldly possessions into two canvas-covered Conestoga, wagons. Each was to be drawn by eight oxen. They also traveled with a buckboard to which a spirited team of horses was hitched.

Then, one beautiful spring morning, they joined up with a train of 40 wagons that was just leaving for the west. Nicholas Earp was elected captain of the small band, so it was with an air of anticipation they rolled out of Pella bound for California and a brave new future.

Their slowly moving caravan of wagons, cattle, mules, horses, and about 150 people passed through Council Bluffs, Iowa, and crossed the Missouri River on barges at Omaha, Nebraska. Before they left Iowa, Nicholas had given Wyatt his first gun. It was a cumbersome "over and under" contraption at best, with a rifle barrel of about forty caliber imposed on a shot-firing barrel. Wyatt's new weapon was a muzzle-loader with an effective range of less than a hundred yards, but within

Westward HO!

that distance he proved it to be deadly. He was a natural marksman whose unerring accuracy was more instinctive than from use of the sights.

At Omaha, Wyatt saw his first killing. Two men had been quarreling in a saloon before shooting it out in the street before his startled eyes. Each was killed. He later confided to a family member, "It made me sick at the stomach."

It was when their wagon train traveled into Wyoming Territory, soon after leaving Ft. Laramie, that Indians first accosted them. A man named Chapman was hunting for game about 500 yards from the wagon train when he was jumped by a war party. He was killed and scalped.

Two days later, when they were at Horseshoe Creek, forty miles from Ft. Laramie, they were attacked by an even larger contingent of Lakota Sioux. The painted, whooping Indians attempted to run off the immigrants' stock while they were eating breakfast. At the time, Wyatt and his younger brother, Morgan, just happened to be out with their father's stock. The two boys were able to restrain some of the animals while stampeding the remainder straight into the attacking Indians. The stampeding herd, and gunfire from the wagons drove the Indians off.

Miles down the road, the wagon train stopped at Ft. Bridger to let the stock rest before making the rough trip through the Wasatch Mountains and into the arid desert beyond. Here Wyatt met Jim Bridger, after whom the fort was named. The 60-year-old scout took a shine to Wyatt and the pair spent a lot of time together. Bridger showed Wyatt the art of catching trout in the "profile holes." It was a restful interlude, but the wagons had to move on and the remainder of the trip to California was to be uneventful.[5] Their slow moving wagon train got underway again, from necessity, and crossed the North Platte River at Bessemer Bend, Wyoming on the 21st of June. The ferry cost $3.00 a wagon. [6]

Wyatt's keen, practiced eye and steady aim had kept them well supplied with fresh game along the way. Aside from hunting, Wyatt also drove one of the wagons and helped care for the livestock. Finally in December, after being on the trail for seven months, they reached San Bernardino County in southern California. Nicholas and his family settled down in the small farming community of Colton, doing what they knew best, farming. (Colton, more-or-less, is now a suburb of Los Angeles.)

The long and difficult journey had tested Wyatt's mettle. He'd grown from a wide-eyed youth into a handsome, rugged, hard-working man. Taller than his older brother James, who stood five feet eight inches, Wyatt was a full six feet and one-quarter inch tall.

Sons Leave Home

1865

Meanwhile, back in San Bernardino, war veteran and farmer James heard of the discovery of gold in Last Chance Gulch at Helena, Montana Territory (Montana). It was said the nuggets were so plentiful that one could actually "shake them out of the sagebrush." Over the years the Earp boys had grown to emulate their father's hard living and wandering ways. In keeping with his spirit of wanderlust and adventure, James heeded the call of the alluring yellow metal.

He left the sleepy little farming community to make his way on horseback north toward Montana.

Montana was a vast, unknown, far-off place described by explorers Meriwether Lewis and William Clark as the land of the shining mountains.[7] James was to live on his disability pension and income from a succession of jobs as bartender, hack or stage driver and card dealer.

June 24-Twenty-two-year-old Virgil was discharged from the Union Army and joined the family in Colton. The Civil War had finally ended on April 9th with Lee's surrender to Grant at the Appomattox Courthouse in Virginia.

Wyatt had also long-since grown weary of the peaceful life of a farmer. He was left troubled and alone when James took off for Montana. But when Virgil showed up from the war, Wyatt saw a way out of his situation. Soon the two brothers left Colton together. They found work with a freight company, at first driving teams of horses and mules that pulled heavy wagons between southern California and Salt Lake City, Utah. They then worked for another line that hauled to Prescott, Arizona. Wyatt learned the work quickly, and he and Virgil took turns swamping, loading, and driving the teams.

Still later, they were hired as stagecoach drivers, shuttling passengers and goods between Los Angeles and San Bernardino. They also drove coaches along the dangerous and lawless routes in Arizona, Utah, and California.

The excitement of driving long teams of straining horses and mules from the seat of a pitching and rolling freight wagon or stagecoach suited Wyatt well. To further add to his

Wells Fargo, San Francisco, CA.
Wells Fargo stagecoach, Trinity, CA, circa 1860s

excitement, scores of outlaws preyed along those routes in the late 1860's. His courage and willingness to fight made him equal to the task, and Wyatt soon built a reputation respected by the criminal element. In later years he would claim to have been attacked by stage robbers six times, but never once arriving late to his destination.

September 12- Newton, the eldest of the Earp brothers, finally mustered out of the service as a fourth corporal. He married a girl named Jennie Adam in Council Bluffs, Iowa, then settled down in Lamar, Missouri, where his father Nicholas still owned some land. They would have several children together, including a baby daughter they named Effie.

1868

These were turbulent times in a war-torn, post-Civil War nation. The rush to lay rails of steel to unite the country brought thousands from the East laborers, gamblers, thieves, and people of all sorts. Rivalry flared between work-crews as flat cars of ties and rails rushed to the end of the track. Towns and camps sprang up along the way. Some settlements lived on, while others were left to the solitude of the elements.

Wyatt and Virgil were hired by the Union Pacific Railroad to take charge of all of the horses and mules in a railroad camp at Bear River City, Wyoming. They were responsible for driving a four-animal plow, loosening up the soil and staying a hundred miles ahead of road graders and the railroad's rapidly advancing steel rails. War veteran Virgil was well suited to the task, but jobs requiring such responsibility and hardship were seldom, if ever, given to a nineteen-year-olds like Wyatt. The hiring boss saw a fire in Wyatt's eyes that he'd seldom seen, even in older men.

Wyatt and Virgil were both good at fist fighting. One night in the railroad camp saloon, they had cross words with two huge Irishmen and a mighty Swede laborer. One of them slugged Virgil and a no-holds-barred fight was on, using fists, feet, heads, chairs, and bottles. Virgil tried his best, but there were just too many of them. After a good fight, they put him down and out in the end.

Wyatt didn't fare nearly as well. He only lasted about half a minute before being knocked senseless, but in that short time he had taken an awful beating. The next day, all battered and limping, Wyatt decided that he'd better learn how to fight and win. He studied boxing from a camp bruiser by the name of John Shannessy.

Wyatt learned how to fight and could soon hold his own with the best of them. Shannessy had not only taught him how to fight but also the fundamentals of refereeing boxing matches. He was to be Wyatt's friend for many years thereafter. Wyatt went on to referee fights throughout the rest of his life, e. g. the highly controversial Sharkey-Fitsimmons fight in 1896 in Portland, Oregon. Boxing became one of both Wyatt and Virgil's great loves. Over the years he and Virgil developed many friendships with boxing champions.

July 4-Wyatt turned up in Cheyenne holding the wagers of a couple of hundred men. It was his responsibility to bet their money on his choice of fighters in a prizefight staged between Mike Donovan, a classy heavyweight, and Johnny Shannessy, a newcomer to the ring. Earp had fought his way into prominence in a number of brawls in the tent towns and was looked upon by the hard-fisted Irish track layers as a good man, honest and a first-rate judge of fighting men.

Earp looked the fighters over, and cast his lot with Donovan. Even though Shannessy had taught him the ins and outs of fighting, Donovan looked like the better man. It's a matter of record that Shannessy took the beating of his life, and that Wyatt returned to Bear River City with his money belt bulging with well-bet money for his friends. Just before he left the railroad camp, he went looking for that big Swede. Wyatt mauled him up badly and was mighty well pleased.[8]

After four adventurous years in California, Nicholas moved his family (himself, Virginia, Morgan, Warren and Adelia) back to the Midwest, to the dusty little town of Lamar, Missouri. There he ran for a seat on the Lamar Board of Trustees, winning on a platform of letting pigs run loose in the city's streets. Nicholas would also later become the Lamar Justice of the Peace.

1869

December-Wyatt joined a government survey team in Springfield, Missouri. Over the years, he'd become an excellent marksman and hunter, and it was his responsibility to keep the engineering party in fresh game. By then, he and Virgil had split up and he was on his own.

Meanwhile Virgil was driving a stage through Council Bluffs, Iowa when he went into the Planters House, a road-side inn where he met waitress Allie Sullivan. They took up together in a common law marriage the following year.[9] (No record of an official marriage has ever been found.)

Wyatt the Lawman is devastated in 1870

March 3-When his work in Springfield was finished Wyatt joined his family in Lamar. At age 21, he was appointed to the position of Lamar Town Constable. Wyatt had finally begun to settle down.

Three months earlier, on January third, he had married Urilla Sutherland and bought his first house. His father, Nicholas, performed the marriage ceremony as the Lamar Justice of The Peace.[10] Wyatt had finally found what he had been looking for all through his young life, the companionship of a beautiful woman. Tragically, though, less than a year later she died in an epidemic of typhoid fever, taking with her the unborn baby whom they'd both so dearly loved. Wyatt was devastated. In utter anguish, he turned to alcohol for comfort. Distraught and in a drunken stupor, he burned their home and all of their possessions. On that terrible stormy night, he swore into the light of the roaring flames, to his beloved Urilla, that he would never marry again. While he kept that promise, he would later have two common law wives.

1871

April-Heart-broken, Wyatt left Lamar to wander aimlessly through the West, falling into a period of lawlessness in Oklahoma. He was arrested in Indian Territory and accused of stealing horses, but was never tried in the case.

In the meantime, his father Nicholas and family again went on the move. They traveled from Lamar, by wagon, to Peace, Kansas, where they stayed temporarily near Wyatt's half-brother Newton and his family. Newton had become a hard-working Christian, a farmer, carpenter and was a community leader. He and his wife were traditional Methodists.

Wyatt and Bat Masterson Hunt Buffalo

That winter Wyatt camped on the Salt Fork of the Arkansas River. It was here that he had a fateful meeting with brothers Bat and Ed Masterson. They were all three professional buffalo hunters who would later become fellow gamblers and lawmen.

The Federal Government encouraged buffalo hunting and paid handsomely for it. Its plan had several purposes. First, to deprive the plains Indians of their main source of food and clothing, thus reducing them to

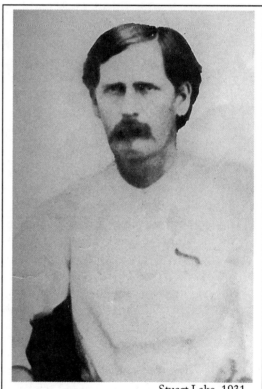

Stuart Lake, 1931
Wyatt Earp in his twenties (1877)

depending entirely on the government for their very existences. Finally, to kill the migrating buffalo herds so as to open up the vast midsection of the country to farming. It was the beginning of the end for the great herds of ancient American bison. Wyatt was once quoted as saying he and Bat saw at least a million buffalo in one herd.

1873

April 18-Wyatt's older brother, James, and a girl named Nellie Bartlett were married in Illinois by a Justice of the Peace. Nellie somehow acquired the nickname of Bessie after that and would be arrested many times for prostitution. But, evidently, James made a good woman out of her as they would have two children together: Frank, who was born in February of 1874, and Hattie, in June of 1875. Frank would die early.[11]

Earl Chafin-Craig Fouts
William B. (Bat) Masterson

August 18-As part of his wandering, Wyatt traveled on to Ellsworth, Kansas. He rode into the little cow town in the midst of a potentially deadly confrontation between famous gunslinger Ben Thompson and town officials. Thompson was holding them at bay with a double-barreled shotgun.

Seeing the stalemate, Wyatt approached the town's mayor and offered to resolve the situation. He borrowed a badge and two revolvers and calmly approached Thompson. Wyatt told him that if he didn't throw down the shotgun, he'd be killed. Thompson threw down the shotgun. This fearless act began Wyatt's reputation as a peacemaker and made him famous all up and down the Chisholm Trail. (This highly controversial story has been a source of debate for Western historians over the years.)

1874

October 26-Wyatt was appointed to the position of temporary officer of the law in Wichita, Kansas. Then the following April he was officially hired as a Wichita Deputy Marshal.

1876

April 13-His tenure abruptly ended, however, when the restless Wyatt traveled on to Dodge City, Kansas to be with his brother Morgan. There, one night, as they were walking across the street, they saw a string of eleven wagons coming toward them. A man on the lead wagon, who turned out to be their father,

Nicholas, hailed them. Happenstance had drawn the family together. Included in the wagon train were also their mother, younger brother, Warren, and sister Adelia, older brothers, Newton and Virgil, and their families.

May-A month after his dismissal as a Wichita Deputy, Wyatt was appointed as a Deputy Marshal for Dodge City. But, being an officer of the law in a cattle town was highly seasonal work; when the cattle weren't running and there weren't any cowboys around, life became woefully peaceful.

September 9-Wyatt had had enough of Dodge. So he and Morgan left with a wagon and team of horses bound for Deadwood, South Dakota. They followed the gold rush to the Black Hills.

Meanwhile their father, Nicholas, and the rest of the Earps remained in Dodge through the remainder of 1876. Then in 1877 they traveled back to San Bernardino County and Colton, California.

The Search for Gold in Deadwood, South Dakota

For some weeks after the two brothers' arrival in the Black Hills, Wyatt and Morgan tried their hand at panning for gold in the different gulches. The brothers finally conceded that all the paying claims had already been taken. But there was so much going on in Deadwood that Wyatt decided there must be some other way to make a living.

Winter was fast approaching and by then they had loaned their team and wagon to miners anxious to lay in their winter wood supply. That gave Wyatt an idea. They started a wood yard, hiring hands to cut logs down to stove size. Wyatt peddled the wood at $10 and $12 a cord. That winter's business netted them a $5,000 grubstake, and, because Wyatt supervised each wood delivery with the team, he earned the moniker, "Wood Hauler."

Winter of 1875-1876

September 25-The first stage had reached Deadwood Gulch and the service ran all winter into 1876 without mishap. But it was a hard winter for the riff-raff. Easy money was fast disappearing along with the lush panning of the placers. Many of the underworld figures grouped together in gangs and began robbing stagecoaches.

The gangs operated with spies in camp and an underground messenger service to the detriment of the stage lines and their insured cargoes. Dunc Blackburn ran one of these road agent gangs. His gang flourished on traffic running between Custer and the Cheyenne River, and the region around Newcastle became known as Robber's Roost. Blackburn knew a winter's cleanup of the sluice boxes had been piling up in Deadwood and that it would make some haul when it was shipped.

One day the stage line's superintendent recognized Wyatt at the Buffalo corrals in the gulch. Earp volunteered to guard the stage in return for the free 300-mile ride to Cheyenne. Meanwhile, Wells Fargo had hatched up a plan to fool Dunc Blackburn by using the "wood hauler" as a greenhorn guard on a seemingly routine trip. Of that trip to Cheyenne, Red Raymond, the stage driver, had much to tell.

"Earp's the shootinist feller I ever seen," Red remarked. "The minute he seen two riders trailing us near the Jenney Stockade end of the run, he says, 'Them's decoys, Red. They want us to keep watching them, which means there's an ambush up ahead.'"

"Earp triggers the rifle down the road and them two riders vamoosed into timber. Next Earp spotted a lookout on a hill, field glassing us, I reckon. The rifle talked his way and he dropped behind a rock and started to chuck lead back at us. The ambush spot was a wooded little gulch that we had to run through. I whipped up the horses. Earp pulls pistols and starts throwing lead into the brush on each side of the road ahead of the leaders."

"Well sir, you orta seen the road agents scramble for bullet proof cover. They blazed away at us as we charged through. The coach is full of slugs. Lucky, no one got hit. There was a yelp from one of them when Earp blasts the shotgun at a whiskered man running for a hitched horse. Then we was through. They started to chase us but they soon gave it up. They didn't want to get within rifle range."

When the coach arrived in Cheyenne and Wells Fargo officials saw that it and its cargo were intact, they touched off a celebration. Wyatt scoffed at their lavish compliments for protecting it. "I had a grubstake to protect (referring to the money he'd gotten for the winter wood business)," Earp said. "I reckon Blackburn didn't know how much I had on me."

"You mean," said a Wells Fargo representative," that Boone's Mayor didn't explain about the secret plan in loading of this coach?" "Nope."

"Come outside," they invited. The coach was being unloaded. There were iron chests built in under each seat and these were full of fat leather bags, amounting to seven hundred pounds of gold. "You brought in $200,000 in dust. Biggest shipment from Deadwood to date." They gave Wyatt a paltry $50 for his part in the trip, but offered him a good job instead. He refused it.[12]

Wyatt later got back together with Morgan and, on one trip through Kansas, they met famous gunfighter and frontier lawman, Wild Bill Hickok. The three men passed each other in the doorway of the Alamo Saloon in Abilene. Wyatt sat down in the chair Hickok had just vacated and got lucky at cards that day. He was to later comment on how flamboyantly Hickok dressed.

Over three million Texas longhorn cattle arrived in Abilene between the years of 1867 and 1872 to be shipped east by rail. Wild Bill became famous in his efforts to maintain law and order on Abilene's legendary streets. Hickok used the Alamo Saloon as his operational headquarters.

Courtesy of Marvin and Margaret Clancy
Stage stop

1877

In the summer, Wyatt, Morgan, and their older brother, Virgil, left Kansas to follow the gambling circuit south to Ft. Griffin, Texas. Wyatt had learned to support himself as a professional gambler, and was especially fond of the game of faro. The Earp brothers had been in and out of Texas so much through the years that they were described as "Texas men" in one contemporary account, despite their more famous association with Kansas's cow towns.[13]

3

Wyatt Meets Doc Holliday

While in fort griffin, Texas, Wyatt befriended a Georgia dentist with a bad cough by the name of John Henry "Doc" Holliday. Doc's constant companion was an ex-prostitute by the name of Kate Elder, known as Big Nosed Kate.

Doc had consumption (tuberculosis) and had come west for his health. Knowing he would eventually die from the disease anyway left him with little fear of death. Doc even came to view his inevitable death as a welcome relief from his constant, painful, and often bloody, coughing fits.[1]

He was to eventually become one of the most infamous figures in the Old West. A gambler, boozer, and quick-tempered gunman, he was said to have put more men in their graves than even the legendary "Wild Bill" Hickok. Doc often claimed that he would eventually be killed in a gunfight with his boots on.

In one of the Ft. Griffin saloons, Doc stabbed a fellow gambler in an argument over a game of faro. The highly volatile situation escalated when word got

Earl Chafin-Craig Fouts

John Henry (Doc) Holliday
1851-1887 dentist, gambler
and gun fighter

out about what he had done. A mob of angry vigilante-minded townsmen formed and was about to string him up when quick-thinking Kate set fire to the back of the hotel building to distract them. The crowd disbanded to fight the fire, knowing full well that it wouldn't be long before all of the tender-dry wooden buildings in their town would be ablaze. In the meantime, Doc and Kate mounted up and galloped out of town in a cloud of dust, headed north for Dodge City, Kansas.

1878

Twenty-two-year-old Bat Masterson, Dodge Marshal Ed Masterson's younger brother, was elected the new Sheriff. They worked the streets together and devised a scheme to cool off Dodge's quarrelsome drunks. They dumped them into an old fifteen-foot deep well. The well didn't contain enough water to drown them, but it was too deep for them to escape from.

Then, on the night of April 9th, a pair of drunken cowboys gunned Ed Masterson down in the street. A bullet had passed completely through the Marshal's body, mortally wounding him, but somehow he still managed to draw his own weapon. He shot one of the cowboys through the body. Then he turned his attention to the second, whom he shot three times, once in the chest and twice in the right arm. The Marshal then staggered into a nearby saloon and collapsed to the floor. Ed was carried to his room where he died about forty minutes later. One of his attackers died the following day and the other was bedridden for months. The badly wounded man eventually vanished into history.

Bat was grief stricken and sent a telegraph to his good friend Wyatt, whom he knew to be in Fort Worth, Texas. Wyatt had previously written to him from there. Indeed, Wyatt was still following the gambling circuit in Texas and he, Virgil, and Morgan were in Fort Worth. James was also in Fort Worth, working as a barkeep in one of the town's saloons.

Bat wrote to Wyatt, describing what had happened to his brother Ed, and offered Wyatt his old job back as Deputy Marshal. Wyatt accepted, and he and Morgan returned to Dodge. When the *Dodge City Times* heard that Wyatt was back in town, they reported, "Wyatt Earp, who was on our police force last summer, is in town again. We hope that he will accept a position on the force once more. He had a quiet way of taking the most desperate characters into custody, which invariably gave one the impression that the city was able to enforce or mandate and preserve her dignity. It wasn't considered policy to draw a gun on Wyatt unless you got the drop and meant to burn powder without any preliminary talk." Wyatt was asked by City Marshal Charles E. Bassett to replace the fallen Ed Masterson.

Wyatt and Bat made a good team. They worked the streets and saloons together and perfected the art of "buffaloing," or pistol whipping, the rowdies, rather than shooting them, and promptly throwing them into jail.

In their search for a good time the hard-riding cowboys got the worst of it. After riding herd on cattle for months on end, they came into Dodge to find female companionship, get drunk, and blow off a little steam. Dodge City's saloon owners and other businessmen were laying in wait for them, and charged the cowboys dearly for the creature comforts they were after.

Sometimes the rowdy cowboys went a little too far in their merrymaking. One such time was when a band of them ganged up on Wyatt in the street out in front of the Long Branch Saloon. Two of the cowboys were holding cocked revolvers on Wyatt, goading him to draw before they shot him down. About twenty others stood nearby, taunting and insulting the enraged, but helpless, Wyatt.

Old West magazine, summer, 1980 by Tom Barkdull
Purported scene of gamblers playing faro, number one is Wyatt Earp.

Doc Holliday just happened to be dealing faro inside the Long Branch at the time, but when he heard of Wyatt's predicament, he threw down his cards and ran for the door. He arrived on the scene with a cocked revolver in hand and loosed a volume of profanity toward the cowboys that they couldn't ignore. When they turned their attention toward him, Wyatt had a chance to draw his revolver in his own defense.

Doc then helped Wyatt herd the group of drunken men to the jailhouse. Wyatt never forgot how Doc had saved his life; the two were bonded together in friendship. Later, when Wyatt migrated to Tombstone, Arizona, Territory (Arizona), he invited Doc to go along.

Lonely Wyatt Hooks Up With Mattie Blaylock

It was around this time that Wyatt met Celia Ann "Mattie" Blaylock, an Iowa farm girl who'd come out west to find a new life for herself. When Wyatt met her, she was a prostitute who had been working in a Dodge City dance hall. Soon afterwards, she moved in with him and for the next eight years they would travel on together as man and wife. Mattie was the first of Wyatt's two common-law wives.

Wyatt was also a deacon at the church and was well respected in Dodge City. The Dodge law firm of Sutton and Colburn even presented him with a Bible. The inscription on its inside cover read, "To Wyatt S. Earp as a slight recognition of his many Christian virtues and steady following in the footsteps of the meek and lowly Jesus."[2]

1879

September 9-Wyatt served as assistant Marshal until well after the trail herds had come in. At that time, he, Mattie, Doc and Kate left Dodge City in two overland wagons bound for the Cimarron Crossing, Santa Fe, and Las Vegas, New Mexico. After spending a short time in northern New Mexico, the foursome traveled on to Prescott, Arizona, where Virgil and his wife, Allie, were living. In the meantime Morgan had gone north to Butte, Montana where, on December 18th, he found a position as a policeman for that city.[3]

Some months earlier, Virgil and Allie had been traveling toward Prescott when they stopped at a mail station to water their horses. As there were no other women living close by, the stations' manager asked Allie to stay and help his pregnant wife through the last part of her pregnancy. This all worked out just fine for Virgil since he only had a half-dollar to his name and this gave them a place to live. Virgil was also given work as a rider on the mail route and even thought of settling down in Prescott. He and Allie filed for several homesteads while they were there.

Tombstone, A town too tough to die!

November 29-A few days after Wyatt and his party got to Prescott, news broke of a great discovery of silver in Tombstone, Arizona. Wyatt and Mattie, James and his wife, Bessie (and their sixteen-year-old daughter Hattie), Virgil and Allie, and Doc and Kate all headed for Tombstone together. Newton and his family had decided to remain in Kansas while the youngest brother, Warren, still lived with his parents in California.

James and Bessie had two children together, a son and a daughter. The boy died young and their daughter, Hattie, ran away from home in Tombstone. Wyatt's sister Adelia was to later say that when Bessie died in 1887, it was of a broken heart.

December 1-The Earps entered Tombstone by wagon, considering them selves to be businessmen. They were hell-bent on cashing in on Tombstone's good fortune. Virgil went right to work prospecting and, five days later, located the Mountain Maid mine.

With all of the new strikes being found in the hills and desert around town, the Earps figured Tombstone's population would soon explode. Events would prove them right. Tombstone's population jumped from 1,000 when they hit town, to 10,000 a little over a year later in 1881.[4]

Gary McLelland, Glendale, AZ
Tombstone looking north-late 1881 or early 1882

1880

Wyatt worked as a shotgun guard on Wells Fargo stagecoaches. Then, in July, he was appointed to the position of Deputy Sheriff for the Tombstone District of newly formed Pima County, serving in that capacity until November.

October-A few months after brother Morgan was appointed as a policeman for the city of Butte, he was dismissed. He then traveled south with his wife, Lou, to be with his brothers in Tombstone. He found work at Wyatt's old job of riding shotgun guard on Wells Fargo stagecoaches.

Morgan's arrival in October brought the count to four Earp brothers in Tombstone. All tall, handsome men with dark mustaches, they looked alike and often dressed alike in black coats, black Stetson hats, white shirts, and black string ties. They were frequently mistaken for one another.

November 1-County officials liked Wyatt's law enforcement record so much that they made him an assistant to Fred White, Tombstone's Marshal, at a salary of $100 per month.

November 15-But, after only two weeks on the job, Wyatt resigned as assistant Marshal to buy an interest in the Oriental Saloon where he operated a game of faro. He would eventually have over $3,000 invested in the Oriental.

His fellow house dealers were Luke Short, Bat Masterson and Doc Holliday, a group of hard cased gamblers and killers if there ever was one. Residents of Tombstone were keenly aware of the presence of four of the West's most notorious gamblers and killers in their town. The four men were dubbed the "Dodge City Gang" because they had all come to Tombstone by way of Dodge.[5]

1881

Earlier, in 1879, Josephine Sarah Marcus, a beautiful nineteen year old, dark-haired Jewish girl had come to Tombstone. Josie was born in New York in 1860 and had two sisters, Rebecca and Henrietta, and a brother, Nathan. In 1869 their father Henry Hyman Marcus and mother Sophia decided to take the family "out West." They traveled by ship around the Isthmus of Panama, to San Francisco. San Francisco was still a miner's town then, even though it had been twenty years since the gold rush of the '49ers.

Because of her mother's influence, as she grew Josie was headed toward the life of a middle class matron. But her thirst for adventure in this new land lured her away. In 1879, the H.M.S. Pinafore craze swept the country. Tunes from the Gilbert and Sullivan opera were being sung, hummed, and whistled everywhere. Completely beguiled by the moment, Josie and a girlfriend ran away from their homes and joined a Pinafore group of actors and musicians. The cast of 26 members went on the road together, performing one night stands in southern California and Arizona. Later that year they reached Tombstone.

It was in Tombstone where Cochise County Sheriff John Behan met and fell in love with Josephine. When her troop of actors and musicians left town and traveled to Prescott, Arizona, he followed. She later returned to Tombstone to live with him as his fiancé.

That summer she came home (to Behan's place) and caught Johnny in bed with his former partner's wife, Mrs. Dunbar. Rather than kick Behan and his ten-year-old son Albert out, she moved out herself.

Meanwhile, Wyatt was beset with problems in his common law marriage with Mattie. He had given his life with her a lot of thought and found that even with her, he was still terribly lonely. Her continuing habit of taking even heavier doses of the opium based-painkiller laudanum had left him essentially alone.

Then one day, while he was dealing faro in the Oriental Saloon, he looked up and saw beautiful Josephine walking past the window. He knew that it didn't make any sense, but he fell head over heels in love with her right then. He later spoke with Josie, and the rest is history. They were drawn to each other and, through lean times and good, their "sweet" relationship would last for nearly half a century. This is where he parted company with Mattie.

July 25-Cowboy leader Curly Bill Brocius shot and killed Tombstone Marshal Fred White on Allen Street. Brocius was later tried in the case, but found not guilty. Virgil was appointed as Marshal White's successor. Due to the dangerous times, Morgan feared for his wife Lou's safety so he sent her to be with the Earp family in Colton, California where she would be out of harm's way.

Wyatt wanted to send Josie back home to her parents in San Francisco as well, but she refused to go. Through all of this desperate fighting and the horrific events to come Josie stood firm in Wyatt's defense. Confrontations between the Earps, with their friend Doc Holliday, and the cowboys had reached near civil war condition, but things were soon to become much worse.

Gunfight at the OK Corral!

October 26-The Earps, backing their brother Virgil, had been having a long-standing feud with four local cowboys: Ike and Billy Clanton and Frank and Tom McLaury. All four were from respectable Arizona families, but were members of a ruthless gang of thieves, rustlers and murderers, known as "The Cowboys." They were a vicious bunch, if there ever was one, and Sheriff Behan operated as their legal backbone, protecting them from the court.

This festering situation between the Cowboys and the Earps finally came to a head on October 26th. That morning Tombstone's Mayor John Clum told Wyatt and his brothers that the Clantons and McLaurys were spreading it all over town that they were going to clean the Earps out.

After a heated discussion as to what to do, Wyatt, Morgan, Virgil and Doc Holliday all strode from the

Arizona Historical Society, Tucson
#76,614
Wyatt's Colt

jail, down dusty Fremont Street toward destiny. They were about to become involved in an event that would change the history of the American West.

Word of what might happen had spread, and many of the townspeople had gathered on the streets to watch the events unfold. A short while later, Wyatt, Virgil, Morgan, and Doc confronted the Cowboys. Once they reached Fly's photography studio, the Clantons and McLaurys backed into a vacant lot next to it. Bordering the lot on the other side was a smaller, private house. The Clantons and McLaurys lined up with their backs to the house. The Earps moved a few steps forward. Virgil, holding Doc's cane in his right hand, stood in front. Behind him were Wyatt and Morgan, and behind them Doc, with the shotgun Virgil had given him clearly visible as his coat flapped open in the breeze. As the two groups eyed each other across a distance of no more than six feet, Sheriff Behan slipped off to the side of Fly's house. The Cowboys' friend, Billy Claibourne, hastily retreated with the sheriff.

The Clantons and McLaurys, without realizing it, had boxed themselves in. Almost immediately, gunfire commenced; within the space of a scant half-minute, thirty shots had been fired. Tom, Frank, and Billy lay dead where they fell. Virgil had received a leg wound, Morgan, a wound in his shoulder, and Doc was seared along his ribs by a near miss. In time, all of their wounds would heal. Wyatt was the only one to remain unscathed.

Their brother, James, didn't participate in the OK Corral fracas. He later said that he was just sitting down to supper when he heard the first shots. He jumped up, grabbing his pistol, and made his way toward the gunfire. However, he arrived late on the scene, just as the last of the Cowboys went down.

Virgil Ambushed by Back Shooters

December 28-As Tombstone Marshal Virgil was crossing 5th Street he was ambushed from behind by blasts from several shotguns. His cowardly assailants then escaped into the darkness of the night. Virgil's left arm was nearly blown off in the melee, even exposing his shattered arm bones. Bleeding profusely, he staggered back into the Oriental Saloon where he'd left Wyatt and Morgan only moments before, and collapsed to the floor in front of them. They frantically tended to his wounds.

Later, a hat marked with Ike Clanton's initials in it was found at the scene of the ambush. Although Virgil did eventually recover from his wounds, he would never again regain the use of his arm.[6]

December 29-At Wyatt's request, U.S. Marshal Crawley Dake telegraphed him an appointment as Deputy U.S. Marshal. Wyatt then caused warrants to be sworn out for the arrest of those suspected in the case: Ike Clanton, Frank Stilwell, and Hank Swilling. But, true to form, cowboy stooge, Sheriff Behan, refused to send a posse after the wanted men. Wyatt reacted by forming his own posse and took out after the men. Fearful of the inevitable vengeance of Virgil's brothers, Clanton and his bunch sneaked back into town and surrendered to Behan.

1882

A mock trial was held on February the 1st, but the Cowboys were found innocent of Virgil's ambush. Gang members corroborated each other's alibis. Wyatt resigned his position as Deputy U.S. Marshal in disgust.

"This is a hard way to Die!"

March 18-In the evening, Wyatt, Josie and Morgan attended a performance of a troupe of musical actors at the Birdcage Theater. As they were leaving, several of their friends approached, warning them to be on guard against some kind of an ambush by the Cowboys. After Wyatt accompanied Josie back to their house, he and Morgan went into Campbell and Hatch's Saloon where Morgan began shooting pool with his friend Dan Tipton and several other men. Wyatt sat across the room watching the game.

It was Morgan's turn, so he walked around the pool table toward the front of the building. He turned his back on the saloon's glass-paned doors and leaned over the table to take aim on the cue ball. Suddenly two rapid-fire shots exploded out of the darkness of the night, shattering the glass in the doors. Everyone dove for the floor, but it was too late for Morgan. The first bullet had passed through his back and come out of his stomach. It lodged in the leg of a bystander. The second hit his spine, passed on through him and lodged in the wall near Wyatt's head.

Wyatt saw that his brother had been hit and, under the threat of even more gunfire, he and Tipton carried Morgan into the safety of another room. Someone ran for the doctor, but Morgan was to live for only one hour more. As he lay there in a state of shock looking up at Wyatt and Tipton, he tried to make light of his situation. He half jokingly said, "Tip, old boy, I have played my last game of pool." Then later, with all expression gone from his face, he slipped off into eternity murmuring, "This is a hard way to die!"

Wyatt stood in shock, looking down at the dead body of his lively young brother, hate welling up from within and his own body screaming for revenge. He vowed that whoever did this would pay with their lives.

Later speculation had it that Wyatt was the intended target of the attack, but he and Morgan looked so much alike they were often confused for one another. When Warren was told that Morgan had been shot, he rushed to his side. By then, poor Morgan was long since dead. Warren, too, was left filled with hate for the back shooters who'd done this to his brother.

The identity of Morgan's murderers was later found out by the confession of Peter Spence's wife. She implicated Spence, Stilwell, some Mexicans, and others. Wyatt also got word that a coroner's jury agreed with her accusations.

Wyatt then insisted that Josie, for her own safety, return to her parent's home in San Francisco. Then he telegraphed Morgan's wife Lou, in Colton, telling her of her husband's death. She came back immediately to Tombstone. (Adelia Earp was to later say that when Lou heard of Morgan's death she slumped to the floor and bawled. "She was a very sad lady.")

March 20-With Warren's help, Wyatt made arrangements to send Morgan's body back to Colton, accompanied by Virgil and the Earp women. They'd dressed Morgan in one of Doc Holliday's suits and placed his coffin on the train. They all boarded in Contention, Arizona.

Wyatt, Warren, and their friends Doc Holliday, Sherman McMasters, Turkey Creek Jack Johnson, Dan Tipton, and Texas Jack Vermilion were all heavily armed and rode along to provide protection. (James and Bessie had left Tombstone two months earlier, by January 23rd, and were already in Colton.)

When the train stopped at the Tucson station, Wyatt happened to spot fugitive Frank Stilwell standing on the platform near a passenger car. Stilwell saw Wyatt at about the same time and took off running down the tracks, in an effort to get away.

Revenge!

Armed with a double-barreled shotgun and two pistols, Wyatt chased after him. A short while later he caught up with Stilwell, who then turned and wrestled Wyatt for the shotgun. With grim determination and looking him squarely in the eyes all the while, Wyatt muscled the shotgun's two gaping barrels up against Stilwell's chest. He saw Morgan's dying face and heard his mournful words, as he jerked back on both triggers. The resulting explosion blew Stilwell's body back away from him. The smoking barrels of his shotgun had set Stilwell's coat afire.

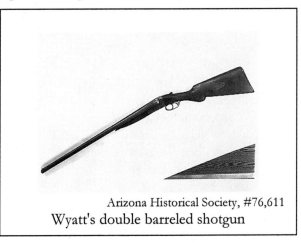

Arizona Historical Society, #76,611

Wyatt's double barreled shotgun

Wyatt stood looking down at the quivering, lifeless body, and was still breathing hard from the chase. He knew the rest of Morgan's killers were out there, somewhere, and that he was going after them to make things right.

Wyatt watched angrily as the train chugged away from the station. It was carrying his broken and murdered family. He and his posse had retrieved the horses they'd had on one of the train's stock cars and they mounted up and rode back toward Tombstone.

Further damage was done to Stilwell's corpse, as testimony to Wyatt and younger brother Warren's unbridled rage toward one of Morgan's murderers. Stilwell's stiffening body was later found sprawled across the tracks. Those who found it noted that six shots had gone into his body—four rifle balls and two loads of buckshot. Both legs were shot through. A charge of buckshot had gone into Stilwell's left thigh and another through his breast, which must have been delivered close, as the coat was powder burned. In all, the corpse was riddled with some twenty-bullet holes. Someone had even stolen his watch. Wyatt was proud of killing him, and would later tell a family member, "Stilwell was the only man I ever *had* to kill."

Later that day, Wyatt and his men were just about to ride out of Tombstone again to continue their search for Morgan's murderers, when Behan approached them on foot. "I want to see you, Wyatt." Wyatt looked down at Behan and angrily returned with, "If you're not careful, you'll see me once too often Johnny." With that, Wyatt reigned his horse around and he and his men rode out of town.

Upon their arrival at Pete Spence's wood cutting camp, they found half-breed Indian Charlie out in the woods. Just before Wyatt shot him to death, Charlie's own terrified confession implicated other members in the Cowboy gang.

March 22-Another member of the Cowboy gang, Florintino Cruz, was shot to death at South Pass in the Dragoon Mountains. At about this same time, back in Tombstone, Sheriff Behan was still holding true to his ways. Acting in favor of the Cowboys, he was busily putting together a posse to go after the Earp bunch. Two of the men in his posse were none other than Cowboy leaders, Johnny Ringo and Ike Clanton. When Pima County Sheriff Bob Paul saw who Behan had in his posse he refused to go with them. Paul retorted, "He persists in cloaking the most notorious outlaws and murderers in Arizona with the authority of the law. I will have nothing to do with such a gang."

March 24-Wyatt and his posse stopped at Mescal Springs in Arizona's Whetstone Mountains to water their horses. In a chance encounter, Curly Bill Brocius, Pony Deal, and others were suddenly upon them.

Dozens of shots were exchanged and most of the Cowboys ran. However, before Curly Bill could get away, Wyatt emptied both barrels into his chest.

During the melee, Wyatt hadn't heard the gunfire or seen the action. He was so intent on killing the murderer of his beloved brother that he was oblivious to the gunfire. After it was all over, he found that his clothing was full of bullet holes from all of the near misses. Cowboy Johnny Barnes received a wound in the fight that eventually would kill him.

Wyatt and his men then talked over their situation and decided to temporarily leave the territory. They knew that warrants had been issued against them, and that Behan and his posse were hot on their trail. They would pick up the chase again later.

From there, they traveled to Trinidad, Colorado, where Wyatt's long time friend, Bat Masterson, kept a gambling parlor and was the town sheriff. Bat had been appointed to that position earlier in the year and, after his appointment, word spread among the locals that "the new Marshal never misses!"

He was popularly credited with the killing of one man for every year of his life, twenty-six in two engagements, in the interest of law and order. Bat had built a reputation with his deeds and courage in the face of seemingly insurmountable odds.

One of these shooting scrapes was described in detail. Two brothers had been killed by a squad of ruffians across the street from the indomitable Masterson. With a revolver in each hand, he jumped against their locked door, with both feet, burst the timbers, and fired right and left. Four dropped; three ran. They got on their horses. Masterson jumped on his pony and had overtaken and killed them all by the time they reached the outskirts of town."[7]

April 15-After a short stay in Trinidad, Wyatt and his posse traveled by train to Albuquerque, New Mexico. They took rooms in an Albuquerque hotel under assumed names. Wyatt called at the city's *Review* and *Journal* offices and asked for interviews with reporters of both newspapers.

During the interview, Wyatt stated that he and his friends had come to Albuquerque to escape persecution. They were waiting for the results of an effort being made by Arizona's Governor Tritle to secure their pardon from the president. He also claimed they were then being sought by their foes and that they would not give themselves up to the Arizona officers without resistance. With these concerns, Earp requested of both papers that their temporary sojourn in Albuquerque should remain unnoticed until they could be assured that the knowledge of their whereabouts would not bring a party of Cowboy avengers down upon them. To back his assertion regarding Governor Tritle's support for them, Wyatt presented the *Review* with several convincing documents. Both papers accordingly honored his request.

The party remained in Albuquerque for a week, their identity being well known to fifty people or more. During their stay, Doc Holliday and Wyatt quarreled. When the party disbanded, Holliday went with Tipton to Denver. Wyatt, Warren, Jack and Sherm holed up in Gunnison, Colorado.[8]

May 5-Doc was promptly arrested in Denver and authorities from Arizona attempted to have him extradited back to Arizona. However, by then Bat had talked with the Governor, telling him about all the double-dealing going on in Tombstone. Colorado's Governor Pitkin refused to extradite Doc, citing "faulty wording" in the extradition papers. In his capacity as a Colorado lawman, Bat then brought fake charges against Doc, so that Colorado could claim him first. Doc was set free, but couldn't go back into Arizona under threat of certain death. (Bat never did like Doc, but put up with him for Wyatt's sake.)

Meanwhile Wyatt and Warren had found their way back to Trinidad, Colorado again.[9]

May 24-Only two months after Wyatt and his posse were chased out of Arizona by Sheriff Behan, a grand jury brought an indictment against Behan. For the next year and more, no inconsiderable portion of Cochise County's criminal docket was devoted to the ex-sheriff's acts while in office. Johnny Behan left Tombstone about two jumps ahead of his successor in office. Behan later became Chief of the Yuma Territorial Prison and eventually returned to Tucson, where he died.

Mid-June-Doc joined Wyatt and the rest of the gang in Gunnison, where he remained for several weeks. The rift between Earp and Holliday had been minor enough so as not to have impaired their friendship.

Gunnison police officer Judd Riley recalled the camp as quiet and prepared for conflict: "The bunch was well heeled and went armed. Earp was a fine looking man, tall with a drooping mustache that curled at the ends. He was quiet in manner and never created a bit of trouble here. In fact, he told us boys on the police force we could call on him if we needed help at any time. He was a dead shot, I guess. He always wore two guns high up under his arms, but he never used them here. Doc Holliday was the only one of the gang that seemed to drink much, and the minute he got hilarious, the others promptly took him in charge and he just disappeared.[10]

Shortly after Wyatt's arrival in Gunnison, he was also singled out to a newspaper reporter, who described him in much the same way. "He is a rather tall, well dressed, pleasant looking stranger who stood leaning against the counter, tapping his boot with his cane." In the interview which followed, Wyatt told the reporter, "I will stay here for a while. My lawyers will have a petition for my pardon drawn up. We look for a pardon in a few weeks, and when it comes I'll go back to Tombstone, but if no pardon is made I'll go back in the fall anyway and stand trial." After leaving Gunnison, Wyatt and his posse moved on to Denver and joined Doc. But Wyatt was still on the hunt for Morgan's last remaining killer, Johnny Ringo. (Neither Wyatt nor any of the members of his posse ever returned to Tombstone to stand trail.)

July 13-Johnny Ringo met his maker in Arizona's Turkey Creek Canyon. His lifeless body was found slumped at the base of an oak tree with a single gunshot wound to the head. A coroner's jury called Ringo's death a suicide, but either directly or indirectly, Wyatt had finally gotten his revenge.

If it was a suicide, Ringo must have pulled the trigger knowing that the rest of his gang of thieves and rustlers had been and were being systematically murdered by the Earps and their gunfighting friends. He therefore must also have known that Earp's posse absolutely would not stop their pursuit of him, no matter how long it took, until he was dead. He knew that it was only a matter of time before he met the same fate.

On the other hand, his worthless life could been taken by someone else. But in either event, long belated justice prevailed. The Cowboy's "enforcer" was finally dead.

Shortly thereafter Wyatt said goodbye to the men who'd helped him avenge Morgan's death. They each went their own way, and a few days later Earp was once again gambling in a Gunnison saloon with his brother Warren.

4

Oh Beautiful Josephine!

Fall of 1882

Wyatt and warren left Colorado to join Virgil in San Francisco. For a short while, the three brothers shared an upstairs apartment on Pine Street.

Even though it had been nearly a year since being grievously wounded back in Tombstone, Virgil was still there seeing doctors about his useless arm. He would later go on with his life, though, and by 1887 had owned his own saloon and become Marshal of Colton, California.

Not long after getting settled in with his brothers, Wyatt went out looking for Josie. She'd told him back in Tombstone where her parent's home was in San Francisco. On that rainy San Francisco afternoon, he finally found the right address. When he saw his beautiful Josie standing in the doorway of her parent's home, the nagging, ever-present feeling of loneliness seemed to suddenly melt away. Her glowing smiles brought him happiness and, somehow, warm thoughts of his youth: Peaceful days of so long ago, back on the farm with Morgan and his brothers.

Josie and her family had been following Wyatt's exploits in the newspapers, and her parents felt as if they already knew him. In the following weeks Wyatt and Josie fell even more deeply in love.

1883

January-They left San Francisco, traveling by train to Gunnison, Colorado, where Wyatt continued to run his faro bank. Josie later said, "Following the killing of Ringo, Wyatt picked me up in San Francisco and we traveled to Gunnison by way of Salt Lake City and Denver."

March-Wyatt and Josie moved high into the Rocky Mountains to the golden boomtown of Silverton, Colorado. For the next three months he continued his practice of dealing faro and running the gambling room in Silverton's Arlington Saloon.[1]

He was later indicted in a massive 1883 "morals sweep" along with scores of other men and women in the gambling and prostitution scene. Nothing ever came of the court actions, which had been filed in order for local authorities to make their point and establish what was basically a long time practice of a local protection scheme. Gamblers and prostitutes paid monthly 'fees' to be left alone by the law. These payments proved to be a reliable source of local revenue and a means of keeping track of who was still in town. It was apparently very effective, and few ever complained, recognizing what the legal and financial consequences of a real "blue nose" push in the courts would have been.[2]

Courtesy of Allan G. Bird

Silverton, CO. showing Arlington Saloon July, 1883

May 26-Bat came into Silverton on a train for a single day in an effort to recruit Wyatt to go back to Dodge City with him to help their mutual friend, Luke Short. Luke was a fellow gambler and was in Dodge in 1876 when Wyatt and Bat were both Dodge Marshals. He'd also spent a lot of time with Bat, Wyatt, and Doc Holliday dealing cards in the gambling parlor in Tombstone's Oriental Saloon.[3]

Bat was well known in Silverton. Eight years earlier, in 1875, Silverton's Green Street had become the principal business artery while the city's notorious Blair Street, just a block south, became the "Honky Tonk" district. Many dance halls and gambling houses were scattered in among the thirty-seven saloons that lined the street. At one period, the underworld gained control of Silverton to run the town from their dens on Blair Street. Irate citizens joined to form vigilante groups, but failed in their attempts to restore order. Then Bat was hired to come in from Dodge City, and was placed in charge of the Police Department. Bat wasn't altogether successful in the attempt, but he did succeed in taming things down a bit. As with most frontier towns, the "taming" process came with the arrival of families and the establishment of churches.[4]

After Luke Short left Arizona in the spring of 1883, he'd returned to Dodge to buy an interest in the Long Branch Saloon. Then he hired a comely blond piano payer who had an angelic voice as well. She drew in most of the boys in town.

That's when Luke found himself in conflict with the town's new mayor who owned a rival saloon. When the mayor saw his business walking out the door headed toward the Long Branch and the angelic presence of Luke's beautiful blond singer, he acted in the capacity of his mayoral office. He declared that singing was promptly outlawed in all Dodge saloons. In all Dodge saloons but his own, that is.

When Luke raised a fuss, a series of arrests and fines ensued for him and his employees. In the end, Luke was forcibly taken to the railroad station and given one of two choices: to go either east or west.

Besides, the Mayor, Dodge City District Attorney, Sheriff, and other leading businessmen were all in cahoots in their efforts to keep the Long Branch shut down tight and Luke Short out of town. In the meantime, the mayor's establishment did a fine business with Luke's former customers, the Texas cattle drovers.

Wyatt agreed with Bat's plan to return to Kansas and help Luke. The next day Bat left on the train and, a day or so later, Wyatt and Josie boarded a train bound for Dodge City. But, before he left, Wyatt wrote a letter to the Denver Press divulging his residence as being in Silverton, Colorado, in an effort to dispel any fears anyone might have that he might be going to Dodge.[5]

May 31-Along the way, he gathered together a small militia of his gun fighting, cutthroat friends to help out in the effort. Once Luke's competition heard that Wyatt, Bat, and a small army of some of the worst killers in the West was about to descend down upon them, they sent an urgent appeal for help to the Governor of Kansas. There was even talk that the infamous man-killer, Doc Holliday, would be with them, as well.

Town officials feared for their very lives, begging the Governor to send in troops to protect them. Their pleas went unheeded, though, because the wily Bat had already told the governor about the state of affairs in Dodge.

The reason town officials were in such fear for their lives? One Dodge newspaper story described Wyatt as:

"Famous in the cheerful business of depopulating the country. He has killed within our personal knowledge six men, and he is popularly credited with relegating to the dust no less than ten of his fellow men." [6]

When the train carrying Wyatt and his heavily armed henchmen arrived at Dodge, the station was empty and they were unopposed. They split up and stationed themselves up and down Front Street. Then Wyatt coolly walked into a prearranged meeting with Short's competition. He was asked, "My God, Wyatt, who are these people you've got with you?" He responded, "Oh, they're just some bushwhackers I've brought over from Colorado to straighten you people out."

Arizona Historical Society, #11,816
Dodge City Peace Commission, Wyatt bottom
row, second from left

The *Evening Star* heralded the event:

"The entrance of the Short party in Dodge was peculiar. First Luke Short arrived. Getting off the train some little distance from the camp he slung a 6-shooter on each hip, and with a double barreled shot gun in his hands walked down the Main street to the Long Branch Saloon, carefully watching the corners. In a day or two Bat Masterson dropped in, armed in a similar manner, and joined Short. Then came Charley Bassett, who simply dropped a Winchester repeating rifle under his arm and walked up the middle of the street. Since then every train has brought fresh delegations, and there are now upwards of 40 or 50 men ready for call at the Long Branch."

But, as it turned out, Wyatt and his heavily armed fellows, who were just itchin' for a fight, never heard a cross word or saw an angry glance. As an afterthought, they learned that Luke was welcomed back into Dodge by a joyous mayor and town council. It seemed that Luke's one-time adversaries couldn't do enough to make him feel back at home. As the result of the peaceful resolution to the trouble in Dodge, Wyatt and the gunfighters he had with him became known as the Dodge Peace Commission. They were in and out of Dodge for ten days in the month of June.

June 23-After leaving Kansas, Wyatt and Josie traveled to Salt Lake City, Utah, where they spent the next several months. In the fall, they returned to Denver, where Wyatt continued to play poker and faro.

November 6-Then in early November, Wyatt, Josie, and Bat returned to Dodge, ostensibly to attend the city elections. Everyone knew the two famous gun-fighting lawmen were in town, so the elections were unusually trouble-free.

While Wyatt and Bat were in Dodge, they sensed that gambling, as they had known it, was fast coming to an end. Their friend Luke knew it too, and sold his interest in the Long Branch. (The Kansas State Legislature was stirring things up.)[7]

Courtesy of White Elephant Saloon, FW, TX
Reenactment of shoot-out between Luke Short and
(Longhair) Jim Courtright

November 16-Wyatt and Josie returned to Denver while Bat and Luke followed the gambling circuit south to Ft. Worth, Texas.[8]

December 28-Luke returned to Dodge City with another Dodge Peace Commission member, Chas. Bassett. Luke would remain in Dodge until after the holidays.[9]

1884

January 15-A few weeks later, Wyatt and Josie left Denver, also traveling to Fort Worth. But by the time they got there, Bat had already returned to Trinidad, Colorado where he was still the Marshal and maintained his own gambling parlor.[10]

Fort Worth served as railhead and passenger center for west Texas. The resulting livery stables and wagon yards occupied much of the town. This notorious-stockyard district was known as "Hells Half Acre," a twenty-four-hour- a-day den of iniquity kept by the underworld and popularized by gambling, fighting, prostitution, murder and crimes of all sorts.

After cattlemen sold their livestock at the stockyards, they proceeded down Exchange Avenue with cash in their pockets looking for entertainment. The crowded street offered saloons, restaurants, hotels, stores, gambling parlors and other forms of amusement   all willing to provide a good time and ready place for cowboys to spend their hard-earned cash.

A favorite stopping place was the up-scale White Elephant Saloon. The White Elephant had the reputation of being the finest in the city, claiming to be the best in Texas, perhaps even in the nation! To back up the claim, it boasted a menu that included fresh fish, oysters and game, and the choicest wines, liquors and cigars.

It was the scene of some of the richest games in town and a gathering place for high rollers like Wyatt and Luke Short. It showed its class all the way from its thickly carpeted floors and staircases to its cut glass chandeliers and forty-foot-long, solid mahogany bar. Its gambling parlors were on the second floor, and the restaurant and saloon on the first. The employees all wore white shirts and dressed formally.[11]

January 16-Wyatt, Luke, and two other men had been playing poker in one of the saloon's two upstairs gambling parlors for most of the night. When play ended in the early morning hours, and the two others had already gone downstairs, then Luke got up, stretched and, tapping his cane lightly against the leg of his chair said, "You know Wyatt...someday I'm going to buy this place...this is nice." Wyatt got up as well and, carrying his cup of coffee, walked with Luke down the stairway. The following year Luke would partner-up with fellow gambler Jake Johnson to buy the White Elephant. [12]

When they arrived at the first floor, Wyatt saw the two men who'd left the game earlier, standing at the bar talking with the barkeep. Luke turned to Wyatt and said, "I'm going on to bed Wyatt," and with that he pushed open the saloon's front door and disappeared into early morning darkness.

Wyatt decided to stay for awhile longer to finish his coffee, so he sat at a table near a front window. It had been a good night. During the game there were gold coins stacked six inches deep on the table and, when it was all over, he'd come out several thousand dollars to the better.

He sat alone, deep in thought, slowly turning the coffee cup with his fingers on the table's dark mahogany top. Memories from the past flooded into his mind. Thoughts of life with his brothers back on the farm in Pella, Iowa. Then to that bitter scene in October of 1881 at the O.K. Corral the sound of gunfire, bullets whizzing by, and Virgil and Morgan falling wounded into the dusty street. In his mind's eye, he could also see the bullet-riddled bodies of the three men whom they'd tried to disarm.

Wyatt's thoughts turned to that terrible night when Virgil was ambushed, and then to Hatch's saloon when Morgan was murdered. Hate swelled within him. He clinched his jaw and tightened his grip on the coffee cup, turning his knuckles white from the pressure. Poor Morgan, he didn't even have a chance. Wyatt still hated the bastards who'd murdered him, even though he and his posse had tracked them down, killing them all.

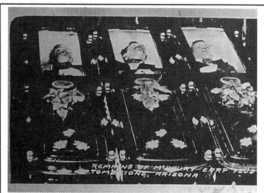

Craig Fouts, San Diego, CA.
Remains of Tom and Frank McLaury and Billie Clanton

Wyatt smiled remorselessly as he remembered the fear in Frank Stilwell's eyes, back on the tracks at the Tucson train station, when he jerked back on both of the shotgun's triggers, blowing Stilwell into the hereafter. Then his grip on the cup eased, as he thought of his beautiful Josephine and that first time he saw her in San Francisco, standing in the doorway of her parent's home. She was probably still asleep in their room, just up the street at the Mansion House Hotel.

Early morning sunlight beamed in through a window to his right, showing dust particles hanging motionlessly in the air. He gazed out at the buildings across the street, thinking of all the moves he and Josie had made in the past few months.

Then laughter erupted from the bar and he looked over that way. The barkeep held out a copy of the Fort *Worth Daily Gazette* and said, "There's gold in Idaho Territory, Wyatt. Says here, a man can get rich in a day." One of the men at the bar brought the paper over to him. Wyatt thanked him, and sat reading it.

A Northern Pacific gold circular stood out boldly on the page, touting the boundless discovery of gold in the Bitterroot Mountains, in the Coeur d'Alenes of north Idaho. It told of the camp town, Eagle City (Eagle), and how $100 a day to the man was being taken out of the rimrock and down in the gulches. Prospectors were panning out from $25 to $40 a day. Nuggets had been found weighing (valued at) as much as $50, $100, $166 and $200. (One ounce of gold was valued at $20 and this was all an absolute bonanza, considering a good day's work only brought in around $1.25.)

The article included with the circular went on to warn against coming into the rugged Bitterroots just yet, because of deep drifting snow, sub-zero temperatures and isolation.

As he read on, he thought of his brother, James, who lived in Missoula, Montana, not far from this new gold strike. James had been trying for years to get him to come up north. A sense of enlightenment came over Wyatt as he read. When he laid the newspaper down on the table, he knew that he and Josie would be going north to Idaho Territory.

Wyatt rose from his chair, thanking the barkeep, as he dropped a silver dollar on the table. The resounding clunk the coin made as it hit the mahogany tabletop could be heard across the room. Then he followed Luke's path, stepping out into cold air and early morning sunlight. Being careful not to slip on the icy boardwalk, he walked the short distance down Main Street to

> **Coeur d'Alene.**
>
> # $100
> # PER MAN
> ### PER DAY
> Are being taken out of the rim rock of the gulches, while
>
> IN THE GULCHES $25 to $40 PER MAN PER DAY ARE BEING PANNED OUT.
>
> These Placers are unequaled in Richness.
>
> They are located in the Gulches of the North Fork of the Coeur d'Alene River, and Eagle, Pritchard and Beaver Creeks, streams flowing into the Coeur d'Alene.
>
> The Pritchard is the chief stream, and it is said
> **DOES NOT FREEZE UP,**
> THE ALTITUDE BEING ONLY 2,400 FEET.
>
> #423-12N65, *Goldfields of the Coeur d'Alenes, University of Idaho*

the corner of Fourth, then into the elegant Mansion House Hotel. A few minutes later he was standing beside the bed in his and Josie's room. She woke up when he came in, and he handed the newspaper to her. As she read, he quipped softly, "How would you like to go up to Idaho and hunt for gold, Josie?" She didn't answer, but only continued to read. Then Wyatt saw a smile slowly come over her beautiful face. She loved the idea.

He started toward the door again, saying, "I'll go get the tickets and wire James telling him we're coming." Then he hesitated, "It's going to be a long trip, so we'll stop off in Trinidad and see Bat on the way through." With that, he closed their room's door behind himself, walking back out to the street again. Wyatt went to the Union Depot, bought their tickets and then sent the wire. His telegram told James when he and Josie would be arriving in Missoula, so James could meet them at the train station.

Josie loved staying at the seven-year-old, 95-room Mansion House. From the window of their room she could watch the street lamps being lit at night and, during the day, children chasing along behind the ice wagon, hoping to grab a piece of ice. Additionally, the Mansion House wasn't far from the White Elephant Saloon where Wyatt gambled.

They took their evening meals in the White Elephant's dining room. Then, after they'd finished eating, Wyatt would disappear upstairs into the gambling parlor for a long night of gambling, often not returning to the Mansion House until one or two in the morning. Josie was left to walk the short distance back to the Mansion House, down lamp-lit Main Street.[13]

Headin' North

January 17-At daybreak the next morning, Wyatt and Josie were at the Union Depot climbing aboard a Fort Worth and Denver City Railroad passenger car.[14] They were bound for Trinidad, which was 558 miles from Fort Worth. Because it was a 36-hour trip, Wyatt had reserved a berth for them on a sleeper car. They would ride in the passenger car during the day and in the sleeper car at night.

A few minutes later a conductor standing just outside their window looked down at his pocket watch and yelled loudly, "All aboard!" The glass window pane somewhat muffled the sound of his voice. Northbound traffic left the station at 7:00 a.m. and southbound at 7:45 p.m.[15]   Then came several shrill blasts from the engine's whistle and a belching cloud of hissing steam. The big driving pistons on the engine's wheels began to move, and the train chugged slowly away from the station. Soon they were picking up speed, passing beyond Fort Worth's city limits into the countryside beyond.

Josie was excited about the prospect of looking for gold in Idaho. She stared out through the window of their car as she talked. The terrain was flat, with occasional rolling hills covered with patches of snow, ice and the gray stubble of dead bunch grass.

Josie asked, "Will this be like Silverton, Wyatt?" He replied, "No, Eagle City is a new camp. There are only a few buildings there now. We'll be getting in on the ground floor."   The glare of the sun on the window made it uncomfortable for her, so he drew the shade.

Hours passed by and the train made many stops as it passed through small Texas and then New Mexico towns. It took on and let off passengers, replenished the supply of coal for the engine, and loaded more water for the engine's boiler. It had gotten dark, and the overhead lanterns were lit in the car. Wyatt and Josie were tired and walked back their sleeping compartment for the night.

January 18-The next morning came and went, and they finally arrived at Trinidad in darkness at 7:00 p.m.. Wyatt got a hotel room for them and, after Josie was settled in, he walked down the street to Bat's gambling parlor, knowing that Bat would be there at this time of night. Wyatt met fellow gambler Johnny Green there as well, and the three friends gambled well into the night.[16]

X-1893, Denver Public Library, Western History Department
Trinidad Saloon

January 19-The next morning Wyatt and Josie had breakfast in the hotel's eatery, sharing the excitement of this new adventure together. Wyatt sat drinking coffee, looking north through a window at the 13,000-foot high, snow capped, Spanish Peaks. It was cold in Trinidad, but there wasn't any snow on the ground. He thought back to the Fort Worth newspaper's warning about terrible winter conditions in the Bitterroot Mountains, and wondered how the weather really was in Montana and Idaho. After breakfast, they returned to the train station to climb aboard a Denver and Rio Grande passenger car. This would be the first of several railroad line changes they would make.

At 7:00 a.m. that morning their train pulled away from the Trinidad station, reaching Denver by 4:00 p.m. in the afternoon. Although it was still early in the day, according to their tickets and schedule of connections, it would be necessary for them to layover for a night in Denver.

January 20-At 1:00 p.m. the next afternoon, they left Denver on Union Pacific's northbound passenger train No. 201, bound for Cheyenne, Wyoming. As their car rolled along Josie looked out through the glass window. Off to the left, the massive Rocky Mountains stood out with all their breath-taking ramparts. She talked about how enormous they were and compared them with the mountains they'd seen around Silverton. Since Wyatt had taken her from San Francisco he'd been presenting her with a seemingly endless variety of new places to see and experience. It was dark at 5:40 p.m. when this leg of their journey ended as their train lurched to a stop in Cheyenne's train yard. Steam hissing from its boilers in idleness.

They had less than an hour to wait for their next connection, though, and Josie was glad of that. They climbed aboard Union Pacific's Passenger No. 1 and, at 6:20 p.m., it left Cheyenne headed west toward Laramie, Wyoming.

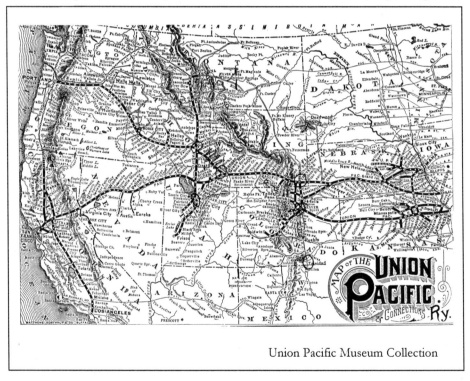

Union Pacific Museum Collection

Hours passed by as the old engine chugged faithfully along. Oil lanterns suspended from the car's ceiling cast a warm glow on the faces and forms of the

Union Pacific Museum Collection, R-1010
Interior of Union Pacific Railroad coach

many passengers. There was silence between them. Wyatt was deep in thought and Josie was just on the verge of falling asleep when he finally said, "You know Josie, when I first came west with the folks back in '64, we were coming right through here when we were attacked by Sioux Indians. One of the men in our train was killed and scalped." His thoughts trailed off. "Seems like it was a running fight for hundreds of miles after that. We were finally able to drive them off, though."

Silence again returned and who knows what her thoughts were as she drifted off into sleep. Perhaps in her dreams she saw the light of a roaring campfire and the distorted forms of evil, dancing red men.

January 21-At around 2:30 a.m. their car suddenly jolted to a stop at Rawlins, Wyoming Territory. That woke Josie up and, straightening herself up and wiping her mouth, she said, "Where are we now Wyatt?"

He'd been watching her sleep, not believing how much joy she brought into his sometimes-troubled heart. He replied smiling, "Rawlins. We'll be here for a few minutes." Then he hesitated, saying thoughtfully, "You know…Calamity Jane once got a divorce here. When the judge asked her, "On what grounds," she said, "For running away. I was after him with an axe." [17] Josie laughed heartily at that and they talked on, even after the train had left the lighted Rawlins station to continue down two ribbons of steel into the darkness.

A few hours later they both awoke to daylight. Much to Josie's surprise, the majestic Rocky Mountains had given way to a low rolling snow-covered prairie. To get an even better view out through the window, Josie wiped away a thin film of ice and moisture with the side of her hand. She was amazed to see hundreds of buffalo standing on a far-off hillside watching them pass by. Vapor from the beasts' great lungs enveloped them in mist, giving a surreal look to the scene.

#157, Haynes

Buffalo herd, near Ft. Yellowstone , Yellowstone Park

Although January temperatures range from thirteen degrees to a high of twenty two degrees, weather conditions can change hourly in response to Wyoming's sometimes-violent winds.

Many of the other passengers had also seen the buffalo, and their voices blended in with the clicking sounds from the car's wheels on the uneven rails beneath. As the train passed by the small herd, it was but a dark smear on the bleak-white Wyoming prairie. This small band of buffalo was but a scant representation of the millions that had been killed by hunters in the past. Wyatt just shook his head at their pitiful number.

At around 8:00 a.m. that morning, they crossed the Green River, passing through its namesake town of Green River, Wyoming. An hour or so later, at 9:25 a.m., the train stopped at Granger. (Green River was the site of the beginning of one-armed Civil War veteran John Wesley Powell's famous 1869 geological survey expedition.)

They changed trains once more at Granger Junction. In no time at all, they were back underway again, and hours later made a brief stop at Pocatello, Idaho. Here they passed by old Fort Hall, crossing over the ruts of the old Oregon Trail.

It had gotten dark, grown progressively colder, and the snow deepened the further north they got. Josie cuddled up against Wyatt for his warmth. Soon the clicking sounds from the wheels and gentle rocking motion of the car sent her off into a deep, untroubled sleep.

Wyatt didn't want to disturb her, so he just sat quietly looking out through their window. Bright moonlight painted a beautiful, snow-covered panorama before him. There were banks of soft-drifted snow and an occasional ice covered river, for an instant changing the sound the car's wheels made on the rails as it crossed over a bridge. Snow-draped pines stood as silent sentinels in the wintry scene.

Cold winds blowing over the car's roof and its movement on the uneven rails sent glittering ice crystals cascading past the window. A cheery, pot-bellied stove stood at each end of the car to keep out the winter chill and occasionally a good-natured conductor came in to stoke their fires with lumps of coal.

Wyatt dozed off from time to time, and even more hours slipped by. In the interim, he'd witnessed the softness of moonlight giving way to the shadowy gray of early morning. Then sunlight shone over the mountains to the east, bringing with it knowledge of the surrounding country. Huge mountains reared up at every side and no colors were to be seen save the brightness of snow.

January 22-It had been fully fourteen and one-half hours since they'd gone through Pocatello, when they arrived at Garrison Junction in Montana at 9:30 a.m. that morning.

Here they changed trains, for the last time, to the Northern Pacific Railroad. They left Garrison Junction at 11:40 a.m. bound for Missoula. Finally at 3:40 p.m., just as it was beginning to get dark again, their train slowed, rolled past a water tower, and came to a stop in front of the Missoula station. The Northern Pacific Railroad had first reached Missoula only the year before in 1883, and its new station was but one of seven buildings situated in a "round house" configuration.

Wyatt gathered up their bags, then he and Josie stepped down from the car into freezing mountain air, to walk the short distance into Missoula's one-room station house where they were met with the warmth of another pot-bellied stove.

Wyatt got the rest of their luggage from the baggage handler as Josie stood near the stove, rubbing her hands together for its warmth. Then she said over her shoulder, "Wyatt where is James...wasn't he supposed to meet us here?"

At that moment, the station's door opened again and in he walked. The train was just pulling away from the station on its way westward, and when the door opened the sounds it made trebled in volume. Wyatt looked up from what he was doing, just as James closed the door behind himself. A short, backslapping greeting between the two brothers ensued.

69-2, K Ross Toole Archives, University of Montana, Missoula
N. P. R. R. roundhouse at Missoula, Montana, 1883

James took them in his buckboard to his house. He and Bessie had come from Colton, California to Missoula in 1882, not long after Morgan was murdered in Tombstone. Wyatt and Josie were careful not to mention their daughter, Hattie, knowing how heart-broken they both still were about her running away from home back in Tombstone. James and Bessie were never to see their daughter again.

That night Wyatt left Josie with Bessie and he and James went into a Missoula saloon where they spent the night playing cards. Wyatt's reputation had preceded him, and everyone he met held him in the highest regard. Everyone, that is, except ex-lawman and roustabout, Bill Houston.

In an article written some years later by columnist Will Cave and published in the **Missoulian Sunday News**, Houston claimed that Wyatt had an altercation with another gambler over cards that night. This is supposedly when "hero" Houston came upon the scene and he and Missoula Marshal E.A. Kenney pistol-whipped Wyatt into submission. Wyatt was promptly thrown into jail where he remained for the next day or so. Then, as the story continues on even further in its sordid detail, Houston, not the marshal, advised Wyatt to leave town, which he supposedly promptly did.

It's interesting to note here that Wyatt had at least four thousands dollars on him at the time, so even if Houston's story were true, he could easily have bailed himself out of jail. Another reason to doubt this tale is that after the people of Missoula "found out" Houston had actually manhandled the famous gunman Wyatt Earp, he was elected to the office of town sheriff.

Taken from the **Spokane Falls Review**, September 1, 1883:

"Last Saturday afternoon a young fellow from the country, who possessed a number of outward characteristics of a cowboy, rode into the city and partook freely of that mixture, commonly called whiskey, and

started out for a trip to the north side of the river. Over the bridge he flew, shooting off his pistol as he went, and adding to the fun by a few yelps that would have done credit to a full blood Indian. Now, one of the laws in vogue expressly states that anyone who drives over public bridges faster than a walk is subject to a fine of $5. And so particular are the authorities to give notice to that effect, that the bridges are decorated with conspicuous signboards to this effect.

"Our officers are generally on the alert for parties who defy the painted law and show their indifference to it by shooting over the bridges with a full head of steam on. Jeopardizing the structures by giving them a terrible shaking up. Once they get their official claws upon such people it is settled in advance that they have to pay the fiddler.

"In this case Marshall Hyde saw the performance, but as the apparent" bad man" was well mounted and a considerable distance off, he was not able to gather him in. Along later in the afternoon the Marshal smiled broadly when he saw the man riding leisurely up Howard Street. He wore the rough raiment of the typical cowboy, with slouch hat and indispensable gun. Appearance would indicate that there would be some trouble attached to the arrest, and the Marshal secured the aid of Deputy-Sheriff Gilliam. The two followed the roisterer, who was peaceful enough by this time, and jailed him.

"He'd treated their request to halt with the utmost contempt, and made no effort to quicken the horse's pace beyond a walk. The officers caught up with the bad man and as Hyde seized the horse, Gilliam grabbed the revolver and yanked the fellow to the ground. By this time he awoke to realize that no one was frightened of him and, not liking the change of affairs, pleaded for mercy. Backing his supplication with copious tears.

70-107, K. Ross Toole Archives, Univ. Mont., Missoula
Bridge near Missoula, Montana...bridge construction was much the same throughout the west

"He declared he had no money, and promised never to do so again. The Marshal took pity on him and when the objects and prisoner appeared before Judge Whitman, Hyde interceded, stating the poverty of the man and his promise to sin no more.

5

Stampede to Idaho Territory

January 24-at 3:45 p.m., Wyatt, Josie, and Jim boarded the northern pacific bound for Rathdrum, Idaho. A few minutes later several shrill blasts came from the locomotive's whistle and the train chugged away from the station. Jim's wife, Bessie, hadn't been in the best of health, so she and Jim decided it best that she not go with them. Jim would send for her when he could.

Jim had been following developments in the Coeur d'Alene gold fields for weeks since Missoula's newspaper, The *Missoulian*, first reported the great discovery. He'd even thought seriously about going himself, but hadn't wanted to leave Bessie's side. At her insistence, though, he did agree to go with Wyatt and Josie to the Coeur d'Alenes. (Three years later, in 1887, Bessie would pass away from an extended illness.)

Jim occupied the seat opposite Josie and Wyatt in a nearly full passenger car. As the train pulled away from the Missoula station, there was excitement in the air. They were headed northward through rolling, snow-covered hills toward bright, shiny gold!

Wyatt told Jim about the newspaper article and gold circular he'd seen in Fort Worth, and was surprised when Josie dug it out of her bag and handed it to him. Jim read it, nodding his head from time to time. Then he laid the paper in his lap, saying, "The reason the Northern Pacific put out these gold circulars in the first place is because of the terrible expense of building the railroad through all these mountains. They're trying to drum up business."[1]

Then he went on to tell them of similar newspaper accounts he'd been reading in the *Missoulian* about the camp "The easiest way to get there is by train to Rathdrum, Idaho and stagecoach to Coeur d'Alene City. Then take a steamboat across Lake Coeur d'Alene to the Old Catholic Mission at Cataldo. Folks spend the night at the Mission and, the next day, rent saddle horses to ride east along the south fork of the Coeur d'Alene River to the Evolution feeding station. From there they ride over the Evolution Trail to Eagle City."

The man sitting with his back to Jim turned around and said, "Pardon me, but I couldn't help overhearing...are you folks going to Eagle City, too? My partners here (he gestured to the two men sitting across from him) and I are going over the Trout Creek trail, we've heard that is the easiest way."

Jim laughed and said, "Oh, yeah some folks will tell you that, but not the prospectors who've taken that route. There are quite a few trails from the railroad over the Bitterroots and according to those who live at each trailhead, theirs is the only way into the gold fields."

Then Jim went on to say, in a sense of enlightened remembrance, "In fact the *Missoulian* just reported yesterday that there is from 20 to 25 feet of snow on the Bitterroots and that both the Trout Creek and Heron Trails are closed. On the other hand, the Evolution Trail over in Idaho isn't nearly as high as the Bitterroots, so there isn't as much snow and folks are riding over it on horses. The only way to get over the Bitterroots, if you even can, is on snowshoes, dragging your provisions behind you on a toboggan."

Jim looked down at the newspaper in his lap and said, "I just saw here." He paused, and then continued, "Oh, here it is. It's even in this Texas paper; listen to this." He began to read:

"The boomers of the so-called Trout Creek trail have succeeded in deluding quite a number into trying this wonderful route to the Coeur d'Alene gold fields. Yet in every instance the poor wretches who have followed this snow trail have returned after a fruitless wandering of several days, cursing the parties who have heaped misfortunes upon them. No sane man will deny that in winter it is somewhat difficult to find your way through a remarkably rough, uninhabited region. With from fifteen to twenty feet of snow, and the whole country covered with a dense forest of timber from seven to twelve feet in diameter and 150 feet high. In fact a region where, when a man once looses his bearings, he will, in all probability, be lost forever. Yet in the face of all the statements of those who have tried and failed to reach the mines via Trout Creek, these human ghouls still claim that their snow trail is not only open but being traveled daily." Jim looked up from the paper with a sadistic smile and said, "It goes on, but you probably get the idea."[2]

Then Jim chuckled and said, "On up ahead, we'll come to Thompson Falls. Well, the train didn't use to stop there…it stopped a few miles on further north at Belknap. So the industrious folks in Thompson Falls threw logs on the tracks. The train had to stop and, while train crews were out clearing the right-of-way, folks from Thompson Falls ran around inside the cars urging the passengers to get off and look the place over. Their efforts must have paid off, because right now there are over a thousand men camped out in tents and shacks at the base of the mountain at Thompson Falls. They're waiting for the weather to clear so they can go up the Trout Creek Trail over the summit (elevation of 6,500 feet) to the gold camp. If they hadn't done that trick with the logs, chances are those men would be camped out at Belknap, instead."

The strangers laughed at Jim's story, thanking him for the information. They decided right then and there to take the Evolution Trail, as well. Then they all laughed at the chance of beating those thousand men, who were faithfully camping out in the cold in Thompson Falls, to the gold field.

H-2050, Haynes Foundation coll., Montana Historical Soc
Thompson Falls, M. T., 1889

The first man introduced himself as J. E. Jack Enright and his partners as Daniel Ferguson and Alfred Holman. In turn, Jim introduced himself, Wyatt, and Josie. When Enright heard with whom he had been talking, he was impressed. The Earp's reputation had spread far and wide, even into these remote reaches of the northwest.

Enright and his two partners had been in Hailey, in the Wood River district of south central Idaho, but came north for this new prospect. The five men would become friends and business associates in the coming months.

It was another bright moonlit night and just then Josie pointed out through the window, asking, "Aren't those the Bitterroots?" An enormous range of mountains loomed ominously to the left (southwest) of the train. After a moment of silent contemplation, Enright said slowly and deliberately, "Whew...I can see what you mean about the snow Jim."

Jim went on to tell them that, according to the *Missoulian* newspaper, mining supplies were best bought from Sam Hayes' Mercantile store in Eagle City. "No sense packing all that-gear up over the mountains if we don't have to, right?" They agreed most heartily.

As the evening wore on, their conversation trailed off and they fell asleep one by one. Meanwhile, the train had passed Thompson Falls, traveling northwest up through the Bitterroot valley, then crossing over into Idaho near Clark Fork, the site of the failure of a glacial dam that created the largest flood in recorded world history. A wall of water nearly half a mile high roared through the Clark Fork canyon, fed by 600 cubic miles of glacial lake water. Had they been awake, they might even have seen the deep scrape marks, on the high cliffs-overlooking the Clark Fork canyon, that were left by passing glaciers.

In their slumber, they passed by Sandpoint, named "Point in the Sand" by famous 1809 explorer, David Thompson. (Thompson Falls, Montana was named for another man with the same last name who lost his life in going over "Thompson" Falls.) In the darkness, their Northern Pacific train's engine pulled them past massive Lake Pend Oreille. The 1,300 foot deep lake is one of the largest fresh water lakes in the world. It was carved out of solid rock by a huge, southward flowing glacier.

January   25-The weary travelers had been sleeping much of the way, but fully awoke to the gray of an early dawn, as their train slowed and came to a stop at the Rathdrum station in Idaho. This marked the end of a very long journey for Wyatt and Josie, but one they had both enjoyed together.

Along with the other passengers, Wyatt, Josie, and Jim

Cheney Cowles Museum/Eastern Washington Historical, Soc., Spokane, Washington, #298-46.1, from N.P.R.R.
Early 1880s N.P.R.R. train

stepped down from the train onto the station's boardwalk. Almost immediately, Jim said, "This is warm, Wyatt. It's a lot warmer here than it was back in Missoula." (January 23rd was the coldest day of the season in Missoula.) Enright and his two friends had joined them on the boardwalk and would accompany them all the way to Eagle City.

After they walked into the train depot to collect their luggage, Wyatt asked the ticket agent how folks were getting to Coeur d'Alene City. The small man behind the counter busily, and almost musically, retorted, "The stage leaves for Coeur d'Alene in about half an hour and costs a buck and a half a head." He then waved his hand, in an impatient gesture, for Wyatt to move aside, saying, "Next please?"

Wyatt hurriedly bought tickets for his party of six from him, stepping aside almost apologetically. Those behind pushed their way forward to the counter. He could see the desperation in these men's eyes and could almost see the lust for gold in their hearts, as well. He mused, "It's the same in all gold camps. The lust for gold is overpowering. So powerful, that it will lure many of these men to their deaths."

H-1917, Haynes Foundation coll., Montana Historical Society
Rathdrum, Idaho, depot, March, 1888

Then he began to get the seeds of an idea. He thought back to when he and Morgan had searched for gold in Deadwood and how hard it was to find. "Maybe it would be better to start a saloon in Eagle and let the prospectors bring the gold to us."

Enright, Ferguson, Holman and Jim paid Wyatt for their tickets and they all walked outside the station house into an even larger field of activity. Even though it was still only 8:00 a.m. in the morning, there were men and horses everywhere. Wagons being loaded with supplies, multitudes of people walking up and down the streets and storefronts pasted with signs of mining supplies. All directed toward the hoard of gold seekers who passed daily through Rathdrum, headed for the gold field. The background was noisy with incessant hammering on new buildings going up all over town.

The wide-awake settlement contained some twenty finished buildings with as many more in all stages of construction. The hotels were crowded: three beds in a room, two in a bed, and the floors covered with sleepers. Four saloons were in full blast as was one Hurdy Gurdy dance hall where four young women and a band of music entertained twenty-five to thirty men.

H-1815, Haynes Foundation coll., Montana Historical Soc.
Street scene, Rathdrum, Idaho, April, 1887

Sure enough, thirty minutes later, U.S. mail contractor McCoy's stage, heavily laden with passengers from the train, left the Rathdrum, Coeur d'Alene Stage Company's station headed south toward Coeur d'Alene City. There were six passengers inside the coach; four more sat on its roof. Josephine sat beside Wyatt, and was the only woman on board.

To urge his powerful team of four horses on, McCoy shouted loudly, "Giddy up there," snapping the reigns across their backsides. As the stage bumped and rolled along the muddy road, Wyatt gazed off to the east at a range of snow-covered mountains. He knew they weren't the mountains they would have to cross at Evolution, but wondered how it would be to cross them all the same.

They traveled across seven miles of level prairie before the stage dropped down through a narrow draw where the road entered a forest of pines. Wyatt heard McCoy shout, "Whoa," slowing his team down, and then, rhythmically, "Haw...Giddy up there." He urged his team on, turning them to the east onto the old Mullan military road. They were paralleling the Spokane River. A few minutes later the stage stopped briefly at the Huetter stage stop to pick up and leave mail.

A few miles further on, Wyatt began to see scattered buildings here and there as the stage entered Coeur d'Alene City just after 10:00 a.m. in the morning. The trip from Rathdrum had taken an hour and a half. They were welcomed by the incessant, far-off sounds of still more hammering. Coeur d'Alene City was also a booming place.

The stage came to a stop in front of the Dividend Saloon on Sherman Street. It was so named in honor of famed Civil War General William Tecumseh Sherman, who'd originally set up the town's mainstay-Fort Coeur d'Alene. To his credit, the fort was later renamed Fort Sherman, as well.

In the summer of 1877, some seven years earlier, the general toured the Coeur d'Alene area, reporting back to the Secretary of War that a greater military presence should be created in the inland northwest. On April 16, 1878, an order from the U.S. Department of the Clearwater officially established Camp Coeur d'Alene on 999 acres of land on the north shore of Lake Coeur d'Alene, at the head of the Spokane River. The small camp was later upgraded to Fort Coeur d'Alene with a complement of three companies of infantry troops (250 enlisted and 15 officers), a school, church, hospital and other out-buildings.

Coeur d'Alene Mines and Gold Fields, 1884

News of Andrew Prichard's discovery of gold in September of 1882 had given seed to this embryo town of Coeur d'Alene City, which, heretofore, had been, essentially, only a virgin forest of pines that stood silently on the banks of a beautiful mountain lake.

When Wyatt stepped down from the stage he glanced up into the sky, noting that it was overcast. It looked like it might even snow. Then he helped Josie down as well. The sign in the front window of the Dividend Saloon read, "Miner's Headquarters on their way to the Gold Camp." Further down it read, "Stages from Spokane Falls, W. T., and Rathdrum stop at our door and we are in easy access to both steamboat landings." That was what Wyatt had been looking for. He wanted to find out more about Eagle City, so he climbed the steps and walked across the boardwalk into the Dividend. Everyone who'd gotten off the stage followed him.

The Dividend Saloon

Museum North Idaho, Coeur d'Alene-CdA 9-3
Coeur d'Alene, circa. 1893 showing Dividend Saloon

The inside was nice. A standup bar graced the wall to Wyatt's right in a spacious twenty-by-fifty-foot room. And there was a glowing-hot, sheet-iron stove against the wall to his left. Two obviously well-used billiard tables occupied its center and, as the sign on the front window had promised, there were large chunks of gold bearing quartz on display in a glass case on the bar. The glimmer of small flecks of pure gold attracted the eye.

John Brown, the saloon's proprietor, stood behind the bar with a towel in his hands. Two glassy-eyed soldiers and several other men stood at the bar eyeing this crowd of newcomers as they came in. In no time at all, the bar was elbow to elbow, conversations were at full flow, and everyone had a drink in his hand. Between orders for more drinks, John busily wiped the bar with his towel.

Wyatt walked up to the bar, to ask him when the next steamboat was going to leave for Eagle City. Meanwhile Josie and Jim had walked on through the saloon back to the Dividend's chop-house (eatery) in the rear of the building.

The crowd grew silent, as they waited for the answer to Wyatt's question. Then John replied, "You just missed it. The steamer, *Amelia Wheaton,* leaves here at around six in the morning. She has to leave early to make it all the way up the Coeur d'Alene River to the Old Mission and back out into the lake again before dark. There isn't as much chance of hitting snags or running up on sandbars in the river that way.

"You'll probably have to spend the night here in town. You folks are lucky to get here when you have, because if it stays as cold as it's been, the lake looks like its going to freeze over and then the steamers can't run. The soldiers who work on the Wheaton come in here and they say the ice is getting bad up the river and along the lakeshore. The *General Sherman* is the other steamer on the lake, but the ice is so bad now that her owners have docked her until the weather warms up."

Then he paused and went on to say, "There's a good hotel just up the street —the Hotel de Landing. They sell tickets for the steamboat next door at Webster's Trading House, too." With that, the crowd of men at the bar sensed adventure, resuming their excited chatter with even more vigor. As Wyatt walked away, John jokingly continued, in a raised tone of voice, "Old Charlie Webster will even sell you a lot or a mine in Eagle City, if you want. He's a realtor too."

Wyatt heard laughter and then a dull thud behind him, so he stopped and turned back toward the bar. There was riotous laughter then, and he saw that one of the young soldiers had fallen to the floor. Several of the men helped him to his feet again and he and his partner staggered out the door and down the street toward the fort. Meanwhile, Wyatt had joined Josie and Jim in the chophouse to sit down to the breakfast that she'd ordered for him.

Wiping the bar where the soldiers had been, John just shook his head. "Some of the soldiers who come in here are real sots. Once in a while, I even find them sleeping in the trees out back. Colonel Wheaton is the fort's commander, and he gets real mad at these poor guys if he finds out about it. So I just let it slide. One reason he gets so mad is a while back one of them was found stabbed to death between here and the fort. That guy had other problems than drinking, though. He used to come in here all the time and he'd turn mean after only a few drinks."

Then he continued, "The steamboat you'll be taking is the *Amelia Wheaton.* She was named after the colonel's daughter. The army thought it needed a boat to patrol the country south of the lake, in case there was any Indian trouble, but there hasn't been any. And...oh, when you get to the Old Mission, Sam Hayes will meet you there. He runs a string of horses from Evolution to Eagle City."

(The following year, in 1885, a 345,000-acre reservation was established for the Coeur d'Alene tribe. Then, in 1906, their so-called "tribal lands" would be cut still further, to a sixth of that, down to 58,000 acres by the grand sounding "Homestead Act." This left the Coeur d'Alene Tribe with a mere pittance of their original 4,000,000 acres. To this day the courts are still battling with them in an effort to gain even more of their nation's lands.)

Cheney Cowles Museum/Eastern Washington State Historical Soc., Spokane, WN, #L88-520

Spokane Falls, W.T., 1884

There was a commotion outside, then the Dividend's front door opened as another group of people came in. They'd just gotten off one of Nelson Martin's Stagecoaches from Spokane Falls. The Martin stage left the Stage office on Main Street, in Spokane Falls, at 6:00 a.m. Monday, Wednesday and Friday for the run to Coeur d'Alene City.[3]

The crowd at the bar doubled in size. Just then Mike Martin, proprietor of the Dividend's eatery who'd served the Earps breakfast, came in through the back door with a load of wood in his arms. He stoked the fire in the saloon's stove.

After they'd finished eating, the Earps walked back outside into a beautiful, and warming day. The morning sun had burned away the fog, leaving a clear, blue sky. As they'd passed by the bar, Ferguson told them that he, Enright and Holman would see them in the morning at the steamboat landing.

Wyatt again heard the sounds of hammering and saw groups of men all up and down Sherman Street toiling over different projects. The rush to the new gold camp had given work to sixty Coeur d'Alene men, who were busy building steamers and houses, regardless of the weather.

Another man had stepped out from the saloon with the Earps and said, "You think this is bad...you otta see 'er down in Portland, Oregon. They are crazy with gold fever down there. A lot of the saloon owners, shopkeeps, and bootblacks are going to close up shop and head up here this spring. It's going to get even crazier around here then."

For the next several hours Wyatt, Josie and Jim walked around Coeur d'Alene City looking things over or escaping from the cold by going inside a nearby business once in a while. Josie was impressed by the sense of urgency. Everybody seemed to be in a hurry.

They'd walked past "Fatty" Carroll's Dance hall, which harbored forty dizzy damsels and women of the underworld. There were fifteen to twenty saloons in town. Many tents and shanties were scattered out through the trees, and several large buildings had already been built, including the Hotel de Landing, which was managed by Henry Stone, and Charles Webster's Trading House.

Webster's choice of locations for his new building was a wise one, in that it was near the waterfront, which was destined to become the point of departure for the Coeur d'Alene Steam and Navigation Company's future steamers. (The company was incorporated in 1885, and operated until 1889.) The company had secured the only deep-water landing on the north side of the lake from Mr. Tubbs. Company officials planned for

Coeur d'Alene Mines and Gold Fields, 1884

their steamers to carry freight and passengers from Coeur d'Alene City to within a few miles of the mines at far off-Eagle City.

Historic Wallace Preservation Society, Inc., SG-0397
Coeur d'Alene, Idaho Territory, between 3rd and 4th Avenues on Sherman, 1889

Mr. Tubbs had laid out the city on the shore of the lake, about a mile from the fort. It was generally accepted that his wise choice of locations had given Coeur d'Alene a glowing future. The city would have a permanent source of support, independent of the gold mines, as being the commencement of navigation through a country of extensive lumber resources. Additionally its central, convenient and beautiful location was bound to attract scores of tourist and sportsman to the region. Coeur d'Alene would gain the legal status of a town in 1887, after the majority of male inhabitants petitioned the Kootenai County Commissioners.

The Earps walked past Webster's building and dow5n to the waterfront where they saw many men working on a new steamboat. One of them looked up and saw the Earps standing on the dock. Sensing their questions about the new boat, he yelled out, "It's the Coeur d'Alene...we'll be launching her in about a month." The enormous steamer/ore hauler, *Coeur d'Alene* would be launched on April 9th and, on her maiden voyage, take the whole town with her on a round trip to the Cataldo Mission. She was piloted by Irvin Sanburn, formerly of Portland, Oregon, and Henry Pape of East Portland was her engineer.

It was good that the *Wheaton* didn't leave until the next morning, because the Earps were dog-tired from all of the traveling they had been doing. They walked into the Hotel de Landing where they were met by its courteous proprietor, Henry Stone.[4] Josie went straight to sleep, but Wyatt and Jim spent some time that night checking out the Coeur d'Alene saloons.

January 26-Very early the next morning Wyatt, Josie and Jim ate breakfast at Webster's trading house. They paid for their meal and bought tickets for passage on the *Amelia Wheaton* at the same time. Charlie Webster said, "If it keeps on as cold as it's been, the lake will freeze over, sure. You folks are lucky to be leaving now. Way it looks...if it doesn't warm up, the Wheaton won't be running more'n a few days."

The Earps left Webster's to walk the short distance down the dock to where the steamer was moored and then climbed aboard. Enright, Ferguson, and Holman came onto the steamer a few minutes later, and they all sat inside the boat's passenger cabin looking out through the many glass paned windows.

The army had given permission for immigrants going to the gold camp to use the *Wheaton* to reach "head of navigation," on the Coeur d'Alene River. This docking point up-river, or "head of navigation," varied throughout the year. In the dead of winter and dry summer months, it was at the Old Mission. In the spring and fall, during high water, it was several miles further up-stream at the small village of Kingston.

Captain Sorenson, the boat's builder, was also its skipper, and there was a crew of four soldiers working with him to service the boiler and run the military boat. Many others, fifty in all, had followed the Earps on board and finally, at 6:00 a. m. in the morning, the *Wheaton* prepared to leave the dock. Josie suddenly screamed with fear at the shrill blast of the steamer's whistle mounted on the rear of the wheelhouse just above their heads.

With Captain Sorenson at the helm, the boat's steam engine groaned and hissed and the large paddle wheel churned the water into white foam. The mooring lines had already been cast off by the soldiers, and soon the *Amelia Wheaton* was underway. It pulled away from the dock to the laughter of Wyatt and others at Josie's fear. By then, the good natured Josie was laughing, as well.

Only the bow of the boat stirred the placid water ahead. The morning sky was again overcast, and a layer of fog-like mist hung at the water's surface, pulled up from deep water by the freezing cold air above. Initially there was silence among the passengers as everyone was absorbed in this new experience, a silence broken only by the heavy mechanical, hissing sounds of the steam engine, the churning of the large paddle wheel and the slapping sound the water made as it hit against the boat's hull.

Then Jim turned to Enright, smiled, and said, "This sure beats climbing over a mountain pulling a sled, doesn't it Jack?" Enright replied enthusiastically, "You've got that right." That broke the silence, and from then on they all shared the experience together.

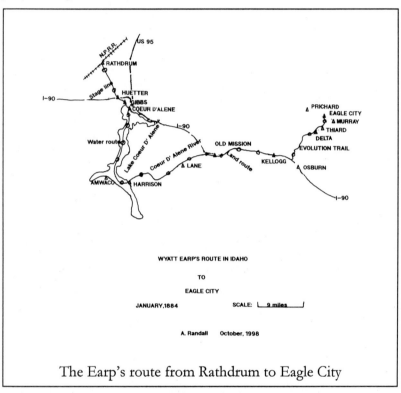

The Earp's route from Rathdrum to Eagle City

It didn't seem long at all before the sun came up. The trees on the surrounding hillsides bowed down from the weight of their burden of snow. An eagle or osprey soared high above, searching for its morning fare.

All fifty passengers aboard were on their way to Eagle City. Several of them had been sitting near the Earps on the train back in Montana and had overheard Jim telling Enright about the benefits of taking the Evolution Trail. Unbeknownst to him, they had also taken his advice.

Some hours later, after the steamer had traveled to the southern-most part of its run on the lake, it suddenly pulled into shore. Its paddle wheel stopped rotating and the big steam engine only hissed in its idleness. Wyatt walked outside to see soldiers up front breaking up the ice with long poles so the *Wheaton* could get close enough to shore to let down her gangplank. He nodded in silent testimony, "The ice is getting bad." Then he asked one of the soldiers, "Why did we stop here? Is anything wrong?" "Oh no," he said. "We have to stop for wood. We'll be here for about half an hour."

The soldier could see the questioning looks he was getting from Wyatt and several of the other passengers standing behind him, so he continued with his explanation. "You see, we're about half way to the Old Mission now. We pay the Indians $2.50 a cord for wood cut to boiler length, and they leave it here at this landing. Then, on the way to the Mission, we stop and load the rest of the wood that was split from the day before, and leave off a man to split up more wood while we're gone. On the way back from the Mission, we'll pick him up and load what wood we'll need of what he's split, and go on back to Coeur d'Alene City. Works out real fine." He hurried off to his chores.

Museum North Idaho, Coeur d'Alene, Trw-4-4
Amelia Wheaton leaving Cataldo Mission

There were still confused looks on some of the passenger's faces, but Wyatt chuckled to himself as he concluded that those folks probably always looked like that. It was fully sixty miles from Coeur d'Alene City to the Catholic Mission via the lake and the Coeur d'Alene River. Even with time spent loading wood, the Wheaton arrived by 1 p.m. in the early afternoon. It had taken seven hours for the trip. Again, the paddle wheel stopped its rotation and the boat drifted to shore. Wyatt's party and many of the other passengers had gotten to their feet and were about to walk outside through the cabin door, but, they held back for a moment, as several of the soldiers hurried by on their way toward the rear of the boat to tie her off. Someone had already broken up the thickening river ice near the landing. The boat's gangway plank was slid out to shore, and the passengers got off.

The Wheaton was an 85 foot long sternwheeler. The first steamboat on the lake, designed and built by Captain C. P. Sorenson in 1880. It was built by the army to provide access to remote areas around the lake in case of Indian troubles. However, it was never needed for that purpose. Its main use was in transporting wild hay, cut on the meadows of the Coeur d'Alene River, to the fort as forage for the army's Calvary horses. After the boat was completed, the army retained Captain Sorenson as its skipper. While so employed, he charted the lake, giving most of its bays, points, and other landmarks the names they still have. Until other boats were completed, the army allowed prospectors to use the Wheaton to reach the new gold field at Eagle City.

Once again on solid ground, they hauled their baggage mightily and made their way up an icy trail toward the massive white Mission building. Wyatt looked back down toward the river to see the steamer pulling away from shore, beginning its long trip back to Coeur d'Alene City. He noticed, too, that the paddlewheel and back of the boat was heavily encrusted with ice and saw all four of the soldiers hard at work chipping away at it. On the way up the river, the soldiers kept the Wheaton's boiler fed with wood. Wyatt smiled wryly at their job, then turned back up the trail again.

Soon they'd gained the high ground and were standing in a group in front of the Mission building. A blast of bitterly cold winter air chilled Josie and she drew her coat's collar up tighter around her neck, stamping her feet. Wyatt heard her say, "Brrrrr." Vapor from the heat of their breath was plainly visible. He put his arm around her, rubbing her back and shoulder to warm her.

Several larger buildings stood nearby, and there were many tents as well. From each chimney, smoke rose lazily up into the cloudy, darkening sky. Wyatt heard the bawling of cattle and the snorts and movement of ever-restless horses within a large corral. He looked over that way just as several men stepped out of the Mission. One was a white man and the other an Indian.

The white man said loudly, "My name is Sam Hayes and I run a string of saddle horses from Evolution to Eagle City. It's twenty five miles from here to Evolution and about twenty four miles from there on over the Evolution Trail to Eagle. In the morning, we'll be leaving here in wagons for Evolution, but we'll have to leave at first light in order to make it there by dark. We'll spend tomorrow night at Evolution and go on over the trail to Eagle City the next day. There are thirty saddle horses at Evolution that we can use for the trip to Eagle. If you want the ride, the cost is six bucks a head for the whole trip. If you're hungry, meals here are fifty cents." He pointed with an outstretched finger, continuing, "You can bed down in one of those tents over there for free."

The crowd of eager gold seekers surged forward, money changed hands, and soon the frozen yard where they'd stood was empty. All of the immigrants had vanished into the tents to escape the intense cold."

Later that night Wyatt and his party ate a meal of rainbow trout, beans and drank hot coffee. It was delicious; freshly caught rainbow trout would be one of the main staples of their diet in the coming months.

Couldn't resist...neat old wagon

January 27-At daylight the next morning, just as Sam Hayes had promised, five wagons-filled with excited gold seekers left the Mission headed for Evolution. Not far from the Mission, the wagons crossed the Coeur d'Alene River on a large ferry, and continued on.

Twenty of the steamer's passengers had elected not to take Hayes up on his offer and most had left the Mission earlier that morning. They were without the means to pay for it and would be making the long dreary trip to Eagle City on foot. The line of wagons passed many walking men and women, dressed as men, along the trail. The walkers were all heavily laden with packs; some pulled hastily built sleds behind them.

Seven miles further on the small wagon train came to a clearing and Tom Irwin's cabin. Locals had affectionately dubbed the cabin "Hunter's Hall," or "miner's cabin," in regard for Irwin's remarkable hunting skills. Thirteen splendid hides were draped on tree branches and bushes around the cabin. They crossed the river twelve times between the Mission and Evolution. It was frozen over and shallow enough so that even when a horse or wagon fell through the ice, it wasn't a problem. It began to snow lightly around dark and shortly thereafter they arrived at Evolution. The settlement was, perhaps, better known as the "Evolution feeding station." It was nothing more than a saloon that herded a large corral and a score of tents. The station stood in a long narrow canyon, flanked on either side by towering snow-covered mountains.

After the immigrants had all gotten down from the wagons, Hayes addressed the crowd once more, "Folks, I know you must be tired. We have a place where you can spend the night," gesturing toward several large tents. "We'll leave for Eagle City at daybreak. It's going to be another long day, the weather is bad on top of the mountains, so I suggest you get some sleep. You're going to need it."

By the time he'd finished talking, Josie was pulling Wyatt toward the tent he'd identified as "a place where you can spend the night." She was exhausted. Wyatt insisted that she eat something first, though, before going to sleep. They went into the cook tent and she ate a scrumptious meal of trout, biscuits and gravy and then disappeared into a sleeping tent for the night.

Wyatt sat with her as she ate, but only had coffee. Then he joined Jim and the other men in the saloon where they played cards and visited for several hours before also retiring for the night.

It turned out that the owner of the string of horses, Sam Hayes, was a businessman from Rathdrum who also had business interests in Eagle City. In fact, he and a man named Bob Horn had originally laid out Eagle City. However, incoming miners from the Black Hills of South Dakota didn't take to the name of Hayes City and promptly changed it to Eagle City in favor of an eagle's nest in a tree on site that local Indians claimed had been there for over forty years.[5]

With the absence of sunlight, the temperature plummeted and the night sky was again filled with millions of brilliant stars. All was quiet in the camp, save for the snorting and pawing of hooves of dozens of restless horses in the corral. Light from the full moon gave a peaceful, almost florescent glow to the surrounding mountains.

January 28-It seemed to Josie that she'd no sooner laid down when, very early the next morning, Wyatt was nudging her to get back up again. It was pitch black in the tent and a new day had begun...one that she wouldn't soon forget. Even though she and everyone else slept in their clothes, the darkness still afforded her some privacy. After she'd gotten herself up and around, Wyatt struck a match to a lantern before hanging it on back on the nail on the tent pole. Josie then saw that the floor of the large tent was strewn with sleeping immigrants. She was alone in the tent the night before, when she'd fallen asleep. Flickering light from the lantern danced eerily across the blanketed bodies on the floor. By then, some of the sleepers had heard Wyatt and were getting up as well. A sheet iron stove standing at the end of the tent had given off blessed, warming heat throughout the night. Josie and Wyatt rolled up their blankets and packed them away. By then Jim, Enright, Ferguson and Holman were ready as well, and they all walked outside into the freshness of a new, bitterly cold, day.

It was a minus fifteen degrees, the coldest day of the season thus far, but Josie was prepared for the cold this time; she was wearing nearly everything she owned. The sun was just beginning to lighten the eastern sky and the star-lit sky had again been replaced by a gray dawn.

Through the early morning darkness, Wyatt saw two men working by lantern light at the corral. It was Sam Hayes and one of the four Indians who worked for him. They walked over to the corral and Wyatt asked Hayes when they were going to leave for Eagle City. "We'll leave in about an hour, at sunup."

Then Hayes grinned and asked, "Are you folks hungry?" They were, and sat down to a scrumptious meal of flapjacks, trout and hot coffee. Meanwhile, the Indians busied themselves in saddling up the horses and readying them for the day's ride. Then, after all was in readiness, 35 horses started away from the camp, climbing up the steep Evolution Trail toward Eagle City. They followed one another in single file.

Five of the horses were serving as pack animals, carrying the riders' bags and supplies for the camp. Hayes rode up front with two of the packhorses to break trail for the others. Then came Enright and his two friends, Jim, Josie, and Wyatt and the rest of the crowd. Three of the Indians were spaced out in the string of riders to help out whenever needed and the fourth bringing up the rear with the other three packhorses.

Wyatt wanted to stay right behind Josie in case she got into any trouble on the trail. They climbed 1,000 feet up the steep Evolution Trail before reaching the first ridge. That gave them a chance to rest their horses. (This was the site of A. J. Prichard's original "Evolution" Mine.) They rode on for nine more miles, climbing steadily for thousands of feet in one of the toughest tests of endurance of horse and rider that could be imagined. The narrow trail wound around trees, large boulders, hillsides, and sheer precipices. The trail had been blazed with axe marks on the trees ahead, though, so their way was clearly marked.

The horses had to jump over many logs as they climbed up the steep trail, causing their packs to shift. Then their riders were forced to dismount, take the packs off the horses, and reload them again before continuing on up the trail.

As they neared the summit, the air grew ever thinner, making it much more difficult to breathe. The temperature had dropped to -45 degrees and, fearful of being frost bitten, the intrepid riders wrapped rags around their faces to cover as much exposed skin as possible.

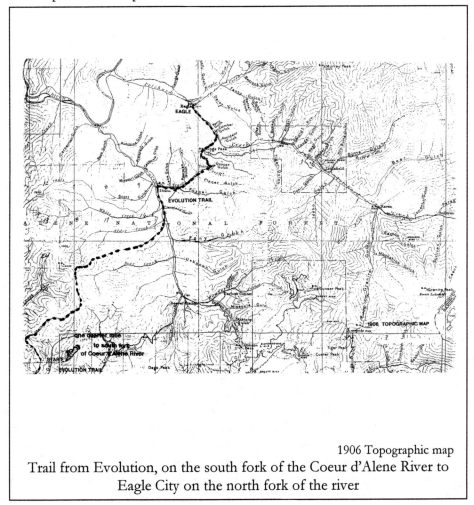

1906 Topographic map

Trail from Evolution, on the south fork of the Coeur d'Alene River to Eagle City on the north fork of the river

They rode over each knoll, fully expecting it to be the last, only to see another, even higher one, off in the distance. The higher they got, though, the less snow there was to deal with, but then the wind began to pick up. Finally utter fatigue set in and, to a man, and woman, their muscles ached and spirits were weakening.

Not complaining though, little Josie was keeping pace with the others. Then she noticed, through the swirling snow, great clumps of ice on the tail and hind legs of Jim's horse. She turned in the saddle, looking down at her own mount's backside and hind legs, to see similar clumps of ice there as well. She was just grateful for the body warmth of the large animal beneath her. Great blasts of vapor came from its nostrils while its head and mane jerked up and down as it climbed and forged on. The well-organized party, that had started out together, was now strung out for a mile back down the mountainside.

Powerful winds howled across the barren mountaintop with eerie moaning sounds, giving voice to the deformed and grotesquely shaped trees that reared from their beds of frozen snow. A ground blizzard blinded them with stinging blasts of ice, making it impossible even to see. But, Wyatt saw plainly that Texas Newspaper article warning them not to come into the Coeur d'Alene Mountains until spring.

Then the unimaginable happened. Enright's horse was suddenly spooked by something or had reached its limit, and began bucking wildly. Hayes pulled his own mount and the two packhorses off to the side of the trail as Enright's mount galloped and bucked past. It disappeared into a cloud of swirling snow with Enright holding desperately onto the saddle horn, cussing at the top of his lungs. The sound of his shouting voice quickly blended in with that of the whistling wind.

It began slowly at first, but exhaustion among his fellows brought on laughter at his predicament. Soon, those who had seen what happened were laughing hysterically while still bracing against the numbing wind. Hayes shouted back, "Don't worry, his horse is ground tied." It was doubtful if anyone heard him, though. (When a horse was "ground tied" it had been trained to stop and stand still if its reigns fell to the ground.)

Sure enough, after they'd topped the final knoll and started back down again they saw Enright's mount standing still on the trail up ahead. The horse was looking at something off to one side. Hayes reached him first, dismounted and with Jim's and other's help, they pulled Enright back up onto the trail again. At first they'd only seen his boots sticking out of a snow bank. Enright's rescuers had to hold back their laughter because of his obvious anger and frustration.

Mounting up again, down the mountain they went, slowly at first to allow the rest to catch up, then nine miles more, down to Beaver Creek. It was late afternoon, darkening quickly and had started to snow again, cutting their visibility still further. So, tired almost beyond exhaustion, horse and rider alike, they camped for the night.

January 29-The next morning seemed to come all too soon for Josie, but a short while later they were back in the saddle and continuing on again. The intrepid bunch rode across another, lower range of mountains. Wyatt hadn't seen another living soul on the journey and thought back to the men and women whom he'd seen alongside the wagon road near the Mission. He wondered if they were going over the Evolution Trail, too, and pitied them if they did. As a rule, walkers went from the Mission over Jackass Trail to Eagle City. Although not fit for horse travel yet, it was a bit shorter.

By the time they'd gotten down off the second range of mountains it was nearly dark again. Their horses forded Prichard Creek and, a while later, Wyatt began to hear music. There were several lights up ahead. A cheer of appreciation raised up from the exhausted riders.

Wide-eyed and absorbing as much of this new place as possible, they entered into Eagle City just as it got dark. Hayes rode into a large, corral and dismounted and one by one the others followed suit. The four Indians immediately set to work unsaddling and caring for the horses.

While they were collecting their bags, Wyatt noticed that it was snowing again. Then the immigrants walked out of the corral to where Hayes was standing. He pointed with an outstretched finger and said, "Folks you can probably spend the night in one of those sleeping tents down the street. Just look for the signs." He saw exhaustion in their faces and laughed. "See, I told you it was going to be a long day." He paused for a second and continued, "Remember now, when you need mining supplies, I carry a complete stock in my store." Then pointing again, he said, "See? That's it over there."

It didn't take long for them all to find a place in one of the sleeping tents for the night. Even the tireless Wyatt and those who'd spent time gambling in the saloon at Evolution turned in early. It had indeed been a difficult day. They ate a meal of bacon and beans for $2 and paid another dollar to spread out their blankets in the tent. Darkness fell, and one by one the sounds and lights from the camp faded into dreams. Only the snores of fitful sleepers could be heard through the thin canvas walls of the tents.

6

Awake In Eagle City

January 30-several quick gunshots broke the quiet mountain air. Sunday morning came with a flurry of excitement and just as suddenly Eagle's streets were filled with half-dressed, sleepy eyed miners. Everyone expected the worst of it and, as if by magic, the camp fairly bristled with shootin' irons. It turned out to be a false alarm, though. Heavy snow in the mountains was forcing deer and elk to search for food in the canyon bottoms. As the result, venturesome early morning hunters had brought down two bull elk, putting fresh meat on the camp's table.

> "The report of a pistol shot will bring a hundred men to their feet for an instant. The saloons will disgorge twice as many more in the same moment, all on the alert to catch a sensation, which has not occurred yet."

Like it or not, the day had begun. It was time for the Earps to get up and make their play in the Coeur d'Alenes. After they'd returned to the warm confines of the sleeping tent, packed up their gear and gotten properly dressed, they ventured back out into the street again. Wyatt was concerned about someone stealing their bags and had talked with the young man who owned the tent. The fellow laughed sadistically and said, "No…we don't have much trouble with thieves around here. The only case of attempted theft we've had in camp was last November. He got caught and had to leave in a hurry." Reassured, the Earps left their bags in the tent and would return for them later. The fellow was referring to the following incident.

November 27, 1883-*Spokane Falls Review-*The first case of attempted theft and punishment occurred last Friday. A party named O'Brien, from Montana, started in on the night mentioned to rob the sluice boxes on the McComber claim, that had not been cleaned up for several days. Newt

Thomas heard someone at the boxes and, stepping out of the cabin with a shotgun, emptied a load of shot in the robber's back.

That individual took the perception a hint that his presence was obnoxious to the owners of the claim and lit out. So great was the 'hit,' thereof, that the punctured prowler ran against and knocked down about forty feet of flume and sprained an ankle in the struggle.

Courtesy of Sprague Pole Museum, Murray, ID
Eagle City jail

O'Brien was found by some parties and conveyed to Hayes City. Thomas heard of the cripple and reported that, if the game was his, the sufferer carried his (Thomas's) trademark in his back. On inspection, O'Brien's back was found to be pretty well peppered with small shot.

Mining law is honorable. Theft is a crime that must be frowned upon. It is a crime that calls for proper measures. In such a community O'Brien was given a certain time to vacate the camp, and the unfortunate fellow struck out on crutches before the allotted time expired; however, the punishment was deserved and it will prove a statuary reason to others.

It turned out that the young man who owned the sleeping tent had left camp with over a thousand dollars in gold dust on him. He'd kept a tidy tent.

After everyone had gotten up and left for the day, he meticulously scraped its dirt floor and reaped the benefit of his tenants carelessness with their dust. He

got the idea one night when he noticed that his tenants loved to show each other up by, in some cases, carelessly displaying the gold they had in their pokes.

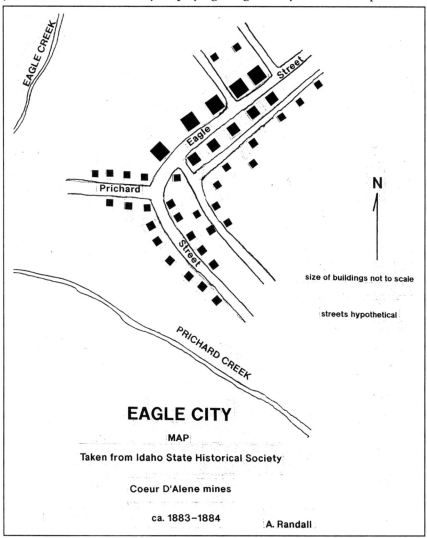

EAGLE CITY

MAP

Taken from Idaho State Historical Society

Coeur D'Alene mines

ca. 1883–1884   A. Randall

It was quiet, very cold, and the sky was overcast because it had been snowing earlier. Frost prevailed, and a thin, gray pall of acrid-smelling wood smoke hung low in the canyon bottom. Wyatt, Josie, and Jim walked north up snowy Eagle Street looking things over. Eagle looked much different by the light of day. They were at the center of town, just a quarter of a mile north of the juncture of Eagle and Prichard Creeks. Fifteen-mile-long Eagle Creek, a tributary of Prichard Creek which flows into the much-larger north fork of the Coeur d'Alene River at a point forty miles north of the Old Coeur d'Alene Mission.

Eagle was a hard looking place. Its structures located on lots from which snow, to the depth of five feet, had been excavated and dumped into the street. This left sheer walls of snow between the buildings and the street. But, in every case, walkways had been shoveled out, allowing entrance into the structures. The hastily constructed camp had been chopped out of a dense forest of immense cedar and pines, leaving large stumps scattered about, many of which were exposed.

Sprague Pole Museum, Murray, ID

Smoking chimneys protruded from the tops of shake-roofed, log cabins and great tents loomed up in a seemingly endless variety. On closer inspection, Wyatt noticed that many of the structures had been marked with charcoal firebrands, and some with gaudily painted signs identifying their respective businesses. Stores, saloons, restaurants, and faro banks were numerous. Even the women in scarlet were there.

"T. F. Cunningham has painted a very attractive sign for Dennell & Co. and another for Sam H. Hayes. In fact he has painted nearly all the signs in Eagle and Murray. In the latter place there are fine specimens of his work at Garrison & Strong's, the Murray Hotel, the Gold Room and at a number of other places."

The cold was intense that morning, but the men were working like beavers. Soon after the earlier gunfire, the mountainsides echoed with the sound of axes chopping wood, the crash of falling timber, and sliding of logs. Logs and whipsawed lumber for new construction and heating fires were in high demand and paid for as soon as they became available.

Men could be seen coming and going in all directions, some with toboggans and others with tents, blankets and cooking utensils strapped to their backs. They came with pack trains, dog teams, sleds and snow shoes. It was an animated picture to the observer. Many, coming, with the intention of remaining, set themselves to the task of clearing snow-off, pitching tents others building cabins, or settling in the different surrounding gulches.

Wyatt also heard the sounds of loud conversation, laughter, and the strains of music coming from within the nearest tent. Even at this early hour the places of public resort were thronged with miners and prospectors. They were waiting for the snow to disappear so they could get off into the mountains to begin prospecting. There were also the packers and transient population, a tough-looking crowd who usually stood around on street corners talking of mines and mining, criticizing ore samples as they passed them from hand to hand, leaving the ground strewn with specimens of quartz from the different claims.

Wyatt looked to the south at the steep and lofty snow-covered mountains that he and his party had come over the night before. It was the same in all directions, even more mountains heavily forested with tamarack, cedar and swaying pines of perennial green, all burdened down with deep snow.

The location and surroundings were ideal for a city of mines. There was plenty of timber and water and Wyatt knew that if the district proved out, as had been speculated, it would be a fair rival to Deadwood, South Dakota or Leadville, Colorado. As he continued looking to the south, he was surprised to see a rag-tag band of people walking out of the timber toward town. Even at that distance, he recognized them as being the ones he'd seen several days earlier, back on the wagon-road near the Old Mission. These walkers had been forced to spend three nights on the Jackass Trail, because of the same furious winds and blizzard conditions that Sam Hayes's horses had faced on the Evolution Trail.

In retrospect:

October 27, 1883-One man who'd come into the camp in the late fall of 1883 was George Henderson, Esq., of Martinez, California, who called upon the *Spokane Falls Review* in Spokane Falls WT:

Among those who understand the most minute principles of mining, and who have studied and learned mining from practical application, is George Henderson, Esq., of Martinez, California. Mr. Henderson is not one of those who take the word of another as to the value of a mine, or who travels with a pick and shovel chancing fortune with a pan. He has been schooled in the diggings of California, Nevada, Colorado and Arizona and is fully competent to pass judgment upon the worth or worthlessness of a mine. When he makes up his mind from personal observations he locates at once if the prospects justifies, and if otherwise, otherwise. He has been mining lately in Arizona, and is interested in the mines there now. He read of the discovery of gold in the Coeur d'Alene Mountains and desiring to learn from actual examination made a trip north. One day spent in the diggings satisfied him of its extent and value. He wasted no time but purchased and located claims. Besides this he had two houses constructed, and has men in his employ to remain all winter. He also has a considerable force of white men and Indians at work packing in a large quantity of supplies.

Wyatt, Josie, and Jim were, by then, walking past the corrals. Sam Hayes and his Indians were mounted on five horses, herding and leading the other twenty-five horses and five mules out of the corral, with sharp whistles from puckered mouths and an occasional "Hey...ho!" to keep their charges in line. The animal's whinnies and snorts could be heard from near and far. Saddle bags and packs empty, they were headed south toward the mountains on the way back to Evolution, leaving behind a trail of vapor that rose from their great lungs into the cold morning air. The oncoming immigrants stepped aside to let the long caravan of steadily moving horses and mules pass-by.

Hayes made the trip to Eagle with his string of saddle horses and mules only every other day, whereas long pack trains of from forty to fifty mules, carrying fresh supplies for the camp, came into town every day, weather permitting.

Just then Josie said, "I smell bacon." Wyatt and Jim smelled it, too, and they entered into the bustling atmosphere of the Nevada Chop House   It was crowded to overflowing, so they first had to wait their turn for a place at a table. The other eatin' places in town were very busy, as well.

Coeur d'Alene Mines and Gold Fields, 1884

"The Pioneer Restaurant is so overcrowded that from 50 to 100 customers are turned away every day, as meals are $1.00 each it can be readily understood that the above indicates a rushing business."

Eagle City was already known to the outside world as the "Capital of the Coeur d'Alenes" but, as word of Prichard's gold discovery spread even further across the country, the town's notoriety was quickly becoming legendary. Its population had increased a hundred fold from the handful of men on-site in the summer of 1883 to well over a thousand by the first snow-fall several months later.

November 9, 1883-*NW Tribune*-"Snow already a foot deep; in hills,
prospecting for quartz will have to be postponed until spring."

The subsequent discovery of free gold in several quartz ledges, and the exhibition of rich specimens in the saloons only increased the life and activity of the place. Before the first of December, 1883, Eagle had grown so as to surprise even the most hardened skeptic.

November 24, 1883-*Spokane Falls Review*-"At present there are 42
buildings in Hayes City and several under way. There are seven stores and ten saloons in full blast."

Through December of 1883, and much of January of 1884, terrible winter storms had dumped many feet of snow in the high Bitterroot and Coeur d'Alene Mountains. This prompted newspaper columnists to warn the foolhardy against coming to the camp until later, thus keeping many would-be gold seekers at home. But, the lure of gold was just too strong. The Earp's entrance into the camp coincided with the overcoming of those fears by the masses, and the flood of humanity was on.

Eagle's growth was phenomenal. All day long, groups of dozens of walkers and riders came down mountain trails into town, following their dream of easy riches, as presented to them by the "gold" circulars put out by the Northern Pacific Railroad Company. (By actual count, 142 souls came into camp in one day.) Everyone wanted to be in Eagle when spring thaws exposed the gold. But, more importantly, they wanted to get to camp "first" to stake out their claims.

Meanwhile, Eagle seemed to be the busiest place of all, busier even than Rathdrum or Coeur d'Alene City. Hundreds of men worked from daylight until dark hammering, whip-sawing lumber, and pushing and pulling freshly cut logs in their efforts to build new structures. It was reported that a thousand houses were being built all up and down the canyon. Eagle was quickly becoming a mining camp of some worth.

January 5, 1884-*Spokane Falls Review*-When we left there was five feet of
snow on the level. Surveyors Hayes and Horn surveyed the town out on January

5th and, at the insistence of 250 miners from the Black Hills of South Dakota, the town's name was changed from Hayes City to Eagle. Its three principal streets were named Gold, Silver and Eagle.

"The recorder of the district, Col. Frank Points, has been kept busy from daylight till dark, and nearly 1,000 claims have been put upon the records. The small boarding houses in tents and log cabins were unable to accommodate their numerous guests, and many were compelled to cook for themselves."

All freight had to be shipped in on pack trains and it was used up much

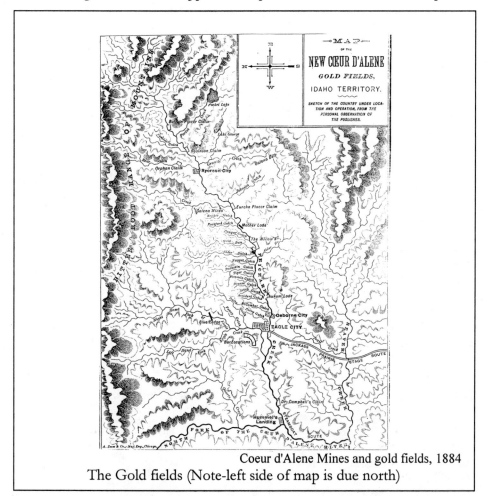

Coeur d'Alene Mines and gold fields, 1884
The Gold fields (Note-left side of map is due north)

faster than it could be brought in. Consequently prices soared, approaching the old California freight scale of $1 per pound. As weather conditions improved, though, packers were faced with stiff competition and the price per pound of freight dropped dramatically.

The first thing Wyatt and Jim wanted to do was to find houses for themselves. They didn't want to spend another night in the sleeping tent if they didn't have to. So, after they'd finished eating a fine meal of bacon, beans, biscuits, and hot coffee, Wyatt asked where one might find a place to rent. He was directed to Wickersham and Butler's realty office, which was located on west Eagle Street.

They left the Nevada Chop House, walking some distance to the realtor's office and passed tents, shacks, and log cabins along the way. Finally reaching a hewn-log cabin with a painted board sign nailed on its front that declared boldly, "Wickersham and Butler's Realty."[1]

Inside they were met with two smiling faces and a cherry-red wood stove. Wyatt told the two men that he and Jim were only looking to rent for now, but would probably be buying houses later. The jocular Wickersham pointed out a town plat map that hung conspicuously on one wall. Another, "claims map," hung there too, as well as a distance chart that read: Belknap to Eagle, 36 miles; Trout Creek to Eagle, 36 miles; Rathdrum to Eagle, 91 miles; and Spokane Falls to Eagle, 109 miles.

Several new log cabins were for sale or rent at a hefty price. Wyatt rented one that stood up against the base of the mountain near Eagle Street while Jim rented another on nearby Lee Street, which he would later buy. When traveling conditions improved, he hoped to bring his ailing wife, Bessie, to the camp, but she would never be able to make the journey.

Then the three made their way back down the street to Sam Hayes's general store, where they bought the necessaries they would need to make their new homes more livable. There were no wagons in Eagle and very few horses, so everything had to be carried and it took several hours for them to get moved in. Later that day Ferguson and Enright moved into cabins near the Earps.

Who'd ever built Wyatt and Josie's cabin went to a good deal of trouble and expense. Due to the difficulty in bringing heavy iron-stoves into camp, they were the highest priced commodities and the cabin was equipped with two. A cook stove, worth $150 and a Sibley sheet-iron wood stove that sold for $30-40. The Sibley heating stove was a simple device with a door and a hole in its top for a stove pipe. A stack of fire wood was piled out back of the cabin at the base of the mountain. (The cost of the stoves was a generous sum of money, keeping in mind that a good day's pay for a farmer was only $1.25 while laborers in the camps made $5 a day.)

Nearly everyone in camp got around on snowshoes if they needed to leave the city. Horses would be in great demand in the spring, but were only a hindrance at this time. Because of the deep snow, they easily got bogged down and their food had to be carried into camp on pack trains.

That night Wyatt left Josie in the cabin and he and Jim walked into the Acion Saloon where they spent time playing poker and faro and getting acquainted. Enright, Holman and Ferguson were already there and had let it be known that Wyatt Earp and his brother Jim were in town. The Earps were afforded the homage of their reputation.

The Acion was a typical gold rush saloon! A large, gable-roofed tent with supporting poles, a door, and a rough-sawn wood floor. In its center stood a large, potbellied heating stove, complete with a stovepipe that snaked its way up into the sloping canvas ceiling and beyond. Scattered across the saloon's expanse were benches, chairs, and poker and faro tables that were, as usual, all filled up. A bar, complete with the trappings, stood along one wall, and lamps and other fixtures were placed in the appropriate places throughout.

As Wyatt and Jim played cards in the warm, well-lit saloon, the men at their table talked about various claims around town and who was doing what. Wyatt recognized one of the fellows at the table as being one of the men whom he'd seen walking into town early that morning.

The man was laughing and began telling the story of his harrowing journey. "We was all lined up wading through chest deep snow and all of a sudden the man in front just disappeared. He sunk like a rock in the soft snow. So's we all gathered round and pulled him back up again. It was like pullin' a cork out of a bottle. We laughed so hard."

He paused for a moment in silent contemplation, then continued, "Seems like that happened a lot. Then, when we got tired for the night, we pitched camp on pine boughs (Idaho feathers). We had to cut the tops off trees and spread the branches out on the snow to put our blankets and gear down on to. If we hadn't, the heat from our bodies would've melted the snow and we'duh sunk like rocks too. Them pine boughs make mighty fine beds. We spread out a lot of 'em for the fire, but when we woke up next morning it was gone. Melted its way clean through. It was like lookin' down a well." The yellow glow of lantern light played over their faces and they all laughed heartily at his fine story.

Another man at the table turned out to be William Keeler, the foreman of the Widow's claim. The Widow was a profitable enterprise, so when Keeler talked, everyone else was silent, hoping to catch some insight on the secret of the Widow's success. Keeler knew that the Earps were new in camp, and invited them both up to see the Widow.

The claim had originally been located by A. J. Prichard, by power of attorney, for widows Mrs. Mary Lane of Illinois and Mrs. Shultz of Michigan. It was not named for the 400 pound woman who was on her way to the camp, but was stuck in Coeur d'Alene City. None of the boatmen, who poled their way upstream, in hewn-log boats, in the swift Coeur d'Alene River for pay, were about to "take her on." There was some confusion by the locals about which widow really owned the claim.

"Widow claim located for Mrs. M. H. Lane by Andy Prichard on March 24, 1883-relocated and recorded on June 11, 1883, page p. 36, book A."

The "friendly" game of stud poker had been going on for several hours and Daniel Ferguson had been loosing heavily. No matter what he did with the cards he was dealt, it always seemed to be wrong.

Now gamblers are as a rule superstitious, believing in secret and mysterious influences at work behind their cards. The callous-hearted Ferguson began looking around for his hoodoo (jinx). He quickly found it in the person of Oregon John, a worthless underworld follower and camp hanger-on. Oregon John, it developed at a glance, had committed the unpardonable offense of watching the game with one foot on the rung of Ferguson's chair.

Ferguson, his hoodoo discovered, rose deliberately from his chair, pulled the .45 caliber Colt revolver from his holster, cocked its hammer back and shot Oregon John squarely in the chest. The deafening explosion set his hoodoo's shirt afire and brought the immediate attention of

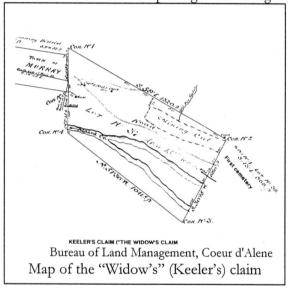

KEELER'S CLAIM ("THE WIDOW'S CLAIM")
Bureau of Land Management, Coeur d'Alene
Map of the "Widow's" (Keeler's) claim

everyone within earshot of the incident. The force of the shot blew Oregon John away from Ferguson and his still writhing body sprawled out dead to the floor. Ferguson then sat back down to the game again. Wyatt just shook his head in disbelief at what he had just seen. There was no demonstration and, without ceremony, someone carted the body out and disposed of it. The incident had given riddance to rubbish and, since there wasn't any law in the camp yet, the matter was forgotten. To the deceased Oregon John's credit, though, Ferguson's streak of bad luck continued on into the evening.

The "lively" game of stud poker ended later that night at around 9:00 p.m. Then, lanterns in hand, the players all returned to their homes and beds. It had gotten colder and was snowing lightly. As Wyatt and Josie snuggled together in their warm cabin, they rejoiced to be back in each other's arms again. They drifted off to sleep truly knowing that they were finally in the Coeur d'Alenes and that their search for gold would begin in the morning.

H-1384, Haynes Foundation Coll., Montana Historical Society
The Widow's claim, 1884

January 31-Monday-The next morning found Wyatt and Jim snow-shoeing up Prichard Creek. They were determined to see the Widow's claim and followed the directions given them by Keeler. Josie had elected to stay in the cabin. It was still snowing lightly and visibility was limited, but three miles above town they finally found it. A narrow strip of placer along the creek, not more than a quarter of an acre that had been worked with sluices before winter snow storms closed the operation down in 1883.

The two brothers made their way to a cabin that stood on the property and were met by the Widow's courteous and accommodating foreman, William Keeler. Keeler had only just arrived himself, as he'd also spent the night in Eagle. After they'd removed their snowshoes and gone into the warm cabin,

Keeler gave them cups of freshly brewed hot coffee. They laughed about their walk up to the claim.

During the course of their conversation, Keeler said, "We've taken a good $18,000 out of the ground so far." (One ounce of gold sold for $18.) A pot of gold stood on the table in the center of the room, among pots of beans, bacon and biscuits. Keeler reached into it and gave them each a small nugget. "Soon as the ground's clear of snow, probably in March or early April, I'm going to hire forty or fifty men to work the claim. She should be a real payer."

He went on to explain the operation, "The Widow divides the gulch into two portions   the one above is known as poor man's country, and the one below will require capital to work. On average, it's two and a half feet down through the gravel to hard pan where the gold is. The money we've got to raise will pay for the crew and equipment it will take to work the claim with hydraulic power. Blasting the gold out of the gravel with high pressure water is the easiest way to get at it and a lot quicker than scraping at the cracks with an eatin' iron and swishing a gold pan around." They laughed some more.

Then Keeler's partner came running up the hill as fast as his snow shoes would allow. After he'd taken them off, he came into the cabin out of breath and clutching something in his hands. "My Gawd Bill," he said, "Look at the size of this'n." He held out a hand-sized slab of white quartz that he'd found laying in the creek-bed that fairly dripped with bright yellow gold.

Jim and Wyatt looked at each other, thanked the two men in the cabin, and hurried back toward town again. Excitement reigned supreme. They returned to Butler and Wickersham's realty office to get a better look at the claims map they'd seen the day before. However, there was a crowd of men going in and out of the building so they had to wait their turn.

There were plenty of places to gamble and drink "likker" in Eagle, but probably the most popular spot in town was in front of the claims map in Butler and Wickersham's realty office. Every time a new claim was staked out it was added to the map.

They finally got their turn and, as they looked the claim map over, Wyatt said, "Jim, looks like about everything in town and most of the surrounding mountain sides has already been claimed. Hmmm, there are a few exceptions out here, though." He ran his finger over a section of the map that remained unmarked. The two brothers would spend the following months probing the earth and chasing after those leads.

That night they returned to the Acion Saloon for more entertainment. They found the place full to overflowing with excited men talking about gold, many standing at the bar with drinks in their hands, while others sat at tables playing cards.

Some 250 miners from the Black Hills of South Dakota were in town and it was reported that 3,000 more were on the way. The Black Hills boys had been on site for some time and had grown restless. On the one hand, they couldn't prospect for gold because of the deep snow. On the other, A. J. Prichard had already claimed most of the good spots for himself and his liberal farmer friends anyway. It was quite a dilemma for them.

Wyatt and Jim sat down to a game of poker. To Wyatt's surprise several of the Black Hills boys at the table recognized him from when he and Morgan were in Deadwood back in the 1870s. These men had bought their winter's supply of firewood from Wyatt and Morgan. A raucous greeting ensued that was so intense that it drew the attention of others in the noisy saloon.

One of the men at the table grinned and said loudly, "Hey boys, this here's Wyatt Earp. Remember when he was back in Deadwood?" Wyatt then saw many smiles of recognition and recognized many of them as well. The two men at the table consoled Wyatt and Jim on the loss of their good brother Morgan. The four men talked for some time. "We plum don't think it's fair that this Prichard feller has all the good ground tied up in 20 acre claims, for other fellers that ain't even here. So a bunch of us is going out in the morning and stake our own claims in case the ones Prichard staked turn out to be no good."

Later that night Wyatt talked with friends Danny Ferguson, John Hardy, J. E. Jack Enright and Alfred Holman. They all decided to throw in together to challenge Prichard's right to tie up his extensive holdings. Others would join their "land syndicate" as time passed on.

Before the evening was over, a popular, if not somewhat inebriated, election was held and Wyatt was voted in unanimously as the new Deputy Sheriff of Kootenai County. It seemed that everywhere Wyatt went he was met by a petition to represent the law and this was no exception.[2]

February 1-Friday-The next morning came with another flurry of activity. At daybreak Wyatt, Jim, their friends, and fifteen to twenty of the Black Hills boys were scurrying about camp staking their own claims over those of A. J. Prichard's. They laughed during the whole larcenous affair and had great sport. Wyatt and his associates would wind up as regular defendants in the Eagle courts, battling claim jumping charges and arguing miners' rights.

Local mining laws deemed it to be illegal to file mining claims by proxy for persons outside the region, which Prichard had done.[3] Still, United States statutes allowed each man to claim twenty acres of placer ground and hold it legally by doing a small amount of work upon it each year. Therein lies the confusion, as many farmers from the Palouse country of Idaho and eastern Washington, whose business wasn't in mining, took advantage of the law to hold the rich ground. In the end, the letter of U. S. mining laws would prevail.

While ownership of mining claims remained in question, there were many speculators in town dealing in real property as well. The price for town lots and the cost of new construction had soared. Frank Reed spent $1,200 building a two-story house that was 20' X 35'. Before it was even finished he leased it for six months at $300 per month. The money was paid to him up-front in cash. Reed was then contemplating building a three-story hotel at the corner of Gold and Prichard Streets as soon as the building materials could be obtained.

Another two-story, 25' X 35' hewn-log house, with double, glass doors, was rented for $100 per month. That money was also paid in advance, even before the snow was cleared away for the foundations to be laid.

Two of the many land speculators in town were at each other's throats. A man known, for obvious reasons, as three-fingered Jack, fought with another man named Nelson over a town lot. Both were injured in the struggle, but both survived. Theirs wouldn't be the only dispute over ownership of town property, either, many more would follow.

The frenzy continued. One enterprising company located a town site on a mining claim owned by Eagle's Judge, Melder and then offered to sell him a choice lot (of his own land) on "Main Street," at a fair price. Needless to say, their fledgling business venture failed miserably. They begrudgingly left the judge's claim, with his laughter, over the whole affair, ringing in their ears.

Heavy snows set in as the month of February began, and there was little or no prospecting being done. So, to pass the time, Wyatt and Jim relied on their skills at dealing cards while beautiful Josie, who was an ex-minstrel actress and singer, tried her hand at singing in the Acion Saloon. She was an instant success. The mostly young, sex-starved placer miners were spellbound by her beauty and charm.

Calamity Jane

Another woman, Martha Canary, better known as Calamity Jane, had rolled into Spokane Falls, Washington Territory in September of 1883 when the Northern Pacific Railroad was building through. Before long she'd proven herself to be one hard lady, around which all the excitement and life of a new town swirled.

She brought with her the rather dubious reputation of being one of the Plains most sensational, old West characters as well as the most reckless and daring rider in the west. Years before, at Goose Creek, Wyoming, Calamity had saved the life of Calvary officer, Captain Egan, who was about to be scalped by Indians. It was he who affixed the name of Calamity to her because whenever there was a calamity, she was always around. It was commonly known that she seemed to invite danger, was the best shot and swimmer in the country, and that even the Indians didn't "mess" with Calamity.

Calamity had been in Spokane Falls dealing faro bank in a wooden saloon building on Front Avenue (now Trent Avenue). Her specialty was regaling the boys with stories as long as they continued to buy five cent glasses of beer.

While dealing, her custom was to peacefully chew tobacco while smoking a cigar. If anyone suggested a drink she was always Johnny on the spot, drinking neat whiskey with relish and buying a return treat with alacrity. Her reputation as a peace preserver and sure shot had preceded her to Spokane. Almost without exception there was order in her place, because the fellers were afraid to even suggest a rough house. Everyone knew that she had killed men in open duels (gunfights) before and nobody evinced the desire to be next. She shot her last husband's arm off in a duel the two had to decide which of them should be leader of the family.

After the excitement of the railroad coming through Spokane Falls had died down, Calamity boarded a train and returned to her house in Livingston, Montana, where she had been living for some time since leaving the Black Hills country.

Molly-B-Damn

The most controversial, yet best loved, woman in the Coeur d'Alenes was a well-formed Irish lass by the name of Margaret Hall. When she rode down the mountain trail from Thompson Falls and entered into Murrayville, she was already a celebrity in the mining camp. Margaret held a child in her arms and the baby's mother sat behind her straddling the saddlebags.

Actually she had begun her long journey to the camp, and eventual destiny, many years before at her birth the day after Christmas in 1853, in far-off Dun Laoghaire, County Dublin, Ireland. Maggie, as she was known to her family and friends, came from a loving household with a Protestant English father and a Catholic Irish mother. (Her mother also bore the name of Margaret Hall.)

She was well schooled and, at an early age, could quote, with feeling, the works of Shakespeare, Milton, Shelley and the Holy Bible. The innocence and excitement of her youth was lost to the harsh realities of life around her, though. As the years dragged slowly on, turmoil between Catholic and Protestant factions lent itself to continued brutal street fighting and near civil war conditions. The sight of death was commonplace.

In fact, eight years before Maggie's birth, in 1845, Ireland had been struck by a blight to its potato crop. In the next two years, three-quarters of a million people would perish from starvation and disease. To make matters even worse, landlords were quick to displace families who were unable to pay their rent. After losing all of their crops, the poor farmers had nothing left to sell in order to get money for food stuffs, let alone pay the rent. These awful circumstances left even more hapless pilgrims to fend for themselves, adding to the grim toll of death.

In the midst of all of this, in 1846, the Irish people's popular leader, O'Connell, asserted Irish rights against an oppressive British rule. But England's King George, the Fifth, refused to even allow the question to be raised.

In the end, O'Connell was murdered by the English and became a martyr to his people. They would be forever grateful to him for his selfless acts of bravery on their behalf. To his honor, many statues would be erected and plaques would be placed. Across the waters in England, the tyrannical reign of King George, the Fifth, ended suddenly and shamefully when he was beheaded by his peers.

Finally all of the violence, death, and hardships became too much for twenty year old Maggie Hall. Early in 1873, in hopes of some kind of future, any kind of a future, she joined with millions of other Irish men and women who were fleeing their beleaguered country for far-off America.

National Gallery of Ireland
The Four Courts Dublin

That early spring morning, she stood on the busy Dublin docks looking about her. The cold fog was lifting and she could see patches of blue sky above. Swarms of snowy, white-breasted seagulls swooped about, landing here and there in hopes of getting a free meal. Multi-story gray stone buildings crowded down to the waterfront dock, which was thronged with a great mass of people-all with their luggage piled nearby.

Maggie stood alone, but, all around her was the constant murmur of many voices. Suddenly the deep bellowing of a ship's horn blared out, echoing back from the Dublin's stone buildings. Then came several quick shrill blasts of a ship's whistle, signaling that it was nearing time to leave. To Maggie's excitement, people began moving slowly toward the nearest ship's gangplank.

She had left home without her parent's blessing and was about to climb aboard one of two ships anchored in the harbor, leaving everything and everyone she knew and loved behind. Maggie was sad and worried about her family, but hoped to some day rejoin them under better circumstances.

She joined in with the throng of people walking up the ship's gangplank and, once aboard, stood near the handrail on the big steamer's deck. Still more time passed. Finally, to another bellow of its warning horn and whistle, the side wheeler's great paddle wheel churned the seawater into white foam. It pulled away from the Dublin docks and slowly made for the open sea. The sky was clear and the north Atlantic was a pretty blue-green color.

The ship's handrails were lined with somber men and women who watched their past-lives fade slowly into the distance behind the ship, knowing full-well that they would probably never see their beloved homeland again. The last bit of Ireland they did see was the long sun-bleached finger of Fastmet Rock, which seemingly reached out, begging for them to come back. Tears were shed by woman and man alike. (This is the same route the ill-fated R. M. S. Titanic took on her way to destiny.)

After many days at sea, though, the mood changed to one of hope and anticipation. Finally the mainland was sighted on a curved horizon and, hours later, their ship docked at New York harbor.

When Maggie and the others set foot on this new land, it was with both trepidation and hope. They passed through Immigrations, walked into New York City and, at last, America. Previously unknown to one another, small groups of excited people clung together as compatriots in a new land.

Soon Maggie was living in an apartment in the Irish-American section of the city, finding work as a barmaid in a local tavern. In the following days and months, her Irish charm and natural beauty earned her many a smile and wink. She'd worked at the tavern for a little over a year when one day her virtues were also recognized by a man named Burdan. His advances toward her were persistent and, after a time, they were married. Deeply in love, Maggie had finally found the one man with whom she would share the rest of her life.

All was not well, though, in that Burdan turned out to be a scoundrel. He'd been living on an allowance from a rich father, but soon that was cut off, leaving them both penniless. Then Burdan's many creditors swarmed in, demanding payment. In desperation, he pleaded with her to prostitute herself as payment of those debts. (Debtor's prisons were in vogue at this time.)

Hardened far beyond her years by the misery she'd witnessed in Ireland, coupled with her deep love for this man, she agreed to do as he asked. But, after a few weeks of her husband's imposed prostitution, Maggie's guilt got the better of her. She visited with a Catholic Priest frequently and finally her morals and council from the church cleared her mind's eye. Maggie saw Burdan for what he was and they parted ways, but not before she was excommunicated from the

Church for her sinful ways. Maggie would never again set foot in a Catholic Church.

After being in New York for four years, Maggie struck out in 1877 for the West on her own. She traveled to Virginia City, Nevada, which was the scene of a wild gold stampede. From there she moved on to San Francisco, up to Portland, Oregon, and back East again to Chicago. She supported herself by selling the pleasures of her shapely body, learning well the trade which Burdan had forced upon her.

Maggie was in St. Paul, Minnesota, on February 3, 1884 when she happened across one of the Northern Pacific gold circulars in a St. Paul newspaper. The article with the circular told a fantastic tale of a great gold strike and the fabulous wealth to be had by all in the rugged mountains of north Idaho Territory. She immediately bought passage on a train bound for Idaho. It was a long uneventful trip across the flatlands of Minnesota and into Montana. The train passed through mountain ranges and many small towns. Then, at Livingston, Montana, an odd-looking man boarded the train sitting across the isle from her. As luck would have it, Maggie was about to have a chance encounter with the most famous woman of the West, Calamity Jane.

February 5-Tuesday-Calamity had tired of the peace and tranquility in Livingston and decided that things would be "heating up" soon in the Coeur d'Alenes. She wanted to get in on some of the excitement, and so was on her way to Thompson Falls where she would ride over the Bitterroots on a pack train into camp.

Maggie studied this new passenger for awhile and finally realized that he was a she. This rough looking woman stood just over five feet tall and looked to weigh around 130 pounds. She wore a man's suit, her nether garments being overalls tucked into the tops of rawhide

Azusa Pub., Englewood, CA
Martha Jane Canary Burke
"Calamity Jane"

boots. She wore a frilled jacket and had a cartridge belt, complete with pistol, strapped around her waist. Her hair was cut man-fashion and rugged "weathered" features made it easy for her to pass as a man.

By then Calamity had noticed Maggie's stares and said simply, "Call me Calamity Jane!" Maggie was startled that her stares had been noticed, but soon regained her composure and returned with, "I'm Maggie Burdan."

An uneasy silence ensued, but a few minutes later conversation flowed freely between the two worldly women. Maggie said, "Are you going through to the Coast?" "Not by a damned sight. I'm going to the Coeur d'Alenes in Idaho. The boys found gold there last year and I hear it looks pretty good. Things 'orta be heatin' up by now." Calamity turned away from Maggie and looked wistfully out through her window-at the passing snow covered scenery. She continued to talk, but to herself, "Soon as this damned snow gets off, that is."

Maggie was very interested and asked, "What's it like in the Coeur d'Alenes?" "Its hell to get to, high mountain passes, deep snow and all that, but there's supposed to be a lot of gold there and the rest don't matter." Then it was Calamity's turn to be curious. She asked, "What's yer line, sister?"

Sprague Pole Museum, Murray
Photo purported to be that of
Maggie Hall

Maggie smiled and looked down into her lap, turning the ball of her right shoe on the car's wooden floor. She replied, "I expect it's the same as yours."

Calamity saw before her a beautiful, well-dressed, shapely, and soft woman whom she knew would be the "belle of the ball" to the young, sex-starved prospectors in the Coeur d'Alenes. Maggie was about 5 feet, 6 inches tall, and weighed 120 pounds. She had a sharp nose, thin lips, and a pleasing face when engaged in conversation.[4]

Calamity felt defensive and challenged, "The hell yer say! That'd put us in competition, now wouldn't it, dearie?" She continued to look Maggie over, carefully, sizing her up. Suddenly Calamity felt very old, and, almost without thought, made a decision. "I'd never spotted yuh, girlie. Yuh got plenty of what I' ain't. An' that'd be downright unfair competition."

Maggie noticed a marked difference in their conversation after that. From then on, nothing was mentioned about the Coeur d'Alenes or gold. Instead,

Calamity talked about her experiences in the west and her stint in Spokane Falls dealing faro bank.

Late in the day, the train finally puffed and snorted its way to a stop at the Trout Creek station, three miles from Thompson Falls. Maggie stepped down from the passenger car into a chilly, but beautiful, moonlit night. The station sat at the base of the majestic, quiet, Bitterroots. Several transport wagons were waiting for the train's arrival at the lantern-lit station. Maggie and several other passengers climbed aboard the nearest one, filling it to capacity. The other wagon was soon filled with passengers from the train, as well. The "hack" driver for Maggie's wagon loaded their baggage into the back, climbed into the seat up front and, snapping the horses reins against their backsides, said, "Giddy up thar!" They were off. A lantern mounted on the pole beside the driver's seat lighted the way and after an exhilarating three mile ride, in freezing night air, they stopped on the main street of Thompson Falls, in front of a hotel. Then the driver carried their baggage to the boardwalk and was soon urging his team off down the street.

Maggie got a room for the night in the hotel, but later walked down the boardwalk looking the town over. There were lights emanating from nearly every place of business. Loud laughter and the stomping of feet to the rhythm of music came from a nearby saloon. She was interested in the festive atmosphere, even looking through a frost-covered window into its lighted interior, but it had been a long trip and she was tired. A few minutes later, she returned to her hotel room and to bed, drifting off to sleep.

February 6-Wednesday-Early the next morning, in front of the hotel, Maggie climbed up onto the saddle of a well-behaved saddle horse. She'd paid for passage on the pack train that was going over the Thompson Falls Trail to the Coeur d'Alenes. Ahead of her, and behind, were other riders who were also mounted and waiting for the ride to begin and at the end of the long string of horses were mules loaded down with baggage and fresh supplies for the camp.

She held the horse's reins loosely in her right hand and adjusted herself in the saddle. The horse shifted its stance easily and the leather saddle beneath her creaked at the shifting of her weight. She looked over and saw the hotel clerk and several other men standing on the boardwalk watching the activity of the pack train. Then she studied the faces of her fellow travelers and was surprised to see that her new acquaintance Calamity Jane wasn't there. Calamity had decided not to compete with her in the camp and had continued on the train to Spokane Falls where she had already established herself as a faro dealer the year before.

Just after daybreak, the long string of horses, and then mules, left town, following along the Thompson Falls Trail up Prospect Creek toward the massive Bitterroot Mountains. It would be an all-day ride. Many who could not afford the high price of a horse decided to make the trek on foot and had already left town. Maggie saw people off to both sides of the trail ahead, carrying or dragging what they could of their possessions.

Although the stampede has scarcely begun, some curious scenes are witnessed on the line of the trail. A gentleman who just came out from Eagle City says he saw several overcoats and bundles of blankets scattered along the trail or hung on branches of trees. The miners start out from Trout Creek City drawing toboggans loaded with their provisions, blankets, etc., and in their eagerness to get ahead never look back, and soon getting warmed up throw their overcoats into the snow and dash ahead. Some were met with bags of flour, cases of coal oil or loads of bacon on their backs, and one man, named Johnson, was actually pressing forward with a sheet-iron stove on his shoulders.

Among Maggie's fellow riders were George Glick, Sam Wilson, his brother Wes Wilson, and brothers Ben and Charley Lafferty. The Lafferty brothers and Glick would later be partners in Murrayville's City Bakery, which they operated from a ten by twelve foot log cabin. They would deliver freshly baked bread to the miner's claims on horseback.[5]

Like the Earps, and everyone else already in camp, they too had been lured into the rugged Idaho wilderness by the Northern Pacific Railroad advertisement which read: "Nuggets weighing $50, $100, $200 of free gold for the picking up; it fairly glistens."[6]

As they rode along, Maggie looked up and saw that it was overcast. She wasn't too cold, but she pulled the collar of her warm fur coat up around her neck all the same. For the sensation of resistance, she pushed forward with her left leg against the carpet bag that she'd tied to the saddle horn. Her other bags were on one of the mules at the tail end of the caravan.

H-1389, Haynes Foundation Coll., Montana Historical Soc.
Miner's traveling bakery, Ben Lafferty stands nearest horse

The snow was four to five feet deep and in places had drifted onto the trail ahead, so the caravan was often halted while packers shoveled out the way. They rode at a slow, steady pace. The scenery was breathtaking to Maggie; she'd never seen mountains this big before and, even though it was broad daylight, the ominous darkness and solitude of the forest and deep snow around them was sobering. The pack train plodded steadily up the trail and later that afternoon it began to snow lightly. As the minutes ticked by the snow fall became heavier and heavier. Soon they were caught in the worst snow storm in the history of the district. Bitterly cold winds swept down over the high mountains upon them. They were caught in a blizzard of swirling snow, dropping visibility down to only a few feet at best. All the while, the pack train's string of saddle horses and riders overtook those less fortunate, who were struggling along on foot.

Then one of the stampeders, riding two horses behind Maggie, thought he saw her suddenly pull off to the side of the trail and dismount. But, the visibility was so bad that he couldn't be sure. When he got up to where she was, he could see that indeed she was down off her horse and helping a woman to her feet. The exhausted woman had fallen into the snow, unable to continue, and she had a three-year-old young'n strapped on her back.

When his horse came plodding deliberately up, Maggie heard the man say, "Kin I help?" She replied, "You sure can, get down here and help this woman up behind my saddle. Then, when I get mounted, hand me the baby." He did.

Once mounted again, Maggie could feel the poor woman behind her shaking violently from the cold. The woman's lips were a light shade of blue. As Maggie urged her horse on with her knees and heels, the woman had her arms wrapped around her for her warmth.

Maggie and the man rejoined the slowly moving caravan, continuing on as before. A while later they came to a lean-to beside the trail where someone had camped. Maggie could still feel the woman's shivering body behind her. She turned to the man who was then riding right behind her, and asked him to help once more. "This woman and her child aren't dressed for this and will surely freeze to death by the time we get to where we're going."

Again they reined their horses off to the side of the trail. The man dismounted and Maggie handed the baby down to him. She also dismounted and tied her mount's reigns to the branch of a tree. Then she walked into the shelter and swept away the snow from its floor with the side of her boot. The man handed the baby back to her and then helped the woman down from Maggie's horse. They both helped the woman into the shelter and Maggie handed her the baby. Then Maggie took off her warm fur coat and wrapped it around the shivering mother and her child.

Maggie thanked the man for his help, saying, "You go on ahead. She can't go any further. We'll stay here for the night." All of this had caught the attention of others in the pack train as they passed by, and they were moved by Maggie's selfless heroism.

The man mounted up again and, a short while later, the string of horses and mules disappeared into swirling snow leaving Maggie, the woman, and her child in near darkness and to the quiet, solitude of the elements. Maggie walked back over to her horse and loosened her bag from the saddle horn. Then she dug down into it and pulled out her other coat and some of her clothing. They would need all of the cover they could get to keep warm through the cold night ahead. Maggie found some dry kindling wood in the shelter and got a fire going. It was a long, cold night for all three of them. (The custom was to leave a stockpile of fresh wood in such places for the next person who might be in just such dire straits.)

H-1379, Haynes Foundation Coll., Montana Historical Society
What Maggie must have seen as she entered Murraysville from
the east, 1884

February 7-Thursday-When Maggie came riding into Murrayville about noon the next day she was welcomed by an enthusiastic crowd. Word had spread about the beautiful woman who'd risked her own life to save those of a mother and her child. The Thompson Falls Trail would remain closed for many days thereafter because of even more blizzards in the high country.

Maggie stopped her horse in front of the courthouse on Main Street. Then she handed the child down to a woman while someone helped the mother get down from the horse. Just then a half-drunken prospector and fellow Irishman named Phil O'Rourke, unmindful of what was going on, came walking by and looked up to see a beautiful woman sitting on great looking horse. He said, "An' who might yez be, me pretty colleen?" Looking him over, her blue eyes wide as she calmly appraised him, she answered, "I am Maggie Burdan." O'Rourke smiled up at her and, in a flirtatious moment, said, "Well Molly-B-Damn!" O'Rourke was fully taken with this lovely woman. Maggie had been renamed by the gold camp and the moniker stuck from then on.

No one batted an eye when she announced to the crowd, in full voice, that she wouldn't require a hotel room or have need of a house in the town. She was moving into cabin number one. O'Rourke beat all the others when Molly asked assistance in dismounting the horse. She immediately took residence in cabin number one on Gold Street in Paradise Alley, the street of dreams for the miners. It was common knowledge that "cabin number one" was reserved for the madam of a red light district.

Molly would go on to own a considerable amount of property and several businesses, some of which were lots in Eagle and Murray. Her Murray lot number 4, of block R, fronted on Gold Street, and ran 150 feet back to Prichard Creek.

During her seven years on the move, since leaving her husband, Burdan, in 1877, Molly had learned well the trade that he'd forced upon her. She would go on to open her own saloon in Murrayville: "With all the comforts a lonely prospector would ask for."

She would also gather a small harem of women around her for the pleasures of the many prospectors. Maggie was good to her girls, protecting them from anyone who wished to exert undue pressure on them. She even looked the other way when a customer would come crying to her after he had awakened in one of the girls rooms and found his "poke" gone. The miners lived by their small leather pokes which contained their walking-around-money, gold they had retrieved from their diggings.

Molly had strange and devious ways of appropriating money. Her philanthropic ways of disposing of it made her a paradox. Molly would "roll" a man as quickly as she would accept a drink. If she were to later learn that the man's pockets were empty or his family was in need, she would see to it that provisions were made for them. At one point, she hit upon an idea that went to extremes...even for her, but it packed in the boys and the money...and besides, it was just too much fun for a rollicking good time! She hit the jackpot, from both sides of the curtain.

The jackpot was a large tin tub, the current mode of dunking dirt, in every way. Her timing was always perfect, for she knew when certain big cleanups from placers were due. That's when Molly advertised her own big cleanup, which would be a naked-bath to be taken in the middle of Main Street. With the sun at a friendly peak, Molly and the sex-crazed boys were ready. There was plenty of glamour to this event. Banter took the place of bubbles, and tin the place of tile.

Out would come Molly, curls piled high, draperies fluttering and flowing, dragging a large tin tub behind her. Molly's glib quips were acid, salty and very funny. Her risqué chatter kept things moving, especially the pouches of pay dirt. "Come on you loiterers! You have too many anxious eyes and not enough anxious energy. Get those leaden paws onto the pouch of pay dirt. I came out here to sit on gold, not tin!"

Sit on gold she did, for it took plenty to get Molly into the tub. Washing her back never came at bargain prices and to get her out of the tub took a well-scraped bedrock of pouches.[7]

Molly was a straightforward woman, quick-tempered, but kind hearted. She is remembered for "riding a high-spirited horse and drinking her whiskey straight."

Her real acts of heroism came when quick consumption (tuberculosis) hit Murray. She willingly provided nursing services, without hesitation, to all who needed them and was an inspiration to others in helping those stricken, rather than abandoning them to their fate. But the disease finally caught up with her as well, and she died January 17, 1888, at the age of 34. A Murray newspaper reported the story: "A woman known all over the coast passes to the Great Beyond. The deceased was known only as Molly Burdan, and as such, she was known all over the coast, from the frozen north to the sunny south. She has been a conspicuous figure in this camp and for good and evil she has drawn more public attention than any other woman in her class."

6-188-1, Historical photo Coll., University of Idaho Library, Moscow

Maggie's final words were in remembrance of her beloved mother back in Ireland. "Maggie Hall is my real name. It was the name of my mother. She was a wonderful and good woman."

Her funeral procession was the largest in the history of the Coeur d'Alenes and Idaho. By 3:00 o'clock that Thursday afternoon, well over a thousand somber people had gathered on Murray's Second Street where the procession followed her casket to its final resting place in the Murray graveyard.

February 8-Friday-Winter had returned to the high mountains with a vengeance. There was a large pack train of mules on the Evolution Trail trying to get down into the city. But, because of the deepening snow, no one believed it would get through.

New construction continued and, like wildfire, new buildings spread for a distance of two miles up Eagle Creek. One of the workmen, named Johnson, received a severe cut to his leg from a misguided swing of his axe. The wound later became infected and he died of the injury.

February 9-Saturday-A stalwart newspaper reporter, working for Montana's *Missoulian News*, came into camp on foot via the Trout Creek Trail. He'd begun his long uphill climb six days earlier at Trout Creek station. On the first day he ate his lunch at eight mile station. Then, footsore and exhausted, before he camped for the night, he made it two miles further up the Bitterroots to the ten mile station. He would indeed face the tiger by going over the Trout Creek route.

> "Second day made only 3 miles. Third day camped at halfway station. Fourth day reached summit after 2 1/2 miles. Snow 5' to 15' foot deep. Fifth day left at 8 a.m. camped at 6.00 p.m.. Reached Eagle on sixth day."

February 20-Wednesday-Still in Spokane Falls, Calamity received a letter from showman and future Eagle Theater owner, J. McDaniels, inviting her to host the first dance and social event in the Coeur d'Alenes. She agreed to his offer, and brought eight women "hostesses" with her from Spokane Falls over the Jackass Trail and into Eagle City. Their arrival in camp came with much fanfare.

February 22-Friday-The dance was held in a long, tented barroom. The outside was banked high with frozen snow; within, the glow from the coal oil hanging lamps fell on a motley assemblage of frontier life: rowdy, rough, tough and noisy!

When someone asked the flamboyant Calamity how her trip was from Spokane Falls, she replied, "Hell, I could have gone to New York and back in the time it took to maneuver transfer points to get to the Jackass Junction and the agony on the trail! Another Hell!"

The warmth for this bibulous occasion was provided by a large, sheet-iron heater, centrally located, full of green timber and, Old Hunter aged in the keg at fifteen cents a drink. The roulette and gaming table and the bar were all in readiness for the star of the evening, Calamity Jane!

An unsmiling, cadaverous looking glum Lum caressed his tightly waxed handle bar and gave his orchestra of four fiddlers the beat. They went into action and, as the red calico stage curtains parted, so did Calamity Jane in her mannish woolens. She did a monologue of her life. Then the, more feminine, girls, danced and the party was on. There was the quid expert who got bounced for pinging the red hot stove. The dehydrated drunk with the quick head turn and roving eye for a free drink, the quick appraisal of who is who by the girls, and the discriminating gentlemen of the arts at the gaming and roulette tables.

A dance was announced. Eight girls were lined up at the end of the long tent. The excess number of Beau Brummell's wishing to dance made a routine imperative. Young, intoxicated prospectors were also lined up in the noisy saloon to dance with real women, which were sorely lacking in camp. Each male was allowed a choice and one turn around the dance floor, then another partner took over. Consequently, many were accommodated.

The ladies' heavily perfumed bodies countered the stench of the camp that wafted from those of the young men. It was all there: the offensive kitchen smells of the heavy woolens, a strong reminder of the skipped ice-cold ablutions of Prichard Creek, and stale breath from the human belly barrels.

Short tempers! Fights! The crimson silhouettes on the snow outside attested to this. The bouncers gave much to their manly art. Old Hunter had fouled the warriors with a rock in his sock! Then inertia; night became day. The hanging lamps cast a ghastly, dull glow. The party was over.[8]

As Calamity was saying goodbye she yelled, "At least we ain't cooking in the hot boxes of hell. We'll be a-wishing we were when we hit the 'Commodious' Jackass Trail. I'll be back when the birds are a twittering in the spring."

In the short time she'd been in camp, she'd seen that there was still no prospecting being done because of the deep snow. Calamity saw only dullness around her, so she left town and traveled back over the Jackass Trail to Spokane Falls. There she boarded the Northern Pacific to return to Livingston, Montana. It was reported that, in early May, she returned to the Coeur d'Alenes to the new town of Wallace, which is about 12 miles cross country from Murray, on the south fork of the Coeur d'Alene River.

February 26-Tuesday-Coy and Hess opened the "Daisy" at the corner of Placer and Eagle Streets; a thousand men were in the house during the evening.

The Daisy was a 30' X 50' tent-covered house and was well furnished with bar, tables, etc. Land speculators were still hard at work. The Daisy's proprietors were offered $750 per month for the empty building the day they opened, but they refused it. They thought their enterprise would be worth much more. The lease would have been for six months, with rent paid in advance.

Meanwhile, Ed Mozart of Spokane Falls leased Joy's Opera House for a term of one year. He was an old timer in the business and would secure many attractions. Among the first would be the Kendall Combination and Callendar's Minstrels, who would appear there sometime in March.

February 27-Wednesday-A warm day that excited the miners. The snow was finally beginning to melt.

February 29-Friday-Winter was finally easing its icy grip on the Coeur d'Alenes. The snow was still deep, but birds were returning to the trees, a very good sign for anxious prospectors.

> Nearly all the claims have been jumped, but the snow being five feet at Eagle no mining is being done. Though the owners of the Widow's claim intend to begin work March first with a force of forty men; on claims not opened, nothing can be done before April. Pack trains leave Evolution every day for Eagle, by which route all freight is carried to the mines, though foot passengers come in every day by way of Trout Creek.
>
> The Judge, however, prefers the first named route as it is the only one by which you can ride in. And the Trout Creek trail is full of hardships and danger; in many places you have to crawl up the steep cliffs on your hands and knees, and the mail carrier who went that way one trip and says nothing would induce him to try it again.

As in any mining camp, most of the socializing was done in the saloons at night. During daylight hours, prospectors roamed the hills looking for anything they could find of value. Then, after darkness fell, they would talk about it for hours in the bars. Lanterns hung on tent poles and store fronts the length of the busy streets, beckoning for all to come on in.

Wyatt and Jim had also been out prospecting that day before they retired to the Acion for a night of entertainment. But, this night was to be a bit different than all of the others. Wyatt was hard at work dealing faro when he heard a commotion at the bar.

A stranger had just come through the tent door, sidled up to the bar and downed his first drink. Wyatt looked up in time to see him fall to the floor. Several of the men standing next to him laughed, thinking he'd only passed out from the excesses of likker, and stooped over to help him back to his feet again. Then one of them stood slowly, still looking down, and shaking his head in dismay said, "This man is dead!"

As it turned out the stranger, William Allen, from Butte, Montana, had only just arrived in town and was a victim of the rigors of the notorious Trout Creek Trail. The poor fellow was quickly removed by the undertaker. Due to the deep snow and frozen ground, his body would be placed with the others out behind the undertaker's establishment, to await the spring thaw and the melting of the snow so the corpses could be properly buried.

Later that night, Wyatt overheard some of the men at the bar talking about another fellow who'd also tried to come to camp over the Trout Creek Trail. He'd gotten lost in deep snow on the Montana side of the Bitterroots, and become so disoriented and frozen on the way that he could not make it the rest of the way in. He remained alone for several days, although every passerby rekindled his fire and gave such assistance as they could tender him. Finally, O. A. Tibbets and Paul Lesueur took him back to the Trout Creek railroad depot. Pitifully, the man later developed pneumonia and also died.

The snow was too deep to do much prospecting, but, in their excitement, men were traveling further and further from Eagle City proper in their search for gold. New towns sprang up, closer to their new diggin's: Littlefield, Osborne City, Ives, Sullivan, and Ellensburg, to name only a few.

This situation persisted for some time. The month before, on January 22nd, other mining activity had begun three miles to the east of Eagle, toward Montana and up Prichard Creek. Surveyors Sam Hayes and Bob Horn, who'd laid out Eagle, also laid out a new town over the snow and named it Curry, in favor of prospector "General" A. P. Curry. A short while later its name was changed to Murrayville after George Murray, a part owner of one of the three creek claims on which the town was built. It was also known as Murraysville for a time.

Originally a dense forest occupied the townsite of Murray, so thick that it was with extreme difficulty that even a woodsman could make his way through it. There were pines, cedars and tamarack that rose 150 to 200 feet high to form a canopy overhead, almost shutting out the sunlight. The snow was four to five feet deep; a more forbidding place for habitation could scarcely be found.[9]

Next to Eagle, Murray was the best physical location for a town. But, as it was with Eagle, the forest was so dense that woodsmen had extreme difficulty in making their way through it to develop the townsite.

Murray's development was a carbon copy of Eagle's. Those who located there were enthusiastic over prospects for its future growth. Every branch of business would be represented, and they would all be making money. The famous Widow claim was located immediately above the town.

The Murray people were active, and enterprising and talked of making the town a lively rival to Eagle. It was speculated, though, that the camp was rich enough and extensive enough to support two or three towns the size of Eagle without their interests conflicting.

Then, just one mile to the east of Murray, persistent men happened across what would later be named the fabulous Mother Lode claim. Like Wyatt and Jim, they were also looking away from the Eagle area for new discoveries. This new claim would prove once and for all that the Coeur d'Alene district was truly the new Eldorado of the west. A fifteen foot wide vein of gold encrusted quartz could be seen in the bed of the creek where the water had laid it bare. It was one of the richest discoveries of the time.

March 1-Saturday-February finally slipped into March and the deep snow continued to melt during the day and freeze again at night. Then, to make matters even worse, some days it snowed steadily. Wyatt and Jim were still dealing cards, and Josie continued to sing. They had run into a bit of bad luck, though, along with the other card dealers in the camp.

> "The faro dealers of Eagle are having a serious time. A number of them were broken by the boys last week, and all of them without exception lost heavily."

The center of the principal mining activity had shifted away from Eagle to the mouth of Alder Gulch in Murray. The discovery of the Mother Lode claim and other new placer claims caused pulse-quickening decisions to be made that brought dozens of prospectors to the scene. They wanted to check it out for themselves to see if there wasn't some adjacent property for the taking. Working prospectors redoubled their efforts on their own claims.

Death of Stumpy Wicks

March *3-Monday-Coeur d'Alene Eagle*-Stumpy Wicks was sure dead. The mountain fever had laid its grip on 'im;..."Gone over the range," the boys said. So they got together and made a coffin out of some boxes, and put Stumpy into it, with a flour sack over his poor dead face. There were forty men in the procession but no woman. Not a woman to drop a tear, as the ex-parson read a few lines of the burial service. If Stumpy's life had any history no one knew it. It was doubtless a sad enough one. In his pocket they found a woman's picture, faded and quite worn out. Maybe that was his history.

There was not a tear at Stumpy's funeral nor a sob. But neither were there any oaths or laughter. They rounded up the mound and put up a flat rock for a headstone. When the ex-parson stepped back from the grave he stumbled over the headstone of Billy Robbins, the gambler that Antoine Sanchez knifed.

The boys were quiet. They were thinking, perhaps. They looked up at the sky which, strangely enough, had no tint of blue. Then the sky, as if in pity that had tear was shed, wept some down on them.

The procession broke up and moved back to the saloons. One man said, "It was the damnedest, mournfullest plantin' I've ever had a hand in." Men wondered what Stumpy was seeing. After a wretched, broken life, what is there for a man "over the range?" The camp didn't get back to its normal condition until the next day.[10]

Trout Creek Trail finally becomes useable for horses!

March 4-Tuesday-Banker Warren Hussey passed through the embryo city of Murray and arrived in the famous town of Eagle. He would later open a drug store in Eagle, as well.

The following is as exactly related in *Warren Hussey's diary* from several days before, on February 29th:

February 29-Friday-Goods all shipped at 11 AM Anderson going up with me Beautiful balmy day with bright sun Off for Trout Creek 9 PM all O.K.

March 1-Saturday-Trout Creek to Bkfst 8 AM Spent day loafing abt & engaging men to haul goods Stuff all in by Ft train at 3:30 & loaded in eveg for an early start tomorrow 11 loads besides Anderson's & mine

March 2-Sunday-Bkfst & off at 1/2 past 8 - 13 of us hitched up horses Warm & sunny Hard days tramp & hard pulling in PM Made 14 miles & camped at the double cabin Very tired but doing well Supper & early to bed Anderson & seven others behind

March 3-Monday-Early start Habian & I leading off Awful pull up the mountain Summit at 3 PM Met McNab Camped on the mountain 6 PM some four of us in all Spread my blankets on some pine boughs rested fairly

March 4-Tuesday-Off early Awful hard pull up Baldy but got through with it Easy going down Eagle Creek at 2 PM and town at three Habian keeping with me-balance all behind Very tired but well McNab glad to see me Two more loads got in eveg Wrote Aunty by Habian

March 5-Wednesday-Habian started back for safe   Anderson in at noon & bal of boys all in by night Cold & blustry day McN getting snow shovelled out for tent

March 9-Sunday-Getting tent in order all day Snowing steadily Very lucky to be in out of the storm   Got counter in place & tent floor partly graded Cold & ugly

March 10-Monday-Opened business for the Bk today   Looks promising Think I can make Charlie some money here Opened a/c with Kountze & Bro NY No letters   Still snowing hard Health still very good except slight cold & cough Safe arrived in evening O K

It took Habin and another man five days to return to the Trout Creek station. They dragged a 250-pound Herring, fire-proof safe on a sled up over the Trout Creek Trail to Eagle. This marked the beginning of Warren Hussey's Eagle Bank.

Meanwhile, Wyatt and Josie talked about the farm house that he'd mortgaged back in Tombstone on February 13, 1882. Wyatt knew this was the day that action was to be held on the property, to recover judgment and for the foreclosure of the mortgage. But he let it go by explaining to Josie, "I don't want anything more to do with that part of my life."

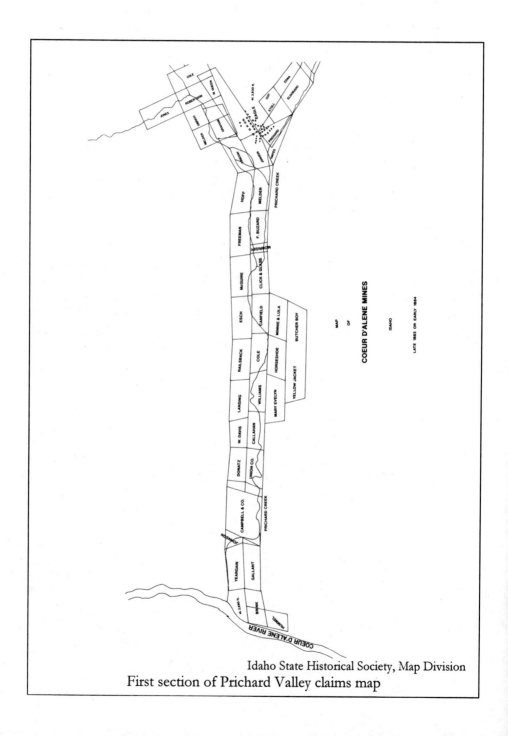

Idaho State Historical Society, Map Division

First section of Prichard Valley claims map

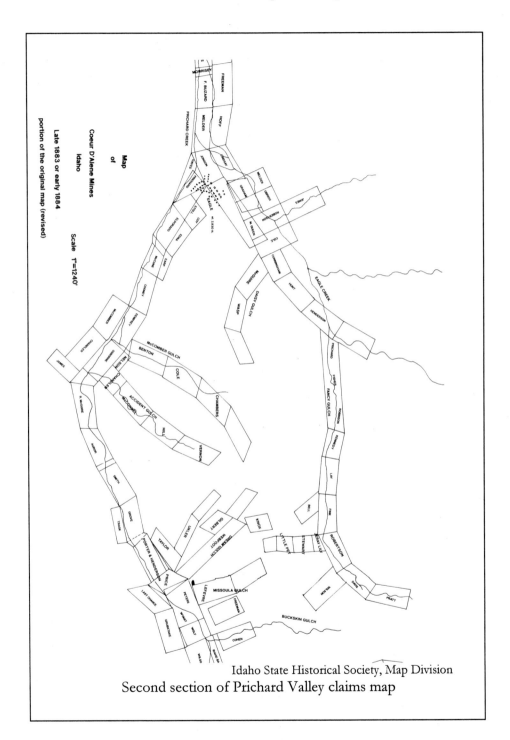

Idaho State Historical Society, Map Division

Second section of Prichard Valley claims map

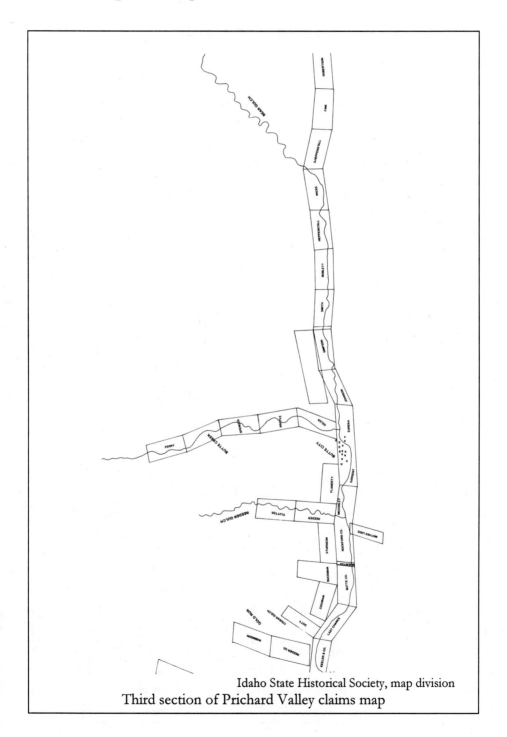

Idaho State Historical Society, map division
Third section of Prichard Valley claims map

7

White Elephant Saloon

MARCH 15-Saturday-in the seven weeks since the town of Murray was laid out on January 22nd, it had grown into a hideous, half-mile-long Main Street with three or four cross streets lined with huts, shanties, and tents. Stumps and half-charred logs encumbered the streets and served as seats for the inhabitants. It had nearly the same "ruffled" look as Eagle City had in her beginnings.

Chairs could only be found in the principal gambling establishments, of which there were many, as every second building was a drinking-saloon. So, for lack of sit-down furniture, folks used stumps to sit on. To escape the threat of getting tree sap on their behinds, they covered them with dirt or "Idaho feathers."

Business was booming as increasing amounts of newly mined gold was shipped out daily via Wells Fargo and Company Express. For lack of coin, gold dust and gold nuggets were accepted as currency in the camps. Heavy canvas bags filled with gold dust and nuggets were hauled by pack train up over the Bitterroots to the rail head at Belknap, Montana. From there the precious cargo was hauled by train to the smelter at Helena, Montana.

Eleven placer claims were down to bedrock, including the Widow, Ives, Wyant, McComber, Murray, Rockford Co. and Allman & Company.

"Freight is from 20 to 30 cents per pound. Coy and Hess opens the Daisy. Wells Fargo has office at Fort Coeur d' Alene. Evolution Trail in service   drove a cow over it."

Immigrant Charles Gay

Many of the miners panning and sluicing the gold from bedrock were dirt-farmers from the plains of eastern Washington Territory. Men used to working the land for its bounty of green with little recompense were now scratching the yellow of gold from crevasses in the rocks and gravel. Some were making as much in a single day as they could have in an entire year back on the farm.

One of those farmers, stampeded into camp from the plains of eastern Washington was Charles Gay. Word had also spread, as it had nearly everywhere else in the west, to Walla Walla, Washington, about the gold rush in the Coeur d'Alenes. Gay was a prosperous farmer with a family and didn't need the gold, but the lure of instant riches was too great for him to resist. So, in the fall of 1883, Charles said goodbye to his family and set out on foot for the Coeur d'Alenes. There was the Tucannon, Snake, and Palouse and other rivers to swim, so with only the sun and his own intuition to guide him, he went the most direct route through the mountains in Idaho.

He later told of a cougar that followed him for two days. In the silence of the forest, he'd heard the muffled cracking of branches and underbrush the cat made and occasionally saw it ahead of him, possibly trying to find a suitable place to stalk his prey. Gay had always contended cougars were natural cowards and that they would only attack when the odds were strongly in their favor.

After his departure, the family had gone about their way of life uncertain of their future. No word was received of him, but little was expected. Then, shortly before the coming of what proved to be a very hard winter, he reappeared as he had gone, afoot, tired, but enthused. The Gay family would dispose of their farm house, 160-acre farm, and the rest of their holdings, and say goodbye to their neighbors and friends during the next few months. In pioneer life, the father made the big decisions and the rest of his family never questioned his judgement.

Finally, in the spring a wagon full of happy, excited, and curious people headed east from Walla Walla for the Coeur d'Alene gold fields. Their wagon rolled along dusty miles of seemingly endless prairie land, crossing the Spokane River at Plante's Ferry (just below where the Spokane bridge now stands) and up the rugged Fourth of July Canyon, camping for the night in the Idaho mountains.

They got underway again the following morning. Charles knew the upcoming Jackass and Evolution Trails were impassable for wagons, having already traversed them on foot. So, at Kingston, he and his family left the older established route, that continued on east to Evolution. They headed north up the narrow sometimes nearly impassable road that followed the banks of the north fork of the Coeur d'Alene River. When they finally arrived at Murray, they were not altogether among strangers since two of Charles' brothers, Evans and Lodowick, had preceded them, coming up from Oregon's Willamette Valley.[1] They all three worked together and would prosper in the coming months.

Indeed, just as Calamity Jane had suspected, more than just the weather was "heating up" in the camps. Claim jumping and property transactions continued at a frantic pace. A suit would even be brought up against Earps on May 20th, claiming that they took forcible possession of a claim. The Earps would win the judgment on July 25, 1884.

Wyatt's business partners Holman, Payne and Ferguson were doing well for themselves, too. They'd purchased a lot, located on the east side of Eagle Street, from Phil Wyman, upon which they erected a small living tent.

M. L. Hedin is going to build a two story house on Gold Street, the upper story to be used as a Masonic Hall. Sid Benton of Colfax, is putting up a mammoth wholesale and retail liquor and cigar house. He will be running inside of a week. Mr. S. W. Ryerson, of Raven City, is authority for the statement that one hundred and twenty miles of claims are marked out and located on the main gulches and their branches above Raven.

Meanwhile, the steady flow of humanity into the camp continued unabated.

A motley throng is to be seen on our streets. Among the three thousand people who have thus early found their way to the Coeur d'Alene mines, a large proportion are businessmen. They are men of means, of energy, of intelligence, who come here to obtain the first opportunities of investment which are so desirable in all new camps.

They are shrewd, toughly informed men, who eagerly compete with each other for the miner's business prizes which are to be drawn in this great mining excitement lottery.

There are hundreds of laborers here, hewers of wood, and men who are content to earn honest wages for honest work. They are stalwart, sinewy fellows, who toil early and late, in snow and storm or sunshine. These are they who are building cities in these desolate mountain wilds. There are gamblers here, of that rest assured. There are hundreds of them. Gamblers of the genuine Bret Harte Style.

Monte Verde

Josie had met and befriended singer Lurline Monte Verde who, for a short while, also lived in Eagle. Josie's new acquaintance had several other stage names including Madam Vestel and Belle Siddons, and had been in Deadwood in the Dakotas at the same time as Calamity Jane. The two show women talked for hours about their common interests.

Lacking other forms of entertainment, pioneers in Montana and Idaho looked eagerly forward to the coming of these show people, who traveled six or seven hundred miles from Salt Lake in spring wagons with scenery to give their entertainment. Aside from the conversant saloons, a few dances in winter, Thanksgiving, Christmas, and, of course, Fourth of July celebrations, the men had little entertainment.

Monte had a log house across the dirt street from A. J. Prichard's cabin on Prichard Avenue. In front of her cabin, she had caused to be erected a small stage for shows which an audience could watch while seated on benches. During such shows, Monte, another woman and a man did stunts, sang and danced. A flute, guitars, and violins made up their accompanying orchestra.

She was a forty-year-old, good looking woman who ran a clean show. To the lonesome miners' delight, Monte sang in a beautifully modulated voice and, with the use of stage props, exchanged dialogue with the other two actors. Their antics at times raised such a fervor in the audience that cheers and laughter could be heard echoing back from the surrounding mountainsides. Some of the songs they sang she'd written herself and were cleverly disguised as musical-tools, with which she told the story of a woman who'd traveled with a show troupe of actors to an out post town.

Another of her songs, sung with guitar accompaniment, had six or seven stanzas and was known as "The Coeur d'Alene Song." It was always greatly applauded by appreciative audiences who often sang along with her. The 160 acres referred to in the Coeur d'Alene song was a dig at the Palouse farmers who came in droves into the Coeur d'Alenes.

"Shoulder shovel, pick and pan, pack your blankets if you can. Take up a homestead of a hundred-sixty-acre claim."[2]

March 22-Saturday-*Coeur d'Alene Nugget***-**Men can batch for $4-$7 a
week. Wanted immediately, ten first-class variety ladies, good dressers and
of handsome figure on the stage. Address J. McDaniels, Eagle City, I. T.
No Chinaman shall ever enter the camp on pain of expulsion or death and
the expulsion of the person importing such Chinaman.

A man popularly known as the Major suggested to people of the camp that he could take his coolies to build a wagon road over the Heron fork of the Coeur d'Alene River about ten miles from Hummel's landing. He would be content, after the completion of the road, to work the celestials on the latter stream in opening up placer diggings. Both proposals were rejected by the miners. In those days the Major had a mental picture of all the bedrock of the creeks being heavily covered with gold dust, as did most other people in the district. He hoped to use the Chinamen's meticulous ways of prospecting to recover that gold.

Shortly thereafter, Major Reed came by train to Belknap with fifty Chinese ready to build a wagon road over the trail into Prichard Creek. The miners warned him then that he could build the road on the Montana side, but white labor would be used on the Idaho side. A noosed rope and sign were fastened to a tree on top the pass. The sign read: "This is for the first Chinaman who crosses this pass into Idaho."[3]

The Major's gang of Chinese workers, under a Chinese boss, began building the road from Belknap, shoveling snow and constructing corduroy (bed of logs) over swampy places. Their labored efforts saw them zigzagging for ten or twelve miles from the base of the mountains up to the summit. It took three or four men, each throwing the snow to the man on the level above, to trench the snow down to the ground twenty to twenty-five feet below. They worked faithfully until the middle of April, when the pay had been promised, but it never came. The Chinese laborers never received a cent for their work. Their rice, tea, and other provisions were sent prepaid from a Chinese firm in Portland. It was piteous to see them come from Belknap carrying their belongings oriental-fashion on sticks over their shoulders.

March 29-Saturday-*Coeur d'Alene Nugget,* Vol. 1, No. 3-"Three sawmills in area-Hood & Co., Browns, and Spokane Mill. Palace Saloon opens. Ainsworth, Hawkins & Co. opens bank in a fine board house. The Leadville opens by Hayes & Laseur."

April 1-Tuesday-*Coeur d'Alene Nugget-*Silver and one dollar bills are so scarce in the mines that it is extreme difficulty to get change for a five. Change is decidedly at a premium and parties coming here would do well to bring in a supply. Merchants and business men are very accommodating to each other, but all are constantly cramped for change in conducting their transactions.

Warren Hussey in town getting ready to establish a bank. Jarrison and Stoll open a saloon, within forty eight hours of the time they began shoveling away the snow for the foundation.

April 2-Wednesday-Wyatt files for the Eagle Creek placer claim. That night he sat in his cabin talking with Josie about their state of affairs. Between Wyatt's dealing faro and Josie's singing in the Acion Saloon, they had been keeping busy during the slack time of the seemingly endless winter months. For some weeks, though, the weather had been warming and he had been spending most of his time prospecting with Jim up in the mountains.

Wyatt picked up the copy of the *Spokane Falls Review* newspaper that he'd brought home with him, and began to read. A few minutes later he laughed aloud and said, "Josie, this is what we need." He read to her:

Beds for the sick rooms

Two narrow beds, with fresh hair or straw mattresses, are the best. These beds are easily moved, and thus the patient will not be compelled to look constantly at the same cracks in the wall, or count the same spots in the corner. You can move him, now into a shaded corner, now to the western window to see the sun go down, again in front of the fire that he may look at the cheerful blaze, and again into the most secluded corner that he may rest and sleep. All this is an immense gain, and is sure not only to comfort the patient, but to shorten his sickness. No matter what malady may be, there is more or less fever, and, in every possible case, the examinations from skin render the bed foul through and through. All the examinations should be got rid of as soon as possible. The only way to manage is to have two beds, and lift the patent from one to the other when the bed which has been in use from four to six hours is replace the mattress and blankets should be thoroughly aired and if practicable sunned. This will not only shorten and ease the graver stages of the malady, but will greatly hasten the convalescence.[4]

Another article caught his eye and he read it silently:

A card
Fort Coeur d'Alene

"In behalf of the officers and ladies of this post who participated in the recent rendition of Pinafore, I take this method of thanking the gentlemen of Spokane who very kindly requested a repetition at that place, and very much regret that circumstances will not allow a fulfillment of this request for some time."

F. T. Van Liew, 2d Lieut. Inf.[5]

April 4-Friday-There had, for some time, been a festering rivalry between two groups of men over ownership of a lot at the lower end of the one solitary street in Eagle City. On the one side was the Earp/Enright faction, as they had become known to the locals, whose members included, among others, J. E. Jack Enright, Payne, Holman and Ferguson. They claimed legal ownership of the land, having purchased it from Philip Wyman, who had built foundations on the front of the property. On the other side of the argument were residents Fay Buzard and three of his associates-who were in the process of building a log hotel on the lot.

The situation finally boiled over when the beleaguered, smaller Buzard pointed a loaded Winchester into the much taller Enright's face and ordered him off the lot. Enright was at a marked disadvantage and saw the wisdom in leaving. He held his temper, though, and as he walked away he angrily vowed to Buzard that he'd be back.

Buzard was by nature a gentle man. He'd arrived in camp several months earlier in the winter of 1883. Later, when George and Frank Heller, with their baby sister, Lily and mother, Elsie, arrived in Eagle City, they became acquainted with him. George Heller, who was later regarded as one of the true local historians of the gold rush days, liked to tell of how Buzard christened his little sister with a sprinkling of snow. He prefixed "Coeur d'Alene" to Lily so as to crown her "Coeur d'Alene Lily" in honor of her being the first baby girl in the mining camp.

The better part of discretion had kept Buzard from firing upon Enright because he was unarmed. The "Old West" frowned indignantly upon shooting anyone who wasn't "heeled." Famous gunman and killer Clay Allison once refused to gun down his unarmed avowed enemy, Ground Owl (Bennington du Pont), as did Marshal Wyatt Earp when he spared the main object of his vengeance, the unarmed Ike Clanton, in the famous fight at the O.K. Corral. In that case, just as the fight broke out, the desperate Ike Clanton rushed to Wyatt and pleaded for his life, declaring that he was unarmed. To which Wyatt coolly replied: "The fight has now commenced; go to fighting, or get away."[6] Ike ran off to safety, leaving his brother, Billie, and friends, the McLaurys, to die in the face of withering fire from the Earps and Doc Holliday. However, there has been some evidence that Clanton was actually armed at the time.

Another case of such "chivalry" was when a fourteen-year-old sheep herder in Colorado was exchanging shots with an enemy cowboy, until the latter said, "Don't shoot. I'm empty." To which the boy responded, "Well then, load up while I wait." Rather than continuing the fight, the cowboy ran away.[7]

Buzard had the right background to defy the Earps and Enright. He and several other hard cases had only recently come to the Coeur d' Alenes from the infamous mining camp of Bodie, California.[8] It was a hell-raising camp with such a reputation of wickedness and whiskey-induced reveille that when a young girl found out her parents were moving to Bodie, she said one last prayer:

"Goodbye Lord…we're going to Bodie."

Buzard had run into their kind before. Some sixteen years earlier, in the late summer of 1867, he was in the town of Bear River, Utah, when the Union Pacific Railroad was being built through. Grading the earth down to a level surface in preparation of the laying of steel rails was a back-breaking job. Ten thousand men of all nationalities, but most Irish, spent their days at the task.

Towns like Bear River City sprang up at every favorite trading point. Bear River was situated in a narrow canyon with just enough room for the river and a grade for the railroad, which was used as a street with buildings on either side.

Most of the structures were built of sawn lumber, but there were a few log houses, as well. One of the latter, at the lower end of town, was designated as a jail and furnished by the citizens, there being no provisional government.

Two of the Irish graders who had robbed and strangled a citizen, nearly killing him, were confined in the calaboose by the town's so-called marshal. A committee from the nearest grading camp waited upon the citizen, bringing him back to health, and demanded the release of the two graders, saying that if the two men were not released, graders would come in sufficient force to release them, burn the jail and the town. However, the two graders were not released by the stubborn townsmen.

The following day, some 5,000 graders quit working to march on Bear River City. They broke down the jail door, released the graders, and then set fire to the building. As the flames overtook the structure, the enraged mob marched through the town to its upper end where the building that housed the town's only newspaper, the *Frontier Index*, stood. The paper, a weekly, was published by L. K. Freeman, a writer of considerable individuality, who later located at Yakima, Washington. They didn't agree with some of his editorials concerning their number and were out to lynch him. Freeman, however, had fled across the river. They burned the office after throwing its contents into the river.

Bill Buzard, an interested citizen, had taken careful note of proceedings and, as the mob was returning from the brightly lit newspaper office, he ran through the town loudly calling for the people to arm themselves and to follow him into Freund's Hardware store. Buzard knew that Freund had just received a case of twelve Spencer rifles (seven-shooters) and a consignment of revolvers.

"Don't be a lot of cowards and whine; defend your property, wives and children!" he yelled. Some twenty to twenty-five of the bravest followed his self-imposed leadership and hurried into the store, virtually packing it with bodies.

But before the guns could be properly distributed, Tom Smith, a giant of a man who led the mob, rushed ahead to the Freund store. He saw the men run into the store ahead of him and close the door. Whereupon he took aim, deliberately firing into the outer wall of the building several times, killing a young merchant outright.

Buzard yelled to the men in the crowded store for all to make a rush for the street and commence shooting. He led the thoroughly aroused men to action and, as they exited the building, they turned the seven-shooters on the rioters who fled, retreating down the street pell-mell.

Forty dead were reported in dispatches to United States Marshal Hosmer at Salt Lake City. How many more were wounded was never revealed. A battalion of regular Calvary made a forced run from Fort Bridger to the bloody battleground and brought the situation under lawful control. Bill Buzard was idolized by the people of Bear City for his heroic conduct during this desperate time in their behalf. He drifted from town to town for the next sixteen years, finally to meet this challenge by the Earps and Enright's in the Coeur d'Alenes.[9]

Buzard and his men had already done a considerable amount of work, shoveling snow from the actual site of the hotel and from the sidewalk in front of it. Their mighty labors had left a seven-to eight-foot-high wall of snow piled all around the perimeter of the property, unintentionally, but effectively, building a fort for themselves. The sight of great heaps of snow along the walkways wasn't uncommon, though, as the owners of other town lots did the same in order to make walking easier and more pleasant.

One fact that neither Buzard nor his associates had considered, as they shoveled the snow, would prove to be significant in coming events. Because the ambient temperature warmed during daylight hours and dropped to well below freezing at night, the great piles of snow had slowly melted into solid, rock-hard walls of ice.

A few minutes after Enright had retreated from the pointed-end of Buzard's Winchester, he returned, but in the company of his friends: Payne, Holman, and Ferguson. The heavily armed men marched up snowy Eagle Street straight for the lot in question. Enright had gone to the Earp brother's gambling house to arm himself and recruit his friends to help displace Buzard.[10]

After Buzard had threatened Enright with his rifle and Enright had gone, he shrugged off Enright's threat of retaliation as a lot of blow. However, a while later, when he happened to glance up and see Enright and three other heavily armed men walking quickly down the center of the street toward him, he knew that he'd seriously misjudged the situation.

Buzard shouted the alarm to his three friends and they hastily prepared for a fight, loading their guns and planning their defense. They would use the partially finished log structure and even the wall of snow in front of it for cover, if need be.

Those bystanders who happened to see what was coming scattered for safety, taking every advantage of good viewing places while still remaining out of harm's way. The only person still in sight was a man sitting on a scaffold erected for whipsawing lumber. He knew nothing of the trouble that was about to take place and the first intimation he had of it was a shower of bullets from the attacking party. Without waiting for a second volley, he tumbled off the scaffold into the deep snow and after he'd regained his feet, struck out into the timber as fast as he could go. This was great sport for the people, who had so arranged themselves as to see the battle without getting hit by a stray bullet.

When the approaching men were about the right distance away, Buzard quickly stepped up onto the log foundation, looked over the snow bank if front of it, drew his pistol and started blasting away. Then he jumped down behind the logs and the fight was on. Smoke from his pistol's first shots hung in the air high above him and his shootin' back friends.

Meanwhile, Enright and his men had dodged for cover to both sides of the street, and returned fire. Gunfire reports cracked through the air, echoing back from the mountainsides, letting the folks in Eagle know that there was a fight. Bullets whizzed past the participants, spinning off like angry bees into the distance. With eight guns blazing, it didn't take long for some fifty shots to be fired (according to a later newspaper report).

Enright and his determined men, while still firing, began to work their way forward from cover to cover advancing on the lot. The shooting had been going on for about ten minutes when Buzard and his associates saw the wisdom of retreat. They ran into a cabin at the back of the lot. Buzard, the last to enter the cabin, had two bullets pass through the crown of his hat. Enright was similarly nearly "crowned" when a bullet zinged past right ear as he continued the advance.

Wyatt had heard the fracas from his and Josie's cabin and armed himself. Then he joined Jim and they made their way to the comical scene. As they approached, Wyatt saw men stooping down behind stumps, logs and telegraph poles shooting into a cabin that was heavily fortified by thick logs and fronted by a solid wall of impenetrable ice. Wyatt knew that there was no way bullets could pass through any of the obstacles between the two groups of men and made light of the situation. Acting in his capacity as Deputy Sheriff of Kootenai County he and Jim stepped into the middle of the fight as peacemakers.

With characteristic coolness, they stood where the bullets from both parties flew about them, joked with the participants upon their poor marksmanship and, although they pronounced the affair a fine picture, they used their best endeavors to stop the shooting.

A few minutes later Wyatt's counterpart, Shoshone County Deputy Sheriff W. F. Hunt, arrived on the scene, as well. He also ordered both sides to stop shooting. Then, working in concert with Wyatt and Jim, Hunt entered the cabin and disarmed Buzard's group, while the Earps ordered Enright and his shooters to put up their guns.

Later, in the true spirit of the American West, Enright and Buzard drank together and complemented each other on their courage. The only casualty of the fight was bystander and carpenter John Burdette, who was shot through the fleshy part of his thigh. His choice of cover hadn't been the best.[11]

Buzard later surfaced in the Shoshone County seat at Pierce, Idaho, on the other side of the divide, and it's probable that Buzard Roost and a nearby spot called Getaway Point got their names from his fight with Enright and Ferguson.[12]

April 6-Sunday- *Warren Hussey's Dairy*-"Nothing special Open until 2 p.m. Closed & went to church Nice day - Dull biz & no profits"

April 7-Monday-This was a day of real estate purchases for the Earp faction. First, Wyatt and Jim, Enright, Holman and Ferguson paid $500 to Florence McCarthy for ten placer acres on Prichard Creek. Next they purchased one-half interest in the Bloomfield placer for $500 and lot 57 on Eagle Street from Fay Buzard for $500. At the same time they also paid Buzard $2,250 for a round, circus-like duck tent that was fifty feet across and stood an amazing forty five feet high. The well-equipped tent had pine board flooring and a wooden stage. It was Eagle City's newest and largest dance hall and would prove to be a lucrative venture for all of its investors.

April 9-Wednesday-_Coeur d'Alene Nugget- Vol. 1, No. 5-_"Golden
Gate Saloon opens, J. E. Jack Enright Pete Webber, managers. Comstock
opens-Tom Wilson, manager. Wells Fargo Express arrives every other day.
Ainsworth's bank still operating."

McDonald Killing

In early April even more gunplay was heard and the ire of Eagle was
raised when T. F. Richards shot and killed Walter McDonald. There as even talk
of a lynching, but cooler heads prevailed and a coroner's jury was convened.
Much to the chagrin of many, because of the testimony of witnesses, the deed
was held as justifiable homicide. Richards was only defending himself against a
drunken McDonald. He was released from custody and returned to the
mountains to his claim.[13]

April 15-Tuesday-Wyatt's group was still busily buying up property and paid
one dollar to W. H. "Fatty" Carroll of Fort Coeur d'Alene for part interest in the
Point of Rock placer on Eagle Creek.

April 16-Wednesday-_Hussey Diary-_"Sent out a big mail this morning
First out of camp Biz quiet but a good feeling in camp & out look bright
Ugly boil in my nose & cold in my head"

The Livingston, MT **Daily Enterprise** "Calamity Jane has successfully
escaped various trials and tribulations incident to a trip to the Coeur
d'Alenes, and is back in Livingston again. She has had enough of the mines
and has had a life's experience in western camps, and is able to size up a
new country pretty intelligently."

April 19-Saturday-The opening of the Golden Gate Saloon yesterday
evening was a decided event in camp. J. E. Jack Enright and Pete Webber are so
well known and so popular that the boys came down from all the towns in the
gulch and gave them a roaring house warming. Standing room could hardly be
obtained inside the large tent at many times during the evening, especially in the
vicinity of the delicious clam chowder which was served out free to all.

Champagne flowed as freely as water in the Golden Gate, and the bar did
an immense business. The faro games were thronged, the limit being as high as
the players could ask. The building is attractively furnished and well lighted and
the bar fixtures tastefully arranged and decorated. Everybody was in the best of
spirits and all present pronounced the opening a grand success. A free clam
chowder will be served again tonight at the Golden Gate, and a cordial invitation
is extended to all in the camp to be present.

Over-flowing business filled the Earp's new dance hall, as well. The boys were eager to dance the night away with whatever and whoever wore a dress.

Exodus Begins

As the snow melted, prospectors were finding that the ground wasn't strewn with free gold as they had hoped and they began to loose heart. While many claims had yielded an ounce of gold a day to the man, and some others had given even larger cleanups, it was found that the greatest wealth of the country was beyond the reach of the poor man. It would take capital to develop lode mines and follow the riches underground. Some effort was made to interest capital in ditch schemes and other developments, and a few enterprises of the kind were begun. [14]

One such enterprise was the Bedrock Flume, meant to furnish water for Murray and for the working of hillside claims, as well as to float mining timbers, lumber, fuel, etc. to points where needed along its course. In October there would be 285 men at work on the bed rock flume at Eagle, an enterprise which claimed to be the most gigantic ever undertaken in the history of placer mining up to that date.

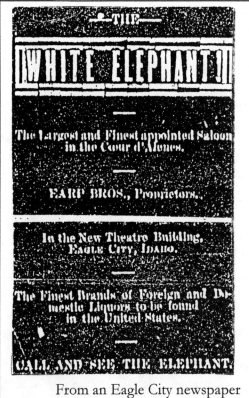

From an Eagle City newspaper

Many of those who'd come to the Coeur d'Alenes for its easy wealth were finding that there was none, at least not for them. The exodus from camp by these disheartened souls picked up in momentum. Most of them were dead broke and were afforded charity by businesses along their way. These unfortunates would sign their name with a D. B., meaning dead broke. Each day, their growing number could be seen carrying packs of blankets toward the mountain trails in much the same fashion as when they'd arrived in the Coeur d'Alenes only months, or in some cases mere weeks, before.

April 26-Saturday-Wyatt remained steadfast, though, in the belief that there were still riches to be had for those who stayed. With this resolve, he paid $132 for a tent with complete furnishings. The long, pointed-roofed tent was located north of and adjoining Sam Hayes' store next door to the Troy Laundry and Bath House. (This was later named the White Elephant Saloon.)

> *Actual deed*: With poles, door and floor situated on lot north of S. H. Hayes' store and immediately adjoining same. The stove pipe chares tables benches. Bar and bar fixtures therein contain together with all stock in said building contained with all lamps chandeliers and their fixtures.

April 30-Wednesday-Wyatt paid W.R. Vaughn $1,000 for five acres in Dream Gulch. W. Payne sued Wyatt over some town land in Eagle. Payne won and was awarded $75.

May 1-Thursday-Wyatt buys Golden Gate claim on east fork of Reeder Gulch. "A dance house is in full blast on Eagle Street, a large number of 'girls' having arrived."

Noah Spencer Kellogg

Fifty-five-year-old Noah Kellogg came into Eagle City, nearly broke, having only $5.00 left of a loan he'd gotten from a friend in order to get there. His wife, Mary, was stricken with paralysis and he'd left her in Dayton, Washington, in the care of her two grown daughters. Like everyone else in camp, he came to the Coeur d'Alenes hoping to better his financial situation. Discovering that there was a great demand for laborers, he found work as a carpenter and roustabout for Murray businessman and builder Origin Peck. He later tried his hand at a shingle mill, but due to mechanical problems, circumstances weren't in his favor. He never sold a shingle.

However, in September 1885, Noah would go on to become the richest man in the Coeur d'Alenes, with his discovery of the famed Bunker Hill lode, on the south fork of the Coeur d'Alene River. It was a discovery that wouldn't have been made by him, but for the aid of a lowly Spanish burro. The resulting town was named Kellogg, in his honor, and the towering mountain that rose above the town was named Jackass Peak in his furry companion's honor.

By December of 1885, the first shipment of high-grade ore was loaded into canvas bags, placed aboard the grand steamer *Coeur d'Alene,* and transported by water to the city of Coeur d'Alene. From there it was loaded onto wagons and hauled across the Rathdrum Prairie to Rathdrum. There it was loaded on Northern Pacific Railway cars, taken to Portland, Oregon and thence by steamer to San Francisco. The first shipment assayed out at an incredible 2,000 ounces of silver to the ton. Noah's Bunker Hill would become the world's largest lead silver mine, making many millionaires in the process.[15]

Among several others who would also be involved in the discovery and become wealthy was "Dutch" Jake Goetz. Dutch was born in Germany in 1853, migrated to the Coeur d'Alene gold fields in 1884, and came to Murray from Eagle to help lay out the town. Later he married Louisa Knuth and theirs was one of the most celebrated weddings in the region. Invites were nailed to trees and circulated widely and the gaily affair was graced by a six-foot-high cake.

May 7-Wednesday-*Coeur d'Alene Nugget*-All the mines have yielded

finely this week. The George B. Ives, H. E. Wolf and the Widow continue to yield over an ounce a day to the man.[16] Missoula Gulch lacks water, but is recognized as ranking among the best paying claims. Lucky Gulch and the Gelatt are getting ready to turn out hansom quantities of dust. This week settles the fact that Eagle Creek is as rich as the most sanguine have predicted. Oregon and all the side gulches are giving first class prospects.

Everybody in camp was excited over quartz. Discoveries were reported daily that are too fabulous for belief. The richness of the placers is universally acknowledged and the day of croaking has passed. Many an old prospector, however, will not condescend to look for placer ground, because such magnificent returns are assured from the quartz. Gen. A. P. Curry has interviewed the bankers and businessmen of Eagle and found that exactly 58 1/3 pounds of gold dust were handled by them in the last two weeks. This is doubtless only a small part of the dust taken out, most miners preferring to keep the dust to themselves.

Buckskin Gulch has given the camp the principal excitement of the past week. Hundreds of men have flocked thither, to witness the very unusual spectacle of men picking gold from the earth instead of washing it out in a pan. This is about what they witnessed: "Robert Williams, David Bryant, John F. Hennessy and Frank Barnes own claim No. 3 and upon striking bedrock got from $2 to $20 to the pan. The entire bedrock averaged $5 to the pan. One nugget weighed $45 (2.25 oz.). The excitement was intensified by Nate Vestal at the mouth of Buckskin finding ounce diggings in the gravel.

Two cleanups on the Widow this week netted 60 ounces and 8 pennyweights and 88 ounces respectively. Work has been commenced on a ditch to be taken from Alder Creek. This ditch will be two and one-half miles long and greatly increase the production of the Widow. From the Webfoot, Gen. A. P. Curry washed $21.50 from one pan of dirt selected at random. The total yield of the Webfoot thus far has been something over 71 pounds or $10, 052. 65.

May 9-Friday-*NW Tribune-*Provisions and labor are now paid for in dust. Laborers are in demand at $5 per day and board. The bankers estimate the daily yield of the camp at $5,000.

The pack trains of Messrs. Burns and Chapman make three trips per week from their wholesale store at Eagle City to their supply depot at the end of the road near Raven.

A man came into Goodchild & Co.'s store Tuesday with $125 in gold dust, bought supplies and went hurriedly back into the woods. He would not tell where his diggings are.

8-N74, Hist. Photo coll., University of Idaho Library, Moscow
Rockford placer, Prichard Creek

W. Friedman grubstaked a man named Newman the other day and he was gone only 6 1/2 hrs when he returned and said excitedly: "Come up the creek and see what your grubstake has done." He went with him three miles up Prospect Creek and saw the ledge his friend had discovered. It is nine feet wide and crops up a distance of 35 feet above the rich loam of the forest. Taking a hatchet, he knocked off a piece that is the prettiest white quartz any one ever saw. It is evidently free milling and is flaked with gold and silver. The ledge is not over three miles from town.

The snow has disappeared from south hillsides and from the bottoms as high up as Osborne's and the mountains are full of prospectors and new discoveries were made every day of both gold and silver lodes. Dream Gulch was producing about 100 ounces of fine gold every 24 hours. On Friday Harvey Howell, a commercial traveler from San Francisco, came in from Murraysville. He saw $1,997 cleaned up from one day's sluicing by ten men in Dream gulch.

A letter from one of the stampeders to his brother:

Eagle City, Shoshone Co. Idaho T.

May, 9th, 1884.

Dear Brother,

I am well at present and in the new "Eldorado." Coeur d'Alene is not what it is represented to be. It may be a good camp after while but it is no good now. We are prospecting and if we find anything, we will be able to sell, any kind of a prospect at all sell here and we are liable to find a $20,000 ledge any day. We will have remarkable bad luck if we don't.

I had a long and tiresome trip in getting to Eagle City. I only reached here 2 weeks ago today, and I had to walk about 40 miles and carry a load the last 30 miles. A load of about 45 pounds over a mountain covered with snow and in the places where the snow was melted the mud was knee deep!

The snow was shoveled off to make a trail and in some places it in was banked up 10 feet on both sides of the trail! We killed lots of deer and grouse when we first came into the country but we don't get any now. A grouse is a fine bird about the size of a game hen and very fat. They are very tame too for a game bird.

There is no wagon road into camp yet or won't be for months to come. The first wagon arrived in Camp about a week ago. (hauled up the river in a boat) and they made more fuss about it than they make in Half Moon Bay on the 4th of July. The trucks used before that, were hand made. The round end of a bed sawed off for wheels. Wooden axles, and pins in the end to keep the wheels from coming off.

I am now staying at Murrayville four miles from Eagle City. But my Post Office address is Eagle, Shoshone Co. Idaho, T.

I have heard no news of the outside world since I came in here. This might be a good place for you to come to after a while but at present I would not advise you to come as a man has got to go through all kinds of hardships and work is scarce and hard.

I can not get any papers in here but I hope it will not be long before papers will be plenty in a month or so.

I have not received a letter from home since I left there but expect one every day. When I first came in here they charged 50 cts for a letter but now there is no charge. The Post Office is the same as any other P.O.

Did Theodore get employment in Oakland or not? Give my love to all the folks at home and any inquiring friends in the city.

Receive the same from you.

John H. Pitcher.

In November, John Pitcher returned to Half Moon Bay, California where he became the Justice of the Peace and for forty years he was known as "Judge Pitcher."[17]

Eagle City had a privileged character who seemingly had a peculiar right or immunity. His name was Ike Trumlea and he was from a well respected family in Salt Lake City where he'd been an auctioneer. In camp, though, the little sixty-year-old Ike was known as "old man Shake 'em up."

He'd built an 8' x 8' hut in the middle of the street in the most frequented place in Eagle, opposite the banks, stores and saloons. Nobody seemed to object, though. Turns out that he was in the second hand business. He was buying everything he could from those who had given up on finding gold and were leaving camp by the drove on their way back to the railroad. So, there in the middle of the street stood old man Shake 'em up waving a shirt, coat or pants on a stick crying, "shake 'em up" in an exciting, mirthful way. This drew the attention of the passing populace, who laughed at his idiosyncrasies.

There were those who hadn't had a bath or change of clothes for weeks. The parasitic creatures that were feeding on their skin, giving them creative sensations, were what the old man was alluding to.

May 10-Saturday-Wyatt locates the Consolidated Grizzly Bear quartz claim. The following day he locates the Dividend claim, two miles up Fancy Gulch. Then Earp, Enright and Northam locate the Dead Scratch claim on the slope of Bald Mt., about nine miles up the north fork of Eagle Creek. Later assays from their newest claim were $103.45 gold and $10.21 silver ledge of free milling ore.

The following *letter* from Rufus Dunlap shows some errors in fact, but can be considered to be source material:

I arrived in Thompson Falls from Townsend, Montana about first of May, 1884, with a carload of potatoes, two cows, and a string of horses belonging to W. G. Stagner. Stopped there for a few days. Pulled out over a snow trail for Eagle City 39 miles with my pack on my back with golden thoughts in my mind. Landed in Eagle 10th of May. Stopped in Cedar Hotel $1.00 a meal for a spud, a little bread and a little

Historic Wallace Preservation Society, Inc., RD-09
Rufus Dunlap at rest in front of his cabin

bacon, one more dollar to spread my blankets on a pole spring bed with balsam bows for feathers.

The first work I did was to fence a marsh for Stagner below Eagle City 1/4 of a mile worked for him until fall then went up Eagle fell in with Archie Smith he was packing up grub for myself and partner James Taylor. We put up a log cabin W. E. Smith and I did not see much of each other until fall. We went to work for a Co. for awhile. They soon broke up and Smith came over and we all three went to work on a claim Taylor and I had. We cleaned up something near $100. Taylor said, "You fellows give me the gold and take the claim." We did then we soon quit the little side gulch called Taylor Gulch lead one follows interest in Eagle Creek we had some good ground. We bought him out, from there on we kept on buying ground for years to come.

Turner passed on last year which was a sad blow for Mr. Guthre. The Earp brothers and J. E. Jack Enright, those fellows were saloon men. Enright's wife Lou was a faro dealer. The boys was crazy to play at her table. She was Queen of Eagle City. There was claim jumping, killing over lot jumping you had better not talk back to a mob that followed up jumping lots and claims. If you had any trouble with them you had better get to work first Bill Buzard and his gang got into a gun battle over a lot that they was building a house on. There was Bill Pain [Payne] whistling Dick, Danny Ferguson, was going to run Buzard off but they was confronted with a volley of 44 bullets. Buzzard and his gang had a pile of logs for breast works. The Payne gang was behind stumps, and telegraph poles which the splinter was flying off lively for a while. But they was poor shots for there was no casualty. Just a few flesh wounds.

Danny Ferguson shot a man one night over a sporting woman and they got him out of it. I was at the inquest and he sat of the head of the corpse, smoking a cigar with his legs crossed. This was in a saloon the sheriff give him a show to escape one eve while he took him out for exercise he stole a boat and went down north fork then he went over to Helena, Montana was shooting off his mouth what he did over in Idaho. The vigilantes gave him 24 hours to get away from town which he did he went over on the Yellowstone Valley got into a cowboy camp was saying he was getting anxious to find another notch on old Betsy's stock. The Cowboys invited him to take a walk with them. The next morning he was found at the end of a rope which was justice.

Pat Flynn shot a man in a saloon in Wallace for throwing a glass of beer in his face. He never served any time. There was a good many killed in here before anyone was convicted of a crime. Smith and I packed grub on our backs for a good may years. We finally got us 5 head of pack horses then we was well fixed. We would send them out to Thompson Falls with nigger Bill to winter them for $10 a head he would bring them back in the spring fat and slick. If you can get any thing out of this trash well and good as ever yours.

Sincerely R. E. Dunlap

May 29-Thursday-Jim locates Jessie Jay on West Fork of Reeder Gulch.

May 31-Saturday-The seventeen ounce nugget, found in Placer Gulch, was brought over to the bank of Murray on Tuesday. It is a companion piece on the counter with the nineteen ounce chunk from the Gelatt claim.

Letter from ex-soldier and road builder John Mullan about the supreme achievement of his life.

June 4-Wednesday-

Washington, D. C., June 4, 1884.

Editor Eagle: I have received your very courteous letter of May 21, 1884. It is exceedingly gratifying to me to view and read of the developments that are now taking place in your section of the country, which for so many years was my camping ground, and where I became familiar with many of the difficulties of opening up so wild a region of our mountain system, and particularly when they are set forth in a sprightly journal like the Eagle, right in the heart of such development.

I am not at all surprised at the discovery of numerous rich gold deposits in your mountains, because both on the waters of the St. Joseph and Coeur d'Alene, all of which indicated the presence of gold. Nay, more, I now recall quite vividly one of my herders and hunters a man by the name of Mose, a French-Canadian (the son-in-law of Louis Brown, then living at Frenchtown, a little village about 15 miles below Missoula) coming into camp one day with a handful of course gold which he said he had found on the headwaters of the north fork of the Coeur d'Alene while out hunting for our expedition. The gold was so pure, so heavy and so free from quartz or matrix rock and weighing several ounces that it attracted not only a great deal of attention, but some degree of surprise at the time. And when he said he had found it his statement was scarcely credited by anyone then in our camp, because it was believed that he had traded for this gold with some parties passing up and down from the Frazer river mines. This was in '58-9.

Further on in our journey another gold deposit was discovered by a member of my party named Spangler, who was my assistant wagon maker, and who is still living in the state of Virginia. This was finer gold and was found on the south bank of the Bitter Root river, between the summit of the mountains and the present town of Missoula. But Spangler, whether justly or not, it is immaterial now to say, was known in our camp to be a sort of Baron Munchausen, and his statement was not credited, there being then no disposition to confirm his discovery and because of the distance from the line of our road, where the alleged discovery was said to have been made.

Further on in our journey, I remember distinctly camping on a certain Sunday on Fline creek, a tributary to Hell Gate river, and while some of my men were engaged in turning the stream in order to catch some of the many trout with which it was known to be supplied, other men went to the hillside and taking up several pans of gravel and dirt washed the same, and in every instance found gold and in some instances considerable, it being however, very fine scale gold.

Passing still farther eastward some of my party made the discovery of gold on what is now known as the American fork, where I am told extensive placer deposits have been worked. Passing still farther eastward, an old miner in my camp, whose name I cannot now recall made the discovery of gold on the waters of the Prickly Pear, where since the rich deposits around Helena have been worked.

The members of my expedition were composed very largely of old miners from California, and having had more or less experience in noticing the indications of mineral deposits, their universal verdict was that the entire country from Coeur d'Alene lake on toward and including the east slope of the Rocky mountains was one vast gold bearing country, and I was always nervous as to the possible discovery of gold along the line of my road, and I am now frank to say that I did nothing to encourage its discovery at that time, for I feared that any rich discovery would lead to a general stampede of my men from my own expedition and thus destroy the probable consummation of my work during the time within which I desired to complete the same. I then regarded it as of the first importance to myself and to the public to open a base line from the plains of the Spokane on the west to the plains of the Missouri on the east, from which other lines could be subsequently opened and by means of which the correct geography of the country could be delineated.

My object at that time and the object of those whose views I was in the field to execute was not so much to discover gold as it was for the purpose of ascertaining whether there was a practical railroad route through the valleys and if there existed any practicable pass in the main range of the Rocky mountains through which, in connection with proper approaches thereto, we could carry a wagon road, to be followed by a railroad line and I did not hesitate to make all other considerations secondary or subordinate thereto, believing then, and knowing now, that if a railroad line was projected and completed through the valleys and the passes of the Rocky mountains, between the 45th and 48th parallels of latitude, that all other developments would necessarily and naturally soon followed.

I am, therefore, not surprised to-day to see, as I saw last September, when going out to assist in driving the last spike on the N. P. railway, countless herds of stock grazing in perfect security from Indians upon the broad plains of the upper Missouri and Yellowstone and the entire road dotted with towns and villages, and being peopled by a hardy population; not surprised to find my old camp on Hell Gate, the site of the beautiful town of Missoula, or to see the broad plains of the Spokane fenced in and reduced to cultivation, or the waste waters of the Spokane at Spokane Falls, harnessed to busy the wheels of industry nor to know that the great waters of the Coeur d'Alene river and lake are being ploughed by steamers, right in the heart of the Coeur d'Alene mountains; and the Hell Gate Ronde in Montana and the Coeur d'Alene lake in Idaho, becoming the sites of two of the most important military posts along our extreme northwestern borders, because all these were foreseen and officially reported by me thirty years ago, and stated as likely to take place. To me it is peculiarly gratifying to know that I have been enabled to live sufficiently long to see these various matters fully realized, and I have no envy whatsoever against any of those persons who are now enjoying the partial development of the results of our early labors.

Your mines, if as rich and extensive as reported are Destined to build up many important interior centers of trade and promise to make the city of Portland, Oregon, a great and busy mart of commerce and an important center of population and industrial development. Fort Benton and Helena on your east are destined too, to be large cities of the plains. Should your mining camps become even one-half what is expected of them, I would not be surprised to see the entire mountain system from Eagle City on the north to Pierce City on the south, becoming the sites of numerous mining camps and towns, connected by a system of narrow gauge railroads, with telegraphs and telephones extending as a network over a bed of mountains, where for so many ages silence has reigned supreme, and whose industrious residents, I hope, may be richly compensated for their arduous occupations, trials and exposures necessarily incident to so rugged a country and so severe a winter climate.

Very truly yours, etc.,
John Mullan

Warren Earp comes into camp.

In early June, Warren came into camp to be with his two older brothers. They had written to him in the southwest, telling him of this new gold strike in Idaho. When he arrived in camp he moved in with Jim in his cabin. Lord knows Jim had the room; he'd been waiting for the camp to get more settled in before sending for Bessie, but seeing prospectors leaving every day made him unsure of the prospects. He knew the trip would be hard on his ailing wife and didn't want to put her through it needlessly.

Warren, Wyatt and Josie, and Jim talked for hours about their past adventures together and those yet to come in this new place. As it had also been in Tombstone, Warren's appearance in the Coeur d'Alenes more firmly entrenched the Earp's activities here, as well. He shared the life of a gambler and prospector with his two brothers.

Judge Buck's Eagle City Court

The Eagle City courthouse was a log structure on Placer Street. At one end of the building, there was a platform for the judge and the clerk of the court, while the jury sat on a bench opposite the judge.

During the proceedings, the lawyers examined the witnesses by gestures and motions and the proceedings were often amusing. Partly because each man was given a flask of whiskey as payment for jury duty, which he drank during the trial. False statements were often heard since juries were drawn from the defendant's sympathizers because there were none others in camp. Sometimes the plaintiffs even had to go home to do their farm work, leaving their case in the hands of the attorneys.

Norman Buck had been appointed by President Hayes as Judge of the First Judicial District Court of Idaho Territory. Some years earlier, during the Civil War, he'd been a Captain of the 7th Minnesota Regiment. At war's end he resumed his law practice and was given the appointment in Idaho. Judge Buck stood five foot, nine inches tall and had a light complexion. He sported an iron-gray beard and carried a walking stick from form rather than use. He was well preserved, affable and kindly, though reserved.

Rules of courtroom procedure were questionable. George McCauley, a gigantic, young man with black hair, defiantly pulled a revolver out of his pocket to menace a lawyer who quizzed him on the witness stand. Soon thereafter McCauley was shot in an argument about ownership of the Crown Point Mine at the head of Milo Gulch on the south fork of the Coeur d'Alene River.

Another hard-fought court battle, which nearly led to disastrous consequences, was when the Golden Chest Mining Company was made defendant in a legal action as trespassing and appropriating unlawfully, ground on an adjoining claim. Judge Claggett and Judge Heyburn were opposing attorneys in that action.[18]

By June, when the Eagle City court adjourned, the population of Eagle had been gradually dwindling and in the following weeks there would be even fewer souls in camp. The *Eagle City Record* was established in February, 1884, but suspended publication by June, for want of subscribers and advertising patronage.

June 9-Monday-Andy Prichard sued Wyatt over claim jumping. Andy won the judgment.

June 18-Wednesday- *Warren Hussey's diary-* "Immense lot of dust up from Dream Clean up over 230 wt [?] Got abt 1/2 of it for Bank Mail in but no cy close run for it Down at Eagle in eveg Back late Clear lovely day Very warm"

June 19-Thursday- *SF Review-* Used Jackass Trail left after breakfast and arrived at Eagle at 4:30 p.m. Cleanup of 72 hours on Dream Gulch yielded 18 1/2 pounds of gold-nuggets.

At this "weakening" state of events in the Coeur d'Alenes, the merchants of nearby Belknap, Montana didn't have anyone to sell their merchandise to.   They soon moved away, leaving their houses as dead investments and the town deserted. Only the train dispatcher, section crew and two or three men remained. During that summer, the Trout Creek, Heron and Belknap Trails also were left deserted.   Clearly the Thompson Falls route was the only naturally suited grade for a wagon road into the mines from the Northern Pacific railroad.

Thomas Steele Murder

It was a soggy, rainy day; not at all unusual for this time of year. Most folks stayed indoors during the heaviest downpour, but occasionally a brave soul would dart from one structure to the next to fulfill some obscure need. Then there were those who, from their heavy intake of likker, were beyond caring if they got wet. They made their way numbly where they would.

Even without the effect of bottled spirits, Thomas Steele was one of those who was beyond caring. A man with a mean streak, he was the agent for the Northwest Mining Company. Earlier that afternoon he'd started out to ride up Prichard Creek to attend to some business matters. However, in his haste to beat an approaching rain squall out of town, he'd forgotten to take some of his companies' papers and had to return to Eagle for them: a decision that would prove to be fatal.

While he was collecting the papers, the ever-present drizzle of rain changed into a steady downpour. Disgusted by his misfortune, he decided to remain in town for the night. He would make the trip the next day.

With the heavily overcast skies, darkness came early and he sought out a fallen woman with whom he had been intimate. He found her, near intoxication, in one of Eagle's many saloons. She said that she was having too much fun and didn't want to leave, so Steele stayed in the saloon with her. He didn't drink that much, but the woman continued to drink heavily and also became one of those who were beyond caring.

June 20-Friday-At about one o'clock in the morning, Steele again tried to get his female companion to go home with him. However, she was still having too much fun, even though by then there were only two other people in the joint.

Finally, disgusted with the affair, Steele grabbed her arm and forced her from the place, outside into the rain. After they'd gone only about fifty yards, though, the fresh air trebled the effect that the whiskey had upon her. At this point, she lay down in the muddy street, declaring flatly that she would remain there for the night. This so provoked Steele that he slapped her face soundly several times.

Meanwhile the owner of the saloon they'd just left and Danny Ferguson stood in the saloon's doorway, watching the pair stagger down the way, and laughed at their labored progress as they slipped and slid in the mud. Then they saw the woman drop to the ground and shortly after heard Steele shouting at her. Even at that distance, they could plainly hear the popping sound his hand made as he mercilessly slapped her face. Without hesitation, the pair ran to the unfortunate woman's aid.

The saloonkeeper arrived on the scene first and asked that Steele not hurt the woman further. Then Ferguson arrived and more forcefully demanded that Steele release her. At this point, Steele left the woman and, advancing toward Ferguson, growled, "Maybe you want some of this...damn you, I'll fix you." At the same time he jerked his revolver from its holster and brought it down hard on Ferguson's head, opening up a bleeding wound in his scalp. In the melee, Steele's gun discharged.

The force of being pistol-whipped knocked Ferguson backward so hard against a tent wall that he bounced off. His ears rung from the blast of Steele's gun and without hesitation, he drew his own pistol and returned fire. Steele was able to get off one more wild shot as Ferguson fired again.

Steele fell mortally wounded into the muddy street, dead almost before he hit the ground. One of Ferguson's bullets had struck Steele just below his ribs, on the left side of his chest cavity, and continued on through his vital organs before exiting out through his back about two inches to the right of his spinal column.

After the shooting, Ferguson holstered his weapon and walked off into the early morning darkness. He made his way to Kootenai County Deputy Sheriff Wyatt Earp's cabin. As he approached the cabin, he found Wyatt standing in its doorway in long underclothes. The light from inside cast Earp's shadow out into the yard to meet Ferguson as he approached.

"Those pistol shots sounded like there was a fight up the street," Earp said. "Yes, I had one," Ferguson answered.

"Did you win it?"

"Yes."

"Well, wait until I get my clothes on, and I'll go up and look over the battleground." A few minutes later Wyatt told Ferguson to stay at the cabin while he went to the scene of the fight.

Shoshone County Sheriff Dunwell and his deputy had arrived on the scene only moments after they heard the reports of gunfire. They found Steele's lifeless body in the street. A contemplative saloonkeeper stood nearby, and the woman sat, sobbing, in the muddy street beside Steele's corpse. Sheriff Dunwell arrested the woman for public intoxication and his deputy led her off to jail.

Upon Wyatt's arrival he told Sheriff Dunwell that Ferguson was the one who'd shot Steele and he would surrender himself at the coroner's inquest later that day. Dunwell agreed with the plan.

When Wyatt returned to his cabin he asked Ferguson, "Now what are you going to do, ride or stay?"

"Stick," Ferguson replied. Then he returned to his own cabin, which was just down the street. Later that morning, a coroner's jury was held into the affair. After hearing testimony from the barkeep, the woman, and Sheriff Dunwell, the jury members returned a verdict that "Thomas Steele had come to his death by a gunshot wound from a pistol in the hands of Dan Ferguson." A warrant was issued for Ferguson's arrest at which time he surrendered himself. Bail was set at $3,000, which Ferguson promptly paid and was released from custody under his own recognizance.

Ferguson left camp with Alfred Holman and the pair traveled south, back to the Wood River area, from whence they'd come with J. E. Jack Enright, before meeting the Earps on the train from Missoula. Enright still had business interests in Eagle and decided to stay on in the Coeur d' Alenes.

During his stay in Eagle City, Ferguson was already known as "a man with a record." He'd come to Coeur d'Alenes with the reputation of being a gunman and of having worked the gambling tables in North Platte, Nebraska. On October 10, 1881, Ferguson had a disagreement with North Platte's notorious Bill Tucker leading to gunplay which both men survived.

Tucker was known as a dangerous man to tangle with since he'd shot it out with famous gunman Ben Thompson's brother, Billy Thompson. In that fray, Bill Thompson had shot away three fingers and the thumb of Tucker's left hand while Tucker emptied both barrels of a shotgun into Thompson's body. Both men survived the encounter. Ferguson left the North Platte country for Hailey, Idaho, in the Wood River mining district.[19]

Wyatt knew that a grand jury would convene in a few weeks, and that many of Steele's friends were hell-bent on getting Ferguson hung. So, he entered the telegraph office and asked John Topliff, who was the telegraph operator and camp assayer, if anyone had contacted Ferguson to warn him of impending trouble. "No, and if they do we will indict them," Topliff responded. Wyatt made a grab for him, but the smaller man ducked under his arm and darted outside.

Knowing that he couldn't catch Topliff, Wyatt picked up a stone and threw it at the fleeing man. The missile glanced of the side of Topliff's head, causing him to trip and fall. Then Wyatt caught up with and roughly grabbed Topliff around the neck. He dragged him back into the telegraph office, angrily shouting, "Now send that telegram or I'll beat you to death." Topliff sent the telegram, giving Ferguson the warning that he could expect to be indicted if he returned to Eagle City.

Upon receiving Wyatt's warning telegram, Ferguson went into hiding and sent Holman to deliver the following letter to Sheriff C. H. Furey at Hailey, Idaho:

Hailey, Idaho, July 16, 1884

To Sheriff Furey:

Dear sir-

My first intentions were to return to Eagle City for trial in case of indictment, but being informed since in regard to underhand work going on in that country, I have concluded to remain concealed until a change of venue to this country can be obtained. I feel that if I were to return to Eagle City for trial (at least for the present), it would be throwing my life away.

I do not wish to evade the law, but simply adopt this course through the advice of my friends, that I may get the benefit of the true letter of the law, which is "justice.

If I am not otherwise apprehended, you may expect me to give myself up to the officers of Alturas county at any time.

Hoping that in the discharge of a public duty, you will still entertain a private regard for the administration of justice.

Yours Respectfully,

Dan S. Ferguson [20]

Ferguson skipped out before the indictment could be completed and would live out his life under the assumed name of Danny Miller.[21]

There had been a good deal of confusion over the issue of which county could claim ownership of the Coeur d'Alenes. Some believed it to be Kootenai County in which Coeur d'Alene City is located, whereas most others believed it was Shoshone County. The believers of the latter prevailed when, in Eagle's Arcade Hall, in the June term of court, the case was decided by Judge Buck to that effect and thus ending Wyatt's tenure as Deputy Sheriff of Kootenai County.[22]

The Shoshone County seat was in Pierce City, some 100 miles south of Eagle and Murray. Pierce remained the county seat until 1885 when it was moved to Murray. Then in 1898 it was moved again to the city of Wallace, on the south fork of the Coeur d'Alene River, where it remains to this day.

"Gold is getting better but sloping bedrock and can't get down to it because of water..."

The year was one of great activity on the gulches of Prichard and Eagle Creeks in developing placer mines, and in all parts of the region in prospecting for both placer and quartz locations. While many claims yielded an ounce of gold per day to the man and some others gave even larger cleanups, it was found that the greatest wealth of the country was beyond the reach of the prospector. Everyone knew that there were mountains of gold to be had, but only by those with the money to install large enterprises. Accordingly, some effort was made to interest capital in ditch schemes and other developments. A few enterprises of the kind were begun.

Murder of John Enright

John Enright (not J. E. Jack Enright, who was a friend of the Earps) had been working as a typesetter for the Murray's *Pioneer* newspaper. Henry Bernard was the newspaper's editor. It appeared, from the testimony at the preliminary hearing, that Enright had been discharged and paid on the afternoon of the homicide. Later that afternoon, he came back to the office for his blankets and personal effects, but instead of taking them and going quietly about his business, he kept complaining to Bernard about the shabby treatment which he claimed had been given him. A heated argument ensued during which Bernard told him two or three times to leave, but Enright still hung around the office. Finally Bernard grabbed a revolver out from under the counter and pointed it at Enright, telling him he must leave or get hurt. Enright received the threats in a jocular manner, and soon the fatal shot was fired. John Enright slumped to the floor in death.

Bernard was immediately arrested for the murder. There was such heated sentiment against Enright's murderer that Bernard's defense attorney asked for and received a change of venue. Bernard was tried two months later in September at Lewiston and the jury found him guilty of manslaughter. Judge Buck sentenced him to eight years' imprisonment. He was confined to the Idaho

State penitentiary for a time, but was eventually pardoned by Idaho Governor Shoup.[23]

Adam Aulbach

July 5-Adam Albauch arrived in Murray with his worldly possession and printing outfit on the backs of forty-five mules and horses. No blare of trumpets heralded the obstreperous printer's coming. In fact, to the lawless he wasn't welcome. They knew he was a scrapper, believed in law and order and had a policy that "transgressors would be published to the full extent of the law."

During the gold excitement of the Coeur d'Alenes, he brought his newspaper to Belknap, Montana, and, as soon as the snow permitted, on to the Murray district. His first paper was printed on July 5, 1884. He'd planned to print on July 4, but the murder of an opposing newspaper publisher, on July the second, caused him to hold the edition to the next day to get all the facts.

Albauch was a pioneer publisher who would have a major hand in developing Murray. He helped develop all branches of government, including a volunteer fire department. He also invented a much needed water system to bring water to the town. To the chagrin of many, he used his prolific hand to dash out stories dealing with area-wide issues, especially the affairs of the lawless. Albauch died in his bed in the home he built on Main Street, with his daughter Ruth Albauch Sellers at his side. She would continue his writing legacy.

July 11-Friday-Mrs. Lane and Mrs. Schultz the rightful owners of the Widow claim are guests of Andy Prichard. E. V. Smalley of *Century Magazine* in town. Warren Hussey has new bank building.

July 18-Friday-The Ben Finnell, John Campbell fight. Mining in Dream Gulch yielded $3,500 in gold. Senate Saloon doing fine business, Lynch is its manager. Civil cases to be tried. W. H. Payne vs. J. E. Jack Enright and Wyatt Earp. Lumber selling for $45 per thousand. Three hundred fine sheep in Eagle were brought in by Indians and selling for 10 cents a pound. Wells Fargo in Rathdrum. Steam pump arrives at Maggie D. (Earps.) Wells Fargo will use Trout Creek Trail. Gelatt claim one of best on Prichard Ck.

Capt. Wooden carries as a watch charm a nugget weighing 5 1/2 ounces which he found on bedrock early this week. The Senate Saloon is doing a fine business as Lynch keeps none but the choicest liquors, wines and cigars, and his long residence east of the Bitterroot Range has made the Senate the headquarters of all the Montana and Black Hills boys in camp Some Indians from Coeur d'Alene brought into Eagle a band of fine American horses and Cayuses for sale Tuesday morning and succeeded in disposing of all of them at good prices before noon.

J. L. Stillwell, the father of the well known W. H. Stillwell, died at Murray last Saturday morning, age 75 years. His death was hastened by an attack of erysipelas in one of his arms which was injured by a blast. He was an old pioneer and had participated in all the great mining excitements of the coast. He was buried on Sunday in the presence of a large attendance.

Wells Fargo & Company Express will travel the Trout Creek route on and after July 20. There is quite a heavy travel between Eagle and Murray and the two express wagons are doing a good business. A tent adjoining the Board of Trade on Prichard Avenue was burned down with all of its contents last Sunday night.

So far as the drift is pushed ahead the Mother lode is as rich as ever. There are now thirteen feet of the ledge exposed.

The grand jury reported to the court Tuesday, having found a true bill against John Leaven for assault with a deadly weapon.

Patrick McGovern and Frank O'Malley were arrested at Murray last Sunday by Deputy Sheriff Frank McDonald for disturbing the peace. In making the arrest both parties attacked one officer, and one of them struck him on the nose; as the affair was getting serious McDonald took a shot at them but failed to connect. They were finally ironed, brought to Eagle and fined $35 each.

Fifteen men were put to work on the projected big ditch up the creek during the week, and it is expected that a large additional force will be put on, on the return of one of the leading spirits of the enterprise, who is expected back next week. The ditch is intended to cover all the old channel diggings on the north side of Prichard Creek, and will undoubtedly prove the best paying property in the camp. The old channel diggings of California have produced $161,000,000 worth of dust and experts say that the Coeur d'Alene wash is much richer than that of California.

Weekly Eagle-"The case of Henry Robbins, the crazed individual who attempted suicide by jumping in the creek some weeks since has been under advisement by his honor who yesterday decided to send him to the asylum."

July 25-*Weekly Eagle, Vol. 1 No. 13-*"Bedrock reached July 23 on the Earp's Maggie D. claim located upstream at Osborne. School district being organized in Eagle 25 or 30 children."

August-*Rammelmeyer's diary-*Donald Cameron came to Murray in August of 1884. Tom Burns had a sawmill below Murray and some lumber piled up near my brewery. Cameron had charge of it and sold it to the customers. He was in my place often and was surprised that I knew his brother whom I had not seen since school age. Sandy was the owner of the Missoula ferry and while Sandy and myself were at Slays helping him putting up some hay the boy he left at the ferry got scared when a lot of Indians came by and took charge of the house. The boy took the ferry across with a pony and notified us. You should have seen us when we rode up to the river took the ferry across and bodily handled the Indians. I did not know his real first name. I have probably forgotten it. He was known as Sandy Cameron all along the river. A stout big man with a large yellow beard and a very sympathetic manner. Donald Cameron was a sort of a blowlast. Sandy went to Chicago to have a growth of cancer removed on his breast and died in the operation. I also knew another brother his name was Jim.

August 15-Friday-*NW Tribune*   "Earp Bros. pump arrived."

September 8-Monday-*Warren Hussey's Diary*-"Off at 6 AM for
Helena   bkfst at Mountain House   Execrable   Quite a head ache
Thompson at 3:30 & had a nap   Head bad off   On time by train"

September 20-They had exhausted all of their gold claims and, just as another cold winter was setting in, Wyatt, Josie and James had finally decided to give up on the camp. (Warren would stay on in the Coeur d'Alenes for a while, at least.) They'd gathered their belongings together and that morning rode rented horses, east, out of town toward Murray and the Thompson Falls Trail. A thin layer of snow covered the high mountains and shone brilliantly in the morning sun.

The Earps were among the last to leave the grand old lady of the Coeur d'Alenes, which had fallen into a sad state of disrepair. They rode silently, single file, down Eagle Street, passing by once busy hotels and saloons that now stood empty. Open windows and gaping doorways stared blankly out at them as they passed. A curtain swayed in a partially opened window from the cold fall breeze and the creak of a door left open wide by its last tenants.

Once they'd rounded the bend, following Prichard Creek toward Murray, Eagle was lost from view. In coming months, attempts would be made to revive the once-booming old town, but she would never regain a substantial population.

Three miles further east, they rode into Murray, to the full voice of laughter and guffaws of dozens of young miners. Pretty little Molly-B-Damn was having another of her famous street baths and they were pouring their hard-earned gold dust into her tin bath tub with abandon. A glad time was being had by all..

Murray had indeed survived the exodus of miners. It would live on as the heart of the Coeur d'Alenes until a year later when Noah Kellogg and his lowly burrow stumbled across what became the world's largest lead, silver mine, the Bunker Hill. As prospectors rushed to the south fork, Murray also fell victim to the progress of shifting times. In later years, a giant dredge that had been shipped in from Alaska would tear down through the canyon, digging for the elusive gold and eating most of the town in the process.

The Earps rode on, following the winding trail up over the Bitterroots to Thompson Falls, Montana. There they boarded a Northern Pacific passenger car and, when the train got as far as Missoula, James said his good-byes and got off. He returned to Bessie, who sadly died shortly thereafter. In later years James would be known by his family as a hack driver in San Bernardino, California, but he would have other adventures with his famous brother, Wyatt Earp.

Meanwhile Wyatt and Josie traveled south to the Colorado gold camps where some say he was shot in the arm during a card game in Lake City.[24]

September 26-Warren had registered to vote in the Coeur d'Alene mining camp's upcoming December elections, but there is no official record that he ever did. He would stay on for a while in the Coeur d'Alenes before making his way to Spokane Falls where he opened a saloon on the east side of Howard Street near Stevens Street.[25]

Warren became involved with two shady characters in Spokane and, in April of 1885, he and his partners jumped what would be later named the Old Dominion mining claim. It was located six miles east of Colville, and one and one-half miles northeast of Chewelah, Washington.[26]

One of the Old Dominion's locators was twenty-three-year-old E. E. Alexander and, by sheer chance, he and his partners had discovered the outcropping of high-grade ore. Alexander remained on-site, to guard their discovery, while his partner rode back to Colville to register the claim.

In the mean time, Warren and his new acquaintances: Tom Fuller, Theodore Erickson, Bob Stokesbury and Charles Sands, rode up and forcibly took possession of the claim. Warren's justification for jumping the Old Dominion, was on the grounds that the owners weren't citizens of the United States which, as it turned out, was not the case. To resolve the heated issue, money changed hands and the matter was resolved.[27] (Over the years, the Old Dominion proved to be a major discovery worth millions of dollars.)

Warren later returned to his father's homestead in California. On July 6, 1900, he was shot and killed by John Boyette at Wilcox, Arizona, and there has been some speculation that Wyatt and James avenged their youngest brother's murder.

December 3-At the invitation of Wells Fargo Express, Wyatt and Josie traveled from Colorado on to Raton, Colfax County, New Mexico, where Wyatt was offered the job of Chief Deputy Sheriff, but he refused the position at Josie's insistence. Wyatt and Josie did attend the Raton horse races on December the sixth. They both loved the ponies. From there, the couple traveled to Cimarron, New Mexico and El Paso, Texas and then on into history together.[28]

December 12-*Raton Comet-*"Wyatt Earp, one of the well known Earp brothers of Tombstone, Arizona, is in town taking in the sights."[29]

December 20-*Murray Sun-*Two packers named W. Taylor and Chris Stone got into a wrangle and Taylor is alleged to have deliberately shot Stone dead. The affair appears to have occurred near the camp of Wm. Irwin, the veteran prospector, twenty five miles from Murray. Irwin, it is said, attempted to arrest Taylor, but he escaped with a slight bullet wound through the left side and made his way to Rathdrum, where he gave himself up.

December 26-Friday-Shoshone County tax sale-Wyatt had failed to pay $8.67 on three lots in rear of Hawkins Bank, value $270 on one tent. Shoshone County paid his fine and took title to the White Elephant Saloon.

December 29-Sunday-*Spokane Evening Review-*Yesterday afternoon a powerful span of gray horses attached to a farm wagon ran straight at a horse car standing at the end of the track, near the turn-table. The driver, seeing them coming, unhitched his horse and ran him into the stable. Just as the runaway team was about to crash into the car, John Oats, a butcher from Spokane Falls, very bravely caught them by the head and succeeded in stopping them. He drove the outfit up Front Street and met the owner, an east side farmer, racing down to look for it. So great was his joy to find his team uninjured and no bill of damages to pay that he bestowed all the change in his pockets on Mr. Oats.

December 31-Wednesday-Last entry in **Warren Hussey's Diary** for 1884:

> Was Very cold morning   Mercury 12 below at 8   3 PM 10 above No biz much   Out to the dance on time & a very nice evening of it Home at 1   Mrs. Marks White & Hawkins to supper with us   To bed at 3 AM.

January 1-New Year's Day-1885-"Temperature at –41 degrees."

City Directories

8

Eagle City

In late January of 1884, Wyatt, Josie and James Earp had to ride horses on high mountain passes over the Evolution Trail to reach the gold camp of Eagle City. But today Eagle can be reached by exiting Interstate 90 at Kingston, Idaho and then proceeding north up FH-9 to Prichard. A right turn follows Prichard Creek for three miles toward Murray and the junction of Eagle and Prichard Creeks.

8-N15, Historical photo coll., University of Idaho Library, Moscow
Eagle City looking east, 1897

At that site, in July of 1882, Tennessee volunteer and Civil War Veteran Andrew Prichard and a prospecting party of three other men were first to discover gold in the fabulous Coeur d'Alenes. This was a discovery that would eventually lead prospectors to the South Fork of the Coeur d'Alene River where they would, in turn, discover the largest mining district on earth. A 40 plus mile-long canyon that is still actively being mined and has produced well over a

159

billion ounces of pure silver, millions of dollars in gold and millions of tons of other highly sought after metals.

But Eagle City was the first of many Hell raisin' gold camps to be chopped out of the rugged mountain wilderness. The foundling camp reached its glory in 1883 and 1884 when its population soared into the many thousands. Helping the boom along, the Northern Pacific Railroad published bulletins proclaiming that $100 per-man per-day could be freely taken from the rimrock and gulches. This was an awesome amount of money and gold at the time, considering that an ounce of gold sold for $18, and a laborer only made $1.25 for a hard day's work.

Construction of the town was furious, with crude board and canvas structures and well-built cabins strung for two miles up Eagle Creek. The Earp brothers and their associates purchased a tent to convert into the White Elephant Saloon. They were also proprietors of a dance hall. Eagle City was a booming town with businesses listed in newspapers and directories:

38- Attorneys and Lawyers
3 - Bankers
12- City buildings which includes the Courthouse
8 - Druggists
26- General merchandise stores
24- Chop and lodging houses
4 - Newspapers
7 - Notary and Justice of the Peace
11- Physicians
24- Saloons

One of the greatest problems in Eagle, though, was getting mail. One could always subscribe to a private mail service, but at a cost of $30.00 per month. Well worth the cost, though, considering that the mail carrier had to carry the mail on his back and walk the thirty plus miles to camp from far-off Fort Coeur d'Alene. Finally, in February of 1884, the United States Postal Department opened a much heralded post office. At first, delivering mail to Eagle and later, after the town's name was changed, successively, to Walker, Union, and Waite.

It was generally conceded that the biggest problem in camp was the lack of mail service. So the Belknap Trail became the mail route when a post office was established in Eagle. Still later an even faster means of communication was established when a telegraph line followed along the trail's length between the two towns.

Setting aside the poor mail service, Eagle was not without its forms of entertainment. Besides the many saloons like the Earp's White Elephant, there were other places of public resort, such as the dance hall in which Calamity Jane hosted the camp's first social event. Shootings and death were all too commonplace, and hard-headed men and women of the night abounded. One man was arrested and chained to a 350-pound stump for the night, since the jail hadn't been built yet. In the morning, he and his stump were gone and everyone figured he had earned his freedom.

Undoubtedly, many of the once hearty pioneers rest in a quaint old cemetery located on a ridge overlooking old Eagle City. A well-preserved tombstone bearing the name of camp-character William Parker is present. However, after all these many years, there are only a few depressions in the earth that can be readily seen and the old graveyard is now on private property. Additionally, the aged landmark was nearly completely destroyed by highway crews digging in the earth for gravel for the highway.

Just the same, a trip through the Eagle graveyard was like a visit to a Civil War burial ground. The company, the regiment and the rank of each was there marking the graves as a grim reminder of an age long gone. When the soft earth gives up its dead, a check list of the states represented will read like a national gathering of the Grand Army of the Republic, along with a few confederates to fill the ranks.[1]

In the summer of 1884, Warren, youngest of the Earp brothers, joined Wyatt and James in Eagle City. It was said of Warren that in a fight he would lower his head and go in with both guns blazing. What wonderful stories of their escapades have escaped the research efforts of your authors.

Wyatt and his brothers, and their partners purchased or staked twelve mining claims in the Eagle City and Murray area. Spending, in the process, over $4,800 for property, mining claims, saloons and gambling tents. (An amount that would today be valued at many times that sum.)

Over the years, the town-plat map of Eagle City has been lost. But, a newly discovered, circa 1883-1884, Idaho State Historical Society map showing the locations of several of the cities' buildings. Also a heavily researched, hypothetical map was drawn by the authors in February of 1998 that shows all street and lot information.

There were ten trails and several wagon roads that led to the Coeur d'Alenes. True, Wyatt and his party did travel over the Evolution Trail, but it and nine others were also used by the flood of humanity that followed them to Eagle City. The names and approximate opening dates are as follows:

Thompson Falls-Winter of 1883

Belknap-February, 1884

Trout Creek-early, 1884

Heron-1884

Martin/Rathdrum-?

Evolution-1878

Jackass-?

Burke-?

Irwin-?

The Idaho Northern Railroad (later known as the Oregon-Washington Railroad and Navigation Company) reached Eagle City at years' end in 1908.

Eagle City Directory

1883-1929

Streets:

"A"
"C"
Eagle
First
Gold
Jackson
Lee
Main
Placer
Prichard Ave.
Reed
Second
Silver
Stevens
Union

Additions:

Hayes
Old Corner
Old Town
New Town
Second

A:

Arion Saloon-Eagle St., C.R. Boyce-**prop.**
Abercrombie-**The Arcade**-Placer St.
Accident-(1884).
Acion Saloon-(1884).
Adams, R.H.-**Druggist**-Three doors north of the **New Theater Bldg.**
Adler, Aaron A.-Parts of lots 11 and 12 on Silver St.
Ainsworth, H.-**Banker/Broker**-Lot 7, on the east corner of Eagle St.
Albert-**Atty.**-Corner of Eagle St. and Prichard Ave.
Allen, William Henry-(Died at age 30).
Allway, J.-Cabin in Eagle City suburbs.

Althoff, Harry-Cabin.

Anderson.

Arcade Saloon and Chop House.

Arlington Lodging and Chop House.

Armstead, Robert W.

Avery & Laumeister-**Sawmill**.

B:

Badger Store-Warren Hussey owned 1/4 interest.

Badgley, Mrs.-**School teacher-**in Eagle.

Baeidenbach, Martin-Cabin on Eagle Cr.

Bair, John-Lot 14, Placer St.

Baker, E.D.

Baker, Jonathan C.-Lot 50 of Old Town-has a $500 log-hewn
  house that's 5-6 logs high.

Baran, Alex.

Barber Shop-Okay-Senate Building-Corner of Eagle and
  Placer St.

Barnard, T.N.-**Photographer**-lot on north side of Placer St.

Barnes, A.M.-Has portions of lots 15, 17, 19 and all of lot
  21 on Jackson St., also lots 26 and 28, west side Eagle St.,
  and **Bull River Merchandise-**June 5, 1884.

Beach.

Bedrock Flume Building.

Beeson, H.D. -**Phys.**-Office in **McNab's Drug Store**.

Behr, John-Lot 14 on Placer St., formerly the **post office,**
  also Reeds cabin on Placer St., Sept 11, 1884.

Bell Restaurant-Epperly & Bemenderfer, **Props**.

Bell, William-On Prichard Cr.

Bemenderfer-**Bell Restaurant**-Next to **Senate** on Placer St.

Bender, C.E.-**Meat Market** on Eagle St.

Benson, John-Cabin on Placer St.

Benton, A.P.-**Real estate**-office with **City Recorder**.

Benton, Sid-**Liquor Store**-Lot 3, Prichard Ave., sold all of
  his supplies.

Bernard, Henry-Killed John Enright, was manager of the
  Coeur d'Alene Pioneer Newspaper.

Bettis, A.-**Atty.**

Bigger, William.

Billings, J.B.

Binkley & Taylor-**Attys.**

Bishop, Andy-Lot borders Unkle's Lot.

Black Hills Headquarters Liquor Store-Corner of Lee and
  Eagle St..

Black, Sam.

Blacksmith-Prichard Ave.

Blossom, Walter L.-**Wardner's Store.**

Blume, H.J.-**Retail dealer-**Prichard Ave.

Board of Trade Bldg.-Prichard Ave.

Boblett, E.A. & Mrs.-She was the first white woman in
Eagle.

Bolander, James C.-**Notary & J.P.**

Boodie, Edmund-Cabin on Eagle Cr.

Boone, D.M.-**Eagle Restaurant** and a **Barber Shop** next
door to **Hayes' Store,** also has interest in **Acion Saloon.**

Boyce, Mrs. C.R.-**Barber Shop** next door to **Hayes Store**
also had **Acion Saloon-**Dec 22, 1885.

Boyer-Prop. **O.K. Barber Shop.**

Bradshaw-**Atty.**

Brenton, Charles-Lot 2, block A., Eagle St.

Britt, A.S.-**Map Maker,** has map of Eagle City, on file with
the **Deputy Mineral Recorder.**

Browers, D.C.-Has lot adjacent to W.H. Payne-West Side of
Eagle.

Brown and Butler-Lot 2, north side Placer on corner of Reed
and Placer St.

Brown, D.C.-Lived at the head of Eagle Cr.

Brown, Felix-**Lodging house.**

Brown, Gustah-**Lodging House.**

Brown, James-Cabin near **Eagle City Post Office.**

Brown, J.L.-**Atty.**

Brown, Matt-On Placer St. Owns **Nevada Chop House and
Hotel.**

Buchan, R.B.-Cabin on Prichard Avenue.

Buchanan, Herbert A.-Lot 2 on Lee St.

Buck, Norman-**Judge-**1884.

Bucahamino, Massomi.

Burdan, Mollie-Sold **Acion Saloon** lot to Mrs. C.R. Boyce.
on Dec 22, 1885, also owned lot 66.

Burdett, John-**Carpenter.**

Burgoine, Felix-Lot 1, Prichard Ave., **Burgoine House,**
Saloon on lot 81, W. Eagle St.

Burke.

Burns, John-Lot in town of Osborne, sold it to Mrs. A. R.
Mills.

Burns, John & Co.-Lot 4, Eagle St.

Burns, W.S.-Had a judgement against Mollie Burdan of
Murray on lot 66-owned a **sawmill** on Prichard Cr.

Burton, E.W.-**City Bakery-**Lot 51, Corner of Eagle and Lee
St.-October 16, 1885.

Burton & Porter-Lot 52, West Side of Eagle St. on corner of
Lee & Eagle St.

Buskirk, Van-**Phys.** in the **Eagle City Drug Store.**

Butler, L.F.-Real estate-**Has town maps; owns lot 1, block A, West Side of Eagle St., lot 2, East side of Eagle St., and lot 5, south side of Placer St. Advertises the town.**

Buzard, William E. (Fay)-Sold lot 57 on Eagle St. to Wyatt Earp, his cabin on Prichard Cr.

C:

Cahan, Frank etal.-Lot 25 Eagle St.

Calavan, J. M.-**Pioneer Lumber Co.**, Littlefield and Raven, (1885).

Caleau.

Callihan, James-Lot 3, block A, Butte City (Littlefield.)

Cam, A.H.-**Saloon.**

Cameron & Nobles-Lot 70, West Side of Eagle St.

Cameron, Dan.

Campbell, Henry L.

Campbell, Heyram.

Campbell, J.H.-Lives down Eagle Cr.

Campbell, R.S.-Lot 80, Eagle St.

Campbell and Webber-Lot 73, East side of Eagle St.

Canutt, Alexander-Rented **Mr. Taylor's Store.**

Cardoner, Daniel-West half of lot 1, corner of Stevens and Eagle St., June 26, 1884.

Carey-**Atty.**

Carlton-**Atty.**

Carpenter, E.D.-West half of lot 10 and east half of lot 12 on Silver St.

Carpenter, J.B.-Cabin near Placer St.

Carpp, Charles-Lot 3, block A, New Eagle City.

Carpp, W.H.-**Laundry** on Gold St.

Carr, A.H.-**Saloon**-Corner of Prichard and Eagle St.

Carrol, W.H.

Carter-**Laundry** on Gold St.

Cedar Hotel-1884.

Chamberlain-Lot 11, Placer St.

Chamberlain, A. M.-Cabin on Union St.

Chambers Bros.-**Palace Saloon**-1/2 lot 7, Prichard Ave., lot 9 w/house, lots 15 & 16 east Union St., lot 24 Prichard Ave., house and lot 3, Eagle St., house on Golden Chief Placer Claim, Prichard Cr.

Chambers, Charles-Lot 9 cabin on Prichard Ave.

Chambers, J.- **Atty.**-Corner of Eagle St. and Prichard Ave.

Chambers, S.T.-Lot 7, block K-First Addition.

Chambers, William H.-Lot 1, west 1/2 on SW corner of Stevens and Eagle St., also lot 67 on Eagle St.

Chandler, M.B.-The first white woman to winter in Eagle.

Channin, J.-Lot 1, Eagle St., lot 11 Placer St. (Mar 3, 1887.)

Charles, Habian-**Burgoine House**.

Chase, J.F.-Main St. in Littlefield.

Child, S.E. etal-Lot 23 Prichard Ave. and Eagle St., opposite Lee St., lot 60 for **saloon**. Lot 62 Eagle St. & Lot 54 Eagle St.

Child, W.E.-Lot 53 corner Lee and Eagle St., lot 60 **City Bakery,** house and lot, corner Lee and Eagle St.

Church.

City Recorder.

Clagget-**Judge.**

Clements, **M.D.**-Judgement for Mamie Stoddard for S. 1/2 lot 44.

Clickman, Frank S.

Cochrane, John.

Coeur d'Alene Brick Co.-C. W. Weber Co.-Osborne (1885).

Coeur d'Alene-Lodging-Carey & Carlton**, Props.**

Coeur d'Alene Nugget-Newspaper, (3-15-84 to 5-7-84).

Coeur d'Alene Pioneer-Newspaper, (4-28-84 to ?).

Coeur d'Alene Supply Co.-One house.

Coeur d'Alene Transportation Co.

Coeur d'Alene Weekly Eagle-Newspaper, (4-12-84 to 8-84).

Cohen, Frank-etal-Lot 25, Eagle St.

Cohen, Simon-**General Merchandise**-Lot 46 Eagle St.-July 5, 1884.

Cole, Asa-Lot 63 Hayes addition.

Cole Bros.-West Side of Eagle, lot 63, W. 1/2 of building.

Cole, Cassius M.-Lot on Eagle St.-site of **Jail and Palace Saloon.**

Collier, J.H.-Lot 21 Jackson St.

Comelays, George-**Atty.**

Comstock, D.C.-Cabin on Eagle St.

Comstock Chop House.

Conkling, James P.-(1883.)

Coughlin, L.P.-**Sign painter**-No. 177 Eagle St. also 1/2 interest in Lot 33 on Eagle St.

Coulter, Charles-Agent for **Wells Fargo Express.**

Courthouse-Lot 8 Placer St.

Cowley, Mike-Cabin on Placer St.

Coy, E.E.-**The Daisy**-Lot 7, and lot 74 Corner of Eagle and Placer St. at the old Corner, also lot on Main St., lot north side of Placer St.

Coy & Hess Clothing, etc.-Lot 62, corner Placer and Eagle St.

Coyle, Frank-Lot on placer St., known as **Frank Coyle and Co.**

Crawford, Joseph B.-Lot 63, Hayes addition.

Cromie, D.-Lot 20 Placer St.

Crossman, Charles-Cabin on Prichard Cr.

Crown, Charles A.-W 1/2 lot 37.

Crozier, Frank.

Cunningham-**General merchandise**-S. half of lot 44 Eagle St. (May 17, 1884), houses on E. Eagle St. and Reed St.

Curtis, S.H.-(1883).

D:

Daggett, F.J.-Cabin on Eagle St.

Dahen.

Daisy Saloon.

Dalton, Louis S.

Dance Hall-Eagle St.

Davis, C.-**Boat builder.**

Davis, Robert M.

Daxon, William-**Pioneer Lumber Co. (**1885).

Day, Charles-Died (Feb. 15, 1884).

Delmonico Restaurant.

Delvin, Andrew-Lived up Eagle Cr.

Demarcho, Angelo.

Demers, T. J.-**General Merchandise**-Littlefield (1886).

Demsey-**Miner.**

Dennee, Tim.

Denner, W.K.etal-Lot 61, West Side of Eagle St. had a **store.**

Denny-**Pioneer Restaurant.**

De Succa, George W.-**Co-owner** of the **Coeur d'Alene Weekly** in Eagle.

Dillard, S.E.-Publisher of the **Eagle Star Newspaper.**

Doherty.

Donnelly, C.-Lot 23, West Side of Eagle St.

Donnelly, J.D.-The **Sazerac Saloon**, east side of Eagle St., also lot 69 on the West Side of Eagle St.

Donnelly, Simon P.-Jan 15, 1889 he purchased 1/2 interest in-**Cahan & O'Brien House** West Side Eagle St., (June 20, 1884). Lot 7 in rear of lot 4 on Placer St., also West Side of Eagle St., purchased 1/2 interest in O'Brien and Cahan home in **Shelton Bldg.** on West Side of Eagle St.

Dorsett, A. K.-Lot 13 Prichard Ave. (July 5, 1884).

Dowd, John-Lot 26 north side of Lee St.

Doyle, W.E.-Lot 50, Eagle St.

Drennan, James-**Pioneer Store.**
Driggs, A.E.-Lot 50, Old Town.
Drummond, James A.-Purchased a house and lot.
Drummond, W.W.-Estate-Purchased a house and lot
Dudley, Charles etal-Lot 7 & lot 48, Eagle St.
Duechesi, Theodore.
Dunlap, Rufus and Smith, Archie-Reed St.

E:

Eagle City Bank.
Eagle City Meat Market.
Eagle City Record-Newspaper. A. Barnard owner
    (February 2, 1884 to ?).
Eagle City Drug Store-R.H. Adam & Fred Quinby, **M.D.**
Eagle Restaurant-D.M. Boone, **Prop.**
Eagle Star-Newspaper, (November 21,1883 to ?).
Earle, Frank-**Assessor.**
Earp Bros-**White Elephant Saloon Props.**-behind **Eagle**
    City Bank in **New Theater Bldg.** Paid $132.
Earp, James-Lot on Lee St.
Earp Warren B.
Earp, Wyatt, etal-Lot 57, Eagle St., had a cabin. (May 1,
    1884.)
Eckert & Wardner.
Eckert, C.C.-**Transportation Co.**-Lot 23, Prichard Ave.
    (August 14, 1884.)
Edwards, W.F.-Editor of **Coeur d'Alene Nugget.**
Elder, J.C.-**Atty.**-Eagle St. in the **Post Office Bldg.**
Elder, J.W.-**Coy and Hess House.**
Elliott, B.M.-Lot adjacent to W.S. James. Had a **laundry** on
    the East (?).
Emerson, Seth, E.-Lot 1, E. side of Eagle St., Jan 15,
    1886. (side ?) of Eagle St. and lot 5 on Eagle St.
Emery, George H.
Enright, John-Killed by Henry Bernard.
Enright, Jack E- Had **stable** on Lee St., also lots 19, 20,
    and 21. Had **Golden Gate Saloon** on Lee St. Had
    judgment on N. 1/2 lot 57. Died July 24, 1884.
Enright, Lou-(Gambler J. E. Jack Enright's wife was known as the Queen of Eagle City)-
    1/2 interest in lots 19 & 21 on Lee St.
Epperly-**Bell Restaurant**-Next door to **Senate Saloon** on
    Placer St.
Erwin, B.C.-Had a cabin.
Evans-**General Store**-On Union St., (April, 1884).
Ewing.

F:

Feinberg, Moses S.-Portions of lots 11 & 12 on Silver St.
Feltman, Louis.
Fender-**The Comstock Saloon**-Eagle St.
Ferguson, D.S.-**Miner**, purchased 1/2 interest in lot
    fronting 25' on Eagle St. (May 21, 1884).
Fidelity and Columbus Co.-Purchased house and lot.
Filipell, Pietra.
Firth, C.C.-**Phys.**
Foley, Charles-**Flemming Store.**
Fornes, Frank.
Fountain, H.T.
Frank, L.J.-**Assayer and mining engineer.**
Frazier, A.J.-Cabin.
Freeman, W.-Lots 17 and 11 on Placer St.
French Bros.-**The Hummel**-Lot is between them and Garry.
French, W.H.-**Atty.**
Friday, Capt.-**Chicago Laundry.**
Fried, Edward-Has a cabin.
Friedlander-W. lot 9 (4-24-1884).
Friend, James-1884.
Frier, W.M. and Co.
Fuller, T.D.-Eagle St.

G:

Gable, Charles.
Gandalfo, Joseph R.-1/2 interest in lot 52, Eagle St.
Gandalfo, Josephine E.-1/2 interest in lot 52 Eagle St.
Garry-Lot between **French Bros. and Hummell's.**
Gavitt, John S.-Prichard Ave.
Gelchrest, Alex M.-Lot 6, 51, block 5 in new addition.
Gem Chop House-George Hagadorn, **Prop.**
George and Human -House on lot 3, Placer St. and lot on
    "C" St.
Ghaghty, Frank E.
Gherry, George-Cabin on Eagle St.
Gibbon, H-**Doctor.**
Gilliland, W.-Lot 13 Prichard Ave.
Gilmartin, Charles-Lot by Kranish, lot 7 on West Side of
    Eagle between Lee and 1st St., lot 10 on north side of
    Prichard Ave., lot 27 on Prichard Ave.
Glass, John-Lot 5, Prichard Ave. (May 15, 1884).
Glider, Peter, etal-Lot 2, Prichard Ave. (Feb. 11, 1888).
Golden Gate Saloon.

Golden King Co-Has a lot.

Goldstein, A.B.-Interest in E. 1/2 lot 33, and lot 2 on Lee St. (June 26, 1884.)

Gondalfo, L.R.-**Delmonico Restaurant**-1/2 of lot 52, Eagle St.(June 26, 1884), lot 50, Old Town (June 4, 1884).

Goodchild & Co.-Store.

Good-**Leadville Lodging House.**

Gove, E.C.-**Wardner's Store.**

Graghty, Frank-Eagle St.

Graham, R.

Graney, Thomas-**Saloon**-Lot 4, Prichard Ave. (June 12, 1884).

Greenfelder, N.B.-Part of lots 11 & 12, Eagle St. (Aug 26, 1891).

Gregory, Henry S.-**Atty.**

Griffith-**Atty.**

Gupano-**Ranch** one mile above Eagle City.

Gutherie, T.B.

Gutherie.W.J.

H:

Haman House.

Hardy, John.

Hagadorn, George-**Gem Chop House**-On Eagle St. adjoins the **Daisy.**

Hanes, Jim-1884.

Hanley, T.F.

Harkness, J.C.-**Justice of the Peace-Prichard House,** registry agent for voting precinct.

Haught, Billy-Has **store and saloon.**

Hawkins, H.J.-Has **store and saloon.**

Hawkins, W.J.-**Banker and Broker**-Corner of Eagle and Placer St. (Nov 8, 1886).

Hay-no location.

Hayes, D.T.-**Leadville Lodging House**-Eagle St., next door to **Ainsworth and Hawkins Bank.**

Hayes, Sam. H.-**General Merchandise**-On Eagle St., Hayes claim-located on Prichard Cr. in rear of **Saloon** building, 80' from rear of saloon. Lot 3, block E. on Main St., 1/2 interest in **Leadville Lodging House.**

Healy, Frank-Lot in town of Osborne.

Heder-**Atty.**

Heflin, M.L.-Gold St., his house used as **Masonic Hall.**

Heller, Frank J.-**Merchants Hotel.**

Henderson, George.

Henry, Sam R.-**Kentucky Beer Hall**-W 1/2 lot 37, on West Side of Eagle St.

Hermany, Charles-Lot with **Golden King Mgr. Co.**

Hess, Herman-**The Daisy**-Lot 74, **Coy and Hess Saloon** on old corner. **The Daisy** on corner Eagle and Placer St., and cabin on Eagle St. (June 25, 1885).

Hilden, Barry John.

Hill, Barry.

Hoffman, Dave.

Holman, Alfred.

Hood and Co.-Eagle Cr. Sawmill.

Horn, Bob-Helped Sam Hayes lay out Hayes (Eagle) City.

Hospital Building-Lot 8 Placer St.

Huey, J.W.-Eagle Cr.

Hummel, John-On Eagle St.**-Black Hills House.**

Humphreys, Sid-lot 65, West Side of Eagle St.

Hunt, W.E.-**Real estate**-Office with **City Recorder**, had a frame building on Eagle St. and house on north side of Prichard Ave. lot 22.

Hussey, Charles-Lots 61-65 on West Side of Eagle St.

Hussey, Warren-**Banker**, banks in Murray, Beaver, Wallace and Spokane.

Hutton, May Arkwright.

Hyde, S.C.-**Atty.**

J:

Jackson, Robert-**Gem Restaurant.**

Jail-On Eagle St.

James, W.S.-Adjacent to B.M. Elliott's lot.

Jarrison-Had a **saloon.**

Jarvis, James M.

Jens, John L.-**Lunch Stand.**

Jenkins, Frank-In town of Osborne.

Jewelry Store.

Johnson, A.P.-In town of Osborne.

Johnson, D.J.-Lot 2 Silver St. in Old Town.

Johnson, F.

Johnson, Lena M. Mrs.-**School Teacher.**

Johnson, Malachi-Died January 24, 1884.

Johnson, S.S.-Lot 36, East side Eagle St.

Johnson, W.F.-**Atty.**-Eagle St., lived in a cabin on lot 14 Lee St.

Jones, A.J.-**Sample Room and Billiards.**

Jones, H.A.-Lot 18 Placer St.

Jones, Thomas A.-Has 25' 7" off lot 80 Eagle St., back of Eagle H.(May 22, 1884.)

Joy's Opera House.

K:

Kadel, W.-**With Coeur d'Alene Restaurant.**

Kaeler, Liene-Lot on Lee St., fronts lot 31 on Lee St., and 62' 7" deep, has a cabin 10' x 12'.

Kamich, William-Lot 13 Prichard Ave., lot 51 corner of Eagle and Lee St.

Kanady,M Ida A.-**Postmistress-**In Union 1916 to 1918.

Kavanaugh, Andrew-Lot 13 Placer St., also lived in Osborne, **assessor and collector** of Shoshone Co.

Keller, Lizzie-Lot 2, Lee St.

Kellogg-**Gem Saloon-**Main St. in Raven.

Kellogg, Noah-**Carpenter.**

Kentucky Beer Hall.

Kerlin, Michael-Lots 15, 17,and 19 on Jackson St.

Kiebler, L.

King, C.B.-Operated **Wells Fargo.**

King Mgr. Co.-Purchased a house and lot.

Kinnaird, J.M. **Notary Public-**Operated **Wells Fargo office.**

Know, W.J.

Kranich, William-North side of Eagle St., bordered on west by a lot owned by Panell and Spalling-Old Town, first addition, corner of Eagle and Lee St., lot 49.

Kuebler, Lewis-**Arlington Chop House**, block A., lot 2, Eagle & Stevens St. (May 13, 1884), also lot 1, block B, First Addition.

L:

Lackie, Henry-On Prichard Cr.

Lake, John K.-West Side of Lee St.

Landoneur, Lewis-Bldg. and lot 54, north side of Prichard Ave.

Landburg, N.O.-Lot 7, block D, Feb 27, 1884.

Lane, F.P.-**Bourgoine House-**Lived in tent on Prichard Ave.

Lange, Melechion.

Lansdale, M.K.-Lot 7 and house, corner of Prichard and Eagle, known as **Lansdale House.**

Larson, Ola.

Lasebo, Charles E.-Up Eagle Cr.

Lassie, Miss-**School Teacher.**

Laumeister-Had a **sawmill.**

Leadville Lodging House-Eagle St., next door to **Ainsworth-Hawkins Bank.**

Lee, George S.

Leester-**Gem Saloon-**In Raven, on Main St.

Levi, A.B.-South side Main St.

Lewis, J.W.etal-Lot 1, Prichard Ave. (May 22, 1884.)

Lewis, Matt-(1883)-has **store.**

Linden, Robert J.-Lot 1, Eagle St. (May 17, 1884).

Littlefield, **Dr. H.L.**-Founded town of Littlefield (Butte
  City.)

Livers, J. W.-**Druggist**-Lot 83 West Side of Eagle St.

Lockies-Lot next to W.H. Payne on Eagle St.

Lonigl, J.H.-Purchased Matterwell lot.

Low, F.P.-**Burgoine House.**

Lowenberg, Bernard-Lot 8 on the north side of Prichard
  Ave., lot 59, West Side of Eagle St., and lot 51 on
  Prichard Ave. Purchased **Sweeny Store** on Eagle St., also
  White Elephant Saloon on Sept. 24, 1884.

Lowenberg Bros-Lots 8, 56, and 59 Eagle St. (lot 8 was on Prichard Ave.)

  Lusha, James H.-**Pioneer Restaurant**-Lot 2, Prichard Ave.,
  also **Lusha's Coffee House**, lot 4 Eagle St., East side
  above 2nd St. (Feb 11, 1886).

Luche, Theordore-Cabin on Eagle St.

Lynch, J.H.-**Senate Saloon**-Corner of Eagle and Placer St.
  and lot 29 north side of Prichard Ave.

Lynch, T.J.-Lot 67 Eagle St. and a wedge shaped in between
  lot 69 on north and lot 65 on south.

Lynch and Meyer-Lot 66 north side of Eagle St., lot 1
  Placer St.

M:

Mackenzie, Roderick-**General Store**-Lot 67, Union St. (June
  4, 1884).

Mahoney, Patrick H.-**Atty., Real estate**-Lot 1, Placer St.
  (May 31,1884).

Malachi, Johnson-Died January 24, 1884.

Maloney, E.-Up Eagle Cr.

Manning, Albert-Lot on Main St. in Raven.

Marker, D.A.-Eagle St.

Markinson, John.

Marshall, Thomas C.-**Atty.**

Mason, Everett G.

Mason John-Died April 1, 1884.

Masonic Hall-Gold St.

Matherwell, J.P.-Lot 1, Prichard Ave. He began working in Murray in March 1884.

Maxwell, L. N.-**Atty.**-Office with **Mineral Recorder.**

Maxwell & Poe.

Mayer, E.B.-1891.

Mayes

McCarthy, Florence.

McCarthy, Timothy-Cabin on Prichard Ave.

McComber-(1884.)

McCormick-(1884.)

McDaniel J.-**Eagle City Theater**.

McDonald, D.-Lot 10 Lee St.

McFettridge, Jack-Shot Nelson.

McGilliwary, Ally.

McGlashan, C.F.-**Publisher of Coeur d'Alene Nugget.**

McGowan, Mike-Cabin on Prichard Cr.

McGrane.

McGuire, Henry.

McIntosh-**Builder-**No. 10, Eagle St.

McLaughlin-Lot 39, West Side of Eagle St.

McLean, Duncan M-**Black Hills House.**

McLin, J.F.-**Carpenter and Contractor**-Eagle St.

McLoud, Thomas J.-**The Pantheron**-Lot 44, Eagle St., north
of Preston's lot.

McNab-**Drugstore**-Tent on lot 30, Eagle St., and lot 36,
Eagle St.

Means, J.K etal-Had judgement on lot 72, on north side of
Eagle St., lot on corner of Eagle St. and
Prichard Ave. called **Means House.** (Oct. 31, 1885.)

Meek, Courtney W.-Corner of Eagle St. and Prichard Ave.,
son of Joe Meek-famous mountain man.

Melder-**Judge.**

Menichino, Gaspera-**Ranch** one mile up Eagle Cr.

Merchant's Hotel.

Merrick, B.A.-Lot 14, Prichard Ave. (July 11, 1884).

Miller S.A.- **Druggist,** Lot 1, Placer St. and lots 10 and
11, East side of Eagle St.

Mills, A.R.-Had lot in Osborne.

Mills, Sydenham-W. 1/2 lot 19, and E. 1/2 lot 12 on east
side of Eagle St., **General Mining.**

Moffitt, Ed. H.-**Meat Market**-Lot 49, Eagle St., cabin on
Eagle St., lot 44 West Side.

Montana Saloon.

Mount House.

Morbeck, A.C.-Ran a **Sawmill**.

Morphy, W. N.-**Atty.**

Morris, John-Died Feb 18, 1884.

Mount, E.B.-Lot 31, Eagle St. and lot 36, West Side of
Eagle St.

Mount, S.J.-Lot 49 Eagle St. (noted on map in **Deputy
Recorder's Office.**)

Murphy, John-**Mine Owner.**

Meyer **Store**-Lot 1, Placer St.

N:

Nash, L.B.-**Notary Public**-Office opposite **Wells Fargo**.
Nason-**Watch Maker.**
Nelli, Panl.
Nelson-Shot by McFettridge.
Nevada Chop House and Hotel-Matt Brown, **Prop.** Placer St.
Noble-**Saloon.**
Nordyke, W.W.-Eagle St.
Northam-(1884.)
Nugget Building.

O:

Oakley, R.S., etal-Lot 3, block A, New Eagle City, north side Placer St., between top of hill on Placer St. and Prichard Ave., old cabin being the 3rd lot east of Prichard's old cabin.
O'Brien, Daniel-1/2 interest in a cabin.
O'Brien, John-Cabin on Lee St.
O'Brien William.
O'Connor, C.-Lot 27, Eagle St. (May 14, 1884).
O'Connor, Michael C.-Lot 27, Eagle St.
O'Connor, Patrick O.-**Boot and Shoe Maker**-Union St., lot on Eagle St. adjoins lots by T.M. Washburn, Small Bros. and Tom Taylor.
O'Mara, William-Cabin on Jackson St.
O'Neil, Charles W.-**Atty.**-Corner of Prichard Ave. and Eagle St., block K, First Addition, lot 7, has lot 71, West Side of Eagle St., Lot 2, block A, Eagle. He buys town lots.
O'Neil, Jeremiah T.-Sweeny's father-in-law, purchased Eagle City from Sweeny for $13,000.
Olsen, L.
Oro Fino Restaurant.
Osborne, S.V.W.-Lived in Osborne.
Owens, John-etal-S. 1/2 lot 57, he purchased the old Wyatt Earp-lot (April 22, 1887).
Oxley-(1884.)

P:

Packer Barber Shop, next to **Hayes Store**.
Palace Saloon.

Palmer, R.A.-Lot 13, Placer St. (April 29, 1886).

Palmer, W.B.-Prichard Ave.

Pannell and Spaulding-Lot 34 and lot 52 on East side of
Eagle St.

Pannell, J.M.-Cabin.

Pannell, W.L.-Cabin in Eagle.

Parker, Aaron F.-Lots 11 & 12 Silver St., April 30, 1887,
and lot 4 on Placer St. First **postmaster-**July 31, 1884.

Parker and Co.-Legal Publishers.

Parker, Austin-Cabin.

Parker, John B.

Parker, John L.-25' 7" off lot 80, back of Eagle St. has a
lot on the East side of Baker's cabin-a man of color.

Parker-**O.K. Barber Shop**-Next door to **Hayes Store**.

Parker, William-Died Nov. 10, 1886, lived in the **Delmonico**.

Parnell, W.L.-Cabin.

Pasters, Frank-**Bar** in Osborne, 1886.

Patterson, J.B.-**Phys. Office**-Next door to S. E. Child.

Payne, W.H.-Lot 51 West Side of Eagle St., lot 55 Eagle
St., opposite **Reed's store, Deputy Sheriff** & lot 12
Placer St., lot 57 north Eagle St.

Perry, James C.

Peterson, Henry.

Peterson, J.S.-S. 1/2 lot 44.

Peterson, Sig.

Peyton, John-25' 7" off lot 80, back of Eagle St.

Pierce, A.B.-Died March 20, 1884.

Pioneer Lumber Co.-Littlefield and Raven-1883.

Pioneer Restaurant-J.H. Lusha, **Prop.**

Poe, J.W.-**Atty.**-office with **Deputy Mineral Recorder** in
Nugget Bldg.

Points, Frank Col.-**Mining Recorder and Justice of the Peace-**Eagle St.

Pomeroy, Richard A.-Corner Eagle and Lee St.-April 22,
1885.

Porter's Building.

Porter, W.J.-**City Bakery**, Lot 12 Placer St., lot 23 West
Side of Eagle St., using his cabin for the **Republican
Club.**

Post Office-Lot 14, Placer St.

Prather, L.H.-**Atty.**

Prestston, A.H.

Preston, N.O.-Lot 46 on Eagle St. in Old Town, McLeod on
the north and Stoddard on the south lot 48 Savage.

Prichard, A.J.-Had **Hotel and Dry works**, wife Catherine
was **Post Mistress** from Apr. 1886 to Jun 1886. Had cabin
located on Prichard Ave.

Purgrine, P.-Corner of Prichard and Eagle St.

Putman, Mary-North side Prichard Ave., lot 76.

Q:

Quinby, Fred-**Physican**-Office in **Adams' Drug Store**, three doors north of the **theater**.

R:

Railroad depot and telephone booth.

Railsback-Lot 5, block A Butte City (Littlefield.).

Rammelmeyer, E.-**Mining engineer**-1884.

Ransom, E.J.-Lot on Prichard Ave., lot 1 on Eagle St., and lot 14 on corner of Eagle and (?), owned the **Pantheon Liquor Store**.

Record (the) Newspaper.

Reed, C.F.-Borders Baker's lot on west.

Reed, Frank-Had a store on lot 4 N.E. corner of Reed and Placer St. between **Pioneer Store** and **Nevada Chop House (restaurant)**, lot 10, Prichard Ave., 1/2 of lot on the corner of Bullion and Prichard Ave., with one house known as **Courthouse**, lot 8 on Placer St., also lot 14 on Placer St. as **Post Office**, lot 6 north Placer St.

Reyton, John-**Real estate**.

Rice, G.E.

Riley, James S.

Riley, W.C.-Osborne.

Rivers, J.A.-**Builder**.

Roaker, E.M.-Lot 3 Eagle St.

Robbins, Henry.

Roberts-**Atty**.

Roberts, Frank-Lot 33 Prichard Ave.

Roberts, J.M.-**General Store in Eagle**.

Roberts, J.T.-**Atty. and trustee for School Dist. 7**, lot 8 on Placer St.

Robinson, Clara D-A deed for ranch improvement.

Robinson, Jack H.-Lot 3.

Robinson, James L.-**Atty**.

Robinson, Jim M.-Lot 12, Placer St. Died July 1884.

Robinson-Office with Singleton.

Ryan John-Lot corner Eagle and Lee St., E. 1/2 lot 12, and west 10' of lot 10 on Eagle St. He lived in Osborne.

Ryman, Caleb.

S:

Sage, Eugene-Part of lots 15, 17, 19, and 21 on Jackson St.
(June 5, 1884).

Salls, Gary.

Sands, Peter-Cabin.

Sanford.

Saray, Alexander-Prichard Ave. (July 30, 1884).

Sargent, C.-Lot 51 West Side of Eagle St.

Saunders, Jack-(1884).

Savage, F.H.-Lot 48, Eagle St.

Sazerac Saloon.

Scallon, William-**Atty.**-A St.-East fork of Eagle Cr.

Schlemline, J. R.-East fork of Eagle Cr.

Schlemline-**Miller Ranch**, 1/4 mile from Eagle City on
Prichard Cr.

School-Lot 8, Placer St.

Scisco, Charles-Lot 42 east Eagle.

Scott, H.F.

Scott, James W.

Scott-**Phys.**

Seinery

Selig, K.-Lot 5, block 13, First Addition.

Senate Saloon.

Sever, Mary-House and cabin.

Sever, Steve A.

Sharp, James-Cabin up Eagle Cr.

Shaw-**The Comstock Saloon**-Eagle St.

Shea, Daniel W.

Sheehey, John.

Shelton, J.L.

Shelton, Nannie-(W.J.'s wife) Lot 1-east side of Eagle St.,
lot 9 on Lee St., lot 53 West Side of Eagle on Eagle and
Lee St., and Lot 68 north side of Eagle.

Shelton W.J.-**Freight Agent**-West Side of Eagle St., lot 53,
Corner Eagle and Lee, lot 31 & 44 Eagle St., was
Postmaster in Eagle City (1885-1886).

Shelton, W.J. and Cunningham S.-Log house on Eagle St., 25'
from Lee St., also a cabin on Reed St.

Shingle Mill-Noah Kellogg, **Prop.**

Shminets, Peter-Cabin.

Shoemaker-Lot 7, block 1, Raven City.

Sibley, Peter-Lot 27 Eagle St.

Simon-**General Merchandise**.

Sinclair, George-(1884).

Singleton, Thomas T.-**Atty.**-Corner Eagle St. and Prichard
Avenue.

Sisea, Charles-Lot 46, Eagle St.

Skeels, C.W.-Cabin up Eagle Cr.

Small Bros.-Lot next to Pat O'Connor.

Smith, Archibald.

Smith, F.B.-**Wardner's Store.**

Smith, Peter-Cabin.

Smith, Jim-1884.

Snyder, William-**Phys.**-Lot 20 Placer St. His office in
   Eagle City Drug Store.

Solam, Ola.

Solomon, Ike-Lot north side of Placer St.

Spalling-Lot next to Kranich.

Stagner, W.G.-**Ranch** near Eagle.

Steele.

Stanemets, Felix-Cabin.

Star Lodging.

Stater, J.R.-Purchased Hummels' lot on Eagle St. and
   Prichard Ave.

Steele, Thomas & Daniel Steel-East fork of Eagle Cr.

Stagner, W.G.

Steinmet, P.-Lot 14, Eagle St.

Steve, George-Lot on Prichard Ave.

Stevens, J.B.-Lot 1, block 13, First Addition.

Stillwell, W.T.

Stinson, Sheridan-In bottom land, 25', T 50 N, R 4 E.

Stinson-**Three Story Hotel.**

Stoddard, Harry-S 1/2 lot 44 Eagle St.

Stoddard, Mamie-S. 1/2 lot 44 Eagle St., bounded on north
   by Preston's lot, May 5, 1884. Mentioned on Britt's
   map.

Stoll and Woods-Lot 39, Eagle St.

Stoll, W.F.-**Atty.** A St., also lot 41 on Eagle St.

Stoner, Elizabeth-Born 1886 in Eagle City.

Store.

Stringham, Berry-Lot on Main St. in Littlefield.

Strong, Martin-Lot 1, east Union St., had a **saloon.**

Sullivan, P.J.-Union St.

Swanton, Edward Lot 72, east Eagle St.

Sweeny, Charles-**General Merchandise Store.** Bought
   wedge shaped lot on Eagle St. from William Stoll. He also
   purchased a lot on Eagle St., next door to **Taylor's
   Store** and opposite **Nevada Chop House,** from T.M.
   Washburn. Sold his store to B. Lowenberg, sold lot 51 on
   Prichard Ave. to Lowenberg, also sold **White Elephant
   Saloon** to him. He had lot 4 on Lee St., lot 56 on Eagle
   St., and Lot 59 on Eagle St.

Sweeny, Nicholas.

Switzer, Homer-Cabin.

Syey, Frank.

T:

Taylor-**Atty.**

Taylor & Co.-Lot 41, West Side Eagle.

Taylor, James -Lot 25, Eagle St.

Taylor, John-Lot 20, Eagle St.

Taylor, Mary-**Laundry**-On Union St., in rear of **Mackenzie and Evans' Store**.

Taylor, Thomas-3rd lot north of Pat O'Connor.

Taylor's-**Store.**

Theston Building.

Thiard, John-1/2 lot 14, Placer St. (former **post office**), had tent in Eagle City.

Thiele, E.-**Physican**-On Eagle St. opposite Lee St., two doors above S.E. Childs.

Thomas, Newt.

Thompson, C.W.-etal-S 1/2 of lot 2 on Eagle St. (July 11, 1884).

Thompson, J.B.

Timmons-**Assayer-**On Prichard Ave.

Todman, J.H.-**Assayer**-Had a cabin.

Tompson, John McL-Cabin up Eagle Cr.

Tonenan, Addison O.-Cabin.

Topliff, James F.-**Real Estate and Notary**-Office in **Porters' Cabin** on Eagle St.

Towers, Ira C.

Town, J.B.-Cabin.

Townsend, W.-Lot 20 Prichard Ave.

Troy-**Laundry**-Eagle St., adjoins **White Elephant Saloon**.

Trumbo, J.R.-**Auctioneer.**

Trumbull-**Atty.**

Trustees for school-Lot 8, N. side of Placer St. (Feb. 19, 1887).

Tucker, George W.-Cabin in Osborne, also lot 35 Prichard Ave.

U:

Unkle, Solomon S. etal-Lot 5, 22' off east part Prichard Ave, also lot north side Placer St., 300' east of junction Bullion and Gold St., bordered by Andy Bishop's lot on the west and A. P. Wright, 30' fronting on Placer St., lot 15 on Placer St.

V:

Van Burg, H.-Cabin.

Van Buskirk-**Druggist.**
Van Dorn-Lot 16 Placer St.
Vaughn, W.R.
Vaux, William B.-Cabin.
Vedder, Arlington-**Chop House**-Eagle and Stevens St.
Velande, Joe-1/3 interest in a lot fronting on Prichard
  Ave.
Verde, Monte-**Singer-(**1884).
Vinsen-**Kentucky Beer Hall**-Eagle St.
Viter, George F.

W:

Wade and Nelson-Lot 46 East side Eagle St., lots on north
  and south Prichard.
Waite, John K.-Cabin on Eagle Cr.
Waite, William-Cabin.
Walker, Ben F.-Parcel of land above W.L. Shelton's house,
  south side Eagle St.
Walls-Lot 1.
Wardner and Company.
Wardner, J.A.-**Transportation Co. store and Wardner's
  Store.**
Washburn, T.M.-Adjoins lot owned by Pat O'Connor.
Watson, J.-Lot 58 north side Prichard Ave.
Watts-Lot 1, block 1, east Raven.
Webber, J.A.-Lot 49 Eagle St.
Webber, P.-**Golden Gate Saloon.**
Webber, F.A.-W. side of Eagle and Placer St. (Sept 17,
  1887). Parcel above W.L. Shelton south side Eagle and
  Placer St., lot 54 on east side of Eagle St., had **Feed
  Livery Stable and Restaurant,** had house and 8 acres near
  mouth of Daisy Gulch, also **Postmaster** in Eagle.
Webster, Charles A.-**Real Estate and Mining** broker.
Weed, D.F.
Weed, E.A.-Corner Eagle and Lee Streets.
Weeks, Judge P.
Welch Dick.
Wells, Fargo-Eagle St.
Wentz, F.W.- East side Eagle and Placer St., lot 36, 4-16-
  84, Old Town. Lot 2 on Silver   St. (July 5, 1884). Lot
  13 south Placer St., East side of Eagle and Placer St.
  Lot 36, Old Town, lot 2 on Silver St., lot 9 south side
  of Placer St. lot 30 south side Eagle St., and lot 7
  Placer St.
Whealan, M.-Lots 9 and 19 on Lee St.

Wheelock, Andrew-Lot 7, block D.

Whistler, Mrs. Kateryn-**Chop House.**

White and Cunningham-Lot 35 West Side Eagle St.

White Elephant Saloon-Earp Bros-**Props.**

White, G.W.-Cabin.

White, Henry.

White Lawrence.

White, W.R.-**Atty.**

White & Wickersham-Lot 35 west Eagle.

Whiteman, Albert A.-**Prichard House**.

Whittle, Frank.

Wickersham, F.A.-**Real Estate/Mining**-Has town's plat
   map.

Wickersham, Pugh.

Wikadel, C.A.-**Arcade Chop House**-Eagle St. and Placer St.

Wilcott, Bill.

Wilcott, Lila S.

Wilcox, Elgin-**Postmaster** (1886-1888).

Williams, John.

Williams, P.B.-**Phys.**

Williams, W.S.-**Atty.**-Next door to **Wells Fargo.**

Wilson, John-Cabin on Lee St.

Wilson, Louis W.

Wilson, Richard-**Assessor.**

Wilson , Thomas B.-**Comstock Saloon**-Cabin on Prichard
   Ave.

Wise-**Meat Market**-Eagle St.

Womaner, Morris-Cabin.

Wooden, Capt.

Woods W.W.-**Notary**-Office opposite **Wells Fargo Office,**
   lot 47 West Side Eagle St.

Woody, Frank H.-**Atty.**-Next door to **Wells Fargo.**

Woolford, Luke D.-**Atty.** (1884).

Worthen, C.C.- Cabin on Prichard Ave.

Wright, A.D.-Borders Unkle's lot on west Placer St.

Wuchins, John M.

Wyant, Lewis-(1884).

Wyman, Phillip -Headwaters of Eagle Cr.

Unknown Landlords

Eagle Street:

lot 5   West Side between Lee and 1st St.

lot 14   One house

lot 15   West Side between Lee and 1st St.

lot 17

lot 19
lot 20
lot 22
lot 23 West Side between Lee and 1st St.
lot 24
lot 27
lot 28
lot 29
lot 33
lot 34 East Eagle St., near lot 4 on Placer St.
lot 36 East Eagle St., west a Bldg.
lot 37
lot 39
lot 40 East side.
lot 44 East side.
lot 46 East side.
lot 49 West Side.
lot 50 East side.
lot 57 One tent on N. 1/2 lot 57 and S 1/2 of same, West Side Eagle St. Lot on West Side between Lee and 1st St.

Lee Street:

lot 1
lot 3
lot 4
lot 5
lot 8
?   Opposite **Montana Saloon.**
lot 14

Placer Street:

lot 1   South on St.
lot 3   South side.
lot 5
lot 7   House south on Placer.
lot 10 North side.
lot 13 South side.
lot 15 South side.
lot 21 Rear lot 4 on Placer.

Prichard Avenue:

lot 4
lot 7   South side Prichard.
lot 11
lot 24 North side
lot 26
lot 28
lot 30
lot 32
lot 35 South side.
lot 37 North side.
lot 42 W. 1/2 lot 42 north side.
lot 44 South side.
lot 50 North side.
lot 54 North side.
lot 56 North side.
lot 61 South side.
lot 71
?   Montana Saloon.
?   Blacksmith shop.
?   Missoula Saloon

Reed Street:

Lot 1   East side
Lot 3   East side
lot 13 East side.
Lot 15 East side.
lot 17 East side.

GRANTORS AND GRANTEES

(Taken from the Records of Deeds-Eagle City)

1884-40
1885-12
1886-10
1887-8
1888-1
1889-0
1891-1
1907-1
1911-1
1928-1
1929-2

A:

Adler, A.A.   1891

Ainsworth, H. & Co.   1884

B:

Baker, J.C.   1884
Baran, Alex.   1884
Barnes, A.M.
Behr, John   1884
Benton, Sid.
Boyce, Mrs. C.R.   1885
Brenton, Charles.
Buchanan, H.A.
Burdan, Mollie   1885
Burns, W. S.   1886
Burton.   1885
Buzard, Fay (William).   1884

C:

Cahan, F.   1885
Cardoner, Dan.   1884
Carpenter, E.D.   1887
Carpp, Charles.   1884
Chambers, S.T.   1884
Chambers, W.H.   1884
Channin, J.
Child, S.E.   1884
Child, W.E.   1885
Clements, M.D.   1885
Cohen, Simon.   1884
Cole, A.   1884
Cole, C.M.   1886
Collier, J.H.   1884
Coy, E.E.   1884
Crawford, Joe B.   1884
Crown, Charles A.   1884

D:

Dennee, T.McK.   1884
Donnelly, Simon P.   1887
Dorsett, A.K.   1884
Driggs, A.E.   1884

Drummond, W.W.	1889
Dudley, Charles	1884.

E:

Earp, Wyatt.	1884
Eckert, C.C.	1884
Emerson, Seth.	1886
Enright Jack	1884
Enright, John E.	1884
Enright, Lou.	1884

F:

Feinberg, Moses S.	1886
Ferguson, D.S.	1884
Fidelity & Columbus Co.	1928
Friedlander, W.	1884

G:

Gandalfo J.R.	1884
Gandalfo Josephine E.	1884
Gelchrest, A.M.	
Gibson, H.	1884
Gillilland, W.	1884
Glass, John.	1884
Glider, Pete.	1886
Goldstein, A. B.	
Graney, Tom.	1884
Greenfelder, N.R.	1886
Gutherie, W.J.	1886
Gutherie, T.B.	1885

H:

Hanley, T.F.	1889
Hayes, D.T.	1884
Henry, Sam R.	1884
Hermany, Charles.	1887
Hess, Herman.	1885
Hussey, Charles.	1884

J:

Johnson, D.J.   1884
Johnson, S.S.   1884
Jones, Tom L.   1884

K:

Kamich, William.   1884
Keller, Lizzie.   1884
Kerlin, M.   1884
Kiebler,L.   1884
Kuebler, Lewis.   1884

L:

Landburg, N.O.   1884
Lansdale, M.K.   1884
Lewis, J.W.   1884
Linden, Robert J.   1884
Lowenberg, B.   1884
Lusha, James H.   1886
Lynch, Tom J.   1884

M:

Mackenzie, Roderick.   1884
Mahoney, P.H.   1884
Matherwell, J.P.   1884
McLeod, T.J.   1884
Means, J.L.   1885
Merrick, B.A.   1884
Miller, S.A.   1884
Mills, S.   1889
Moffitt, Ed.   1884

O:

O'Brien, D.   1885
O'Connor, M.C.   1884
O'Neil, Charles W.   1884
Oakley, R.S. etal.   1884
Owens, John.   1884

P:

Palmer, R.A.	1886
Parker, John B.	1884
Parker, Aaron F.	1884
Payne, W.H.	1884
Peterson, J.H.	1885
Peyton, John.	1884
Pomeroy, R.A.	1886
Preston, A.H.	1884

R:

Ransom, E.J.	1884
Reed, Frank.	1884
Robinson, Clara D.	1907
Ryan, John	1887

S:

Sage, Eugene.	1884
Selig, K.	1884
Sever, Mary.	1929
Sever, Steve.	1929
Shelton, William J.	1884
Sibley, Peter.	1884
Stevens, J.B.	1884
Stoddard, H.	1884
Stoddard, N.	1884
Sweeny, Charles.	1884

T:

Thiard, John.	1885
Thompson, C.W.	1884

U:

Unkle, S. S.	1884

V:

Velande, Joe.	1884

W:

Walker, B.F.	1887

9

Murrayville

There were ten trails that led over the mountains into Eagle. True, Wyatt and his party traveled over the Evolution Trail, but it and nine others were also used by the flood of humanity that followed them into the Coeur d'Alenes. The names and approximate opening dates are as follows:

Thompson Falls-Winter of 1883
Belknap-February, 1884
Trout Creek-early 1884
Heron-1884
Martin/Rathdrum-?
Evolution-1878
Jackass-1883
Burke-?
Irwin-?

8-X348 Barnard-Stockbridge Collection, University of Idaho, Moscow
Murray Idaho in 1890

The Idaho Northern Railroad (later known as the Oregon-Washington Railroad and Navigation Company) reached Eagle City at year's end in 1908.

More recently, the Yukon Gold Company established their base of operations in Murray and first worked Prichard Creek with six small dredges in an effort to get the gold. But, finding the small dredges inadequate for the job, in 1917 the company shipped a massive wooden gold dredge down from Alaska. It was state of the art of its day. All of the natural obstacles, gave company officials a devil of a time in getting the massive wooden structure to the camp, even in pieces, let alone putting it all back together again. But, having finally accomplished that, for the next nine years it chugged, ground and whistled its way day-and-night dredging up Prichard Creek for a distance of seven miles, between Eagle City and Paragon. Murray residents were incensed by all of the racket, but a job is a job, after all.

Work finally stopped in 1926, but not because of the lack of gold. On the contrary, the shiny bits of pure gold were becoming more plentiful, but the dredge went out of business when steeply sloping bedrock made it impossible for the dredge to reach it. In the interim, the Yukon Gold Company had made a net profit of over a half million dollars and, in the process, had destroyed much of the old town of Murray. They abandoned the site, leaving behind broken machinery parts and great heaps of tailings. (The company paid kids to sit on the bank and yell whenever they saw something yellow come out of the conveyor belt. The machinery's recovery of gold was geared toward dust and the smaller nuggets. Operations would then shut down and men would look for the lost gold.)

Then, in the 1960s, an enterprising Murray resident and business owner, Chris Christofferson, decided that since his tavern was one of the original buildings in town, there must be gold in the undisturbed ground beneath it. He then went into his bedroom, closed the door and promptly sank a shaft down to bedrock. It was another paying proposition, but only during times of low water.

In later years, Mr. Christofferson's niece, Lucille, appeared on television's old Gary Moore show "What's My Line?" Turns out that she was the only person in the country with a gold mine in her bedroom.

Interestingly enough, the bones of four ghost towns are located between Eagle and the base of Thompson Falls Pass to the east. And the bumpy old wagon road that once ran along the route has recently been replaced by a freshly paved roadway that stretches all the way over the mountains to Thompson Falls, Montana.

The once active little towns of Butte City (Littlefield), Osborne, Raven, and Paragon (Sullivan) lie today in silent ruin. "Metal detector don't fail me now!" (Additional data on Eagle City and Murray can be obtained from the authors.)

Murrayville Directory
(Ives addition)

1883 to 1997

Streets:

Alley
Cromie
First
Gold
Incline
Keeler
Main
Murray
Second
Third (Alder Gulch)

A:

Ainsworth & Hawkins-**Bankers,** 1885.
Alexander, Rova-**Phys.,** 1902.
Allen, Albert-**Atty.,** 1886.
Allen, Frank-1905.
Allison, J. L.-**Photography,** Lower Main St., 1885.
Almquist, Harry-1997.
Almquist, Walter-Lots 6, 7, 8, 13, and 14, block 6, 1997.
Argyle, J. T.-**County Commissioner,** 1888.
Arion-**(Red light district with Mollie Burdan),** 8-6-1885.
Assayer's Office-Lot 7, block 4, 1896.
Athey, M. C.-1885.
Aulbach, Adam-**Newspaper editor,** 1884.
Aulbach, Rose-1905.

B:

Baer-**Saloon,** 1886.
Bakery-Lot 5, block 4, 1896.
Bank-Lot 1, block 6, 1884-1886.
Bank Exchange-Garrison & Strong-S.E. corner of Main & first
  St.

Bank of Murray-Charles Hussey, **Sec.** (1885); Dahler,
   President, 1888.
Bank Saloon-Felix Brown & Co. Prop's.-S.E. corner Main &
   second.
Bank of Northern Idaho-Johnson, **Cashier** (1890-1891).
Barber Shop-Lot 8, block 9, 1896.
Barber Shop-Lot 2, block 9, 1896.
Barber Shop-Lot 8, block 10, 1896.
Barnard, T. N.-**Photographer,** W. Main St., 1889.
Barnes-On hillside, 1st St., also part owner of **Skating
   rink,** corner of Main & 1st St.
Barnham, Frank-1905.
Barrett & Zeiglers-**Restaurant,** 1884.
Barroil-**Hardware,** 1886.
Bartlett, Elmer-1905.
Barton and Smith **Daily Stage and Mail**-1890-1891.
Bass and Ingalls-**Drugs,** Main near 2nd St., 1884.
Bass, C. T. P.-1885.
Bean, James H.-Lots 17 & 18, block 12, 1996.
Beartop Mining Co.-1905.
Beatty, George-1905.
Beckwith, C.D.-**Photographer,** 1885.
Bedroom Bar-Grebil's lots, 1997.
Beehner, Duane & Kristi A.-1996.
Bellinger, Coner-**Drugs**-1886.
Bennington, J. S.-**Restaurant,** NE. corner of First & Main
   St., 1884. S. side Main St., near 1st St., 1885.
Bennington & Waite Saloon, 1886.
Bennington Chop House-1885.-J.S. Bennington, **Prop.**-Main
   near first.
Bernard, Henry-Shot & killed John Enright in 1884.
Bill, Panama-1905.
Billiards-Garrison and Strong Prop., SE. corner of Main St.
   Sept. 22, 1885).
Black, J. E. -**Blacksmith** (1886).
Blackman.
Blackwell, Mrs. Anna-(1905).
Blaine & Emmett **Mining Co.**-(1910-1911).
Blossom, W.L.-**General Store** (1886).
Boarding House-Lots 11, & 12, block 11 (1896).
Boblett-(1884).
Bolander, L. C.-**County coroner** (1888).
Bossie, W.-Main and Second St.
Brace, Charles E.-**Postmaster** (1885-1886).
Brackett, L. B.-**Prop. Merchant's Hotel** (1886).
Brien, D. H.-**Phys.** (1886).
Brile, Alfred-**Hardware, Mgr. Kentucky Mining Co**. (1886).
Brile, J. J.-**Assayer** (1888).

Brown-(1948).

Brown, Bros.-Lodging (1885).

Brown, Felix-**Saloon** (1885).

Brown, F. W.-**Fruits, Nuts, etc.**, Main St. (1885).

Brown, H. S.-**Furniture** (1886).

Brown's **News Depot** (1884).

Bruch & Co.-(1884).

Brunswick **Restaurant**-Main St., between 1st and 2nd, Sept. 22, 1885.

Buck-**Judge**, 1885.

Burdan, Maggie-**Mollie-B-Damn** (Maggie Hall-maiden name), 1884.

Burgoine, M.-Lot 3, block F. on Main St., 1886.

Burk, H. S.-Keeler St., 1886.

Burke, John M.-**Fire Dept.**, upper Main St., 1885.

Burke, Mary Cannary-**Calamity Jane**, 1884.

Burke, Paddy-1910-1911.

Burke, X. S.-**Placer Mining Recorder,** 1886.

Burmeister, Deloris, J.-Lot 12, block 1-Ives Addition 1996.

Burnell, Athalie-1949.

Burnell, Charles-1949.

Burns, W.R.-**Sawmill,** 1888.

Burton, Edward W.-**Bakery/General Store,** 1884.

Burton, George-**Photographer,** 1910-1911.

Burton, Mrs. Susan-1905.

Burton & Porter-**Bakery & Lodgings.**

Bush, Ben-**Insurance,** 1888.

Bush, Edward-1996.

Bush, Lean-1996.

Bushea, Joseph-Corner Gold & 2nd St., 1886.

Butler & Kennedy-Lot 2, block D., W. Main.

C:

Cahan, Frank-1905.

Calavan, J. M.-**Pioneer Lumber Co.**, Littlefield and Raven 1885.

Caldwell & Co.-Lot 1, block A., corner of Main & 1st. St.

Calver, Helen C.-**Postmistress,** 1959.

Cameron, J. B.-1884.

Campbell, Henry-1905.

Campbell, W. R.-**Saloon,** 1886.

Canby-**Post of G.A.R.**, 1905.

Cardon S.-1884.

Cardoner, D.-**Produce and Fish Market,** 1886; **Fruits Etc.** 1888; above **Wolf's Cosmopolitan Saloon.**

Cargill, J. F.-**Mgr. Nye Vacuum Pump,** 1886.

Carlise, H.-**Saloon**, 1885.

Carpenter, Ed.-**Lumber**, 1888.

Carpenter Shop-Lot 9, block 7, 1896.

Carpenter Shop-Block 13, 1896.

Carpenters-**Laundry**, 1884.

Carten, John-1885.

Cavanaugh, Andrew-1885.

Center Market-Harris and Miller Prop., Main St. near 2nd
   1889.

Chamberlain.

Chambers & Barrell-**Hardware**, 1884 & 1896.

Charboneau & Knuth-**Clothes**, 1888.

Chemodurow, Betty-1996.

Chevalier, H.-**Restaurant**, 1888.

Childress, Randy L. & Claudia.-Lots 1 through 4, block 6,
   & Lots 15 & 16, 1997.

Christofferson, Chris & Lucille-Lots 26 through 29, block
   12, 1997.

City Beer Hall-John C. Knuth, **Prop.**, S. side of Main
   1889.

Claggett, Thomas-**Judge,** 1885 & 1908.

Claggett, W.H.-**Lawyer**, 1886.

Clark & Co. Clothing-S. Main above 2nd, 1885.

Clark J.-1884.

Cleary, Mrs. E. B.-**Notions, Art Gallery, and Photo Studio,**
   opposite **Wolf's Cosmopolitan Saloon,** 1886,
   Club Saloon-Next door to **Greenleaf Saloon,** 1886.

Clutter, J.F.-1883.

Cobbler-Lot 8, block 4, 1896.

Cobbler-Lot 5, block 13, 1896.

Coeur d'Alene Brewery-Mallon and Rammelmeyer, **Old Bank
   Bldg.**, center Main St., 1885.

Coeur d'Alene Brick Co.-C. W. Weber & Co., Osborne, 1885.

Coeur d'Alene Manufacturing Co.-1905.

Coeur d'Alene Mining Co.-J.F. Murphy, **Supt.**, 1910-1911.

Coeur d'Alene North fork Mining Co.-E.P. Spalding, **Manager**
   1910-11.

Coeur d'Alene Record-O.H. Culver, **Prop.**, 1886.

Coeur d'Alene Sun-Lt. E. Harson, **Publisher,** 1910-1911, Adam
   Aulbach, 1885.

Coeur d'Alene & Thompson Falls, Tel. Co.#1-Dutton **Manager,**
   1888.

Collins, Joseph

Collins, Joshua-E. 1/2 lot 6, block A.

Comique Theater-1884.

Condon, Mike-1996.

Cone, Geo. M.-**Druggist & Probate Judge**, 1885.

Conellard, I.W.-1885.

Conison, L.-Lot 2, block C.

Conkling, George-Murray St.

Cookindale, H.M.-**Prop. Palace Hotel,** 1886.

Coons & Paskill's **Place**-1896.

Cooper and Peck-**Express Office** upper Main St.

Cooper, M.H.-1905.

Cooper, **Dr. J. T.-Phys.**, office at **Burke & Co.** on upper
  Main St., 1885.

Corder, Dan-1996.

Corder, Donald E. & Shirley F.-Lots 9 & 10, block 9, 1996.

Cornellis, Joe-1905.

Cosmopolitan Saloon-Wolf **Prop.,** e. Main St., 1885.

Cotter, June-Lots 1, 2, 3, block 9, 1996.

Coulson & Co.-**Express Line (stage),** 1886.

Coulter, Jesse-**Manager, C.J.A.W. & M. Co.,** 1886.

Coumerilh, Mrs. John-**Ice Cream Saloon.**

Coumerilh, John-**Blacksmith and Iceman,** 1886, **Blacksmith and
  Co. Treasurer,** 1888.

Courthouse-Lot 1, block 12, 1896, S. 1/2 lot 1, & lots 2 &
  3, block 12.

Courthouse Tavern-Lot 1, block 12 (circa 1950's).

Cox, Edith H.-1885.

Craig, Andrew & Andora-**Saloon,** 1888.

Craig, George-1883.

Craven, C. B.-**Bank cashier,** 1891.

Cromie-1885.

Cromil, David-1884.

Cronin, James-1885.

Crossley-1948.

Culver and Co. Clothing-S. Main above 2nd, 1885.

Culver & McKelvy-**Printing.**

Culver, G. N.-**Fire Dept.**

Culver, O. H.-**Prop. Coeur d'Alene Record,** 1886.

Cummings, Richard-1886.

Cummings, R. R.-Lots 6, block D, 1884.

Cunningham, A.-**Mgr. Griggs & Foster.**

Cunningham, C.-1884.

Cunningham, R. A.-**Sheriff,** 1890-91.

Curry, A.P.-**Town was named for him   only for a short time**
  1884.

Curry, J.-1884.

Cusack & Wood Co.-Prop. Palace Saloon, 1886.

D:

Daddy Gold Mining Co.-R.T. Horn, **Manager,** 1910-1911.

Dahler, C.L.-**Banker,** 1884.

Darling, L. W.-**Prop. Louisville House,** 1886.

Dave's Place Saloon-1885.
Davis, George H & Son-**Meat Market,** 1910-1911.
Davis & Hackelman-**Saloon,** 1886.
Daxon, William-**Pioneer Lumber Co.,** Littlefield and Raven.
Dean, Parrish-(Circa. 1880's).
Dee **Prop. Brunswick Restaurant**-1886.
Delta and Wardner Express-1886.
Demarco, Angelo-1905.
Dennce, W. McK.-Hillside on 2nd St.
Dennell & Co.-General Merchandise, 1885.
Devore, Walt & Christine V.-Lots 1, 2, 3, 4, 5, 6, & 7,
   block 3, 1996.
Diamond Chop House-Doc & Dick Gelineaux **Props.,** next door
   to **Cosmopolitan.**
Ditmar, Madame-1884.
Docktor, John-1905.
Doherty, L. A.-**Banker,** 1891.
Doherty, Mrs. Maggie-Lot on Gold St. & Main.
Donnelly, J.-Keeler St., has 3 lots, 1885.
Donovan, C.-1905.
Doyle, Biddy-**Dairy,** 1886.
Doyle & Comerihl **Dairy**-1888.
Doyle, W. E. **& Co.Meats**-1886.
Dressmaker-Opposite **Sun Printing Office,** Mrs. J. D.
   Milintock, one door west of **J. R.**
   Drugstore-Lot 9, block 6, 1896.
Dry Goods & Notions-Lot 11, block 6, 1896.
Dunavan, Chasteen-1905.
Duncan, L. R.-Near Buckskin Gulch.
Dunlap, Rufus-1908.
Dunlap &, Smith-1905.
Dunn, Charles-1905.
Dunn, G. H. & wife-**School teachers,** 1902.
Dutton, Fred D.-**Postmaster,** 1888 to 1889.

E:

Eaton, Frances Bogert-Wife of Charles, 1909 to 1910.
Eaton, Charles-**Mining Engineer for Monarch Mine,** 1909-
   1910.
Eck, H. J.-**Prop. of Murray Hardware Co.,** 1910-1911.
Eckert and Wardner-**Groceries,** 1884.
Edith, Terrible (Edith McCorkindale)-1884.
Edwards, Thomas E.-**Edwards & Pollick,** 1910-1911.
Edwards, W. F.-**Publisher of Murray Sun,** 1884.
Eggleston, Ben-**Feed & Stable,** 1885.
Ehlers, J. H.-Mouth of Dream Gulch.
Ellarson, J. T.-**Published Coeur d' Alene Sun,** 1910-1911.

Emacio, Wilber J. and wife Emily J.-Bought the **Murray Court House** from Van Berg-1959.

Emmerson, Seth & Ira-1/2 lot on Main St.

Emmett-1910-1911.

Endicott, W.O.-1894.

Enright, John J.-Shot by Henry Bernard in 1884.

Episcopal Church (Catholic)-Lot 12, block 1, 1896.

Erdman, Michael W. & Sherly K.-Lots 4, 5, & 6, block 9, 1996.

Ervin, A.-**Boots & Shoes,** West Main St., next to **McKenzie,** 1886.

Ervin, Mrs. J.-**Postmistress,** 1910-1911.

Erwin, Josephine-**Restaurant,** 1902.

Excelsior-**Assay office-**H. G. Lougee, **assayer.**

F:

Farrar, Elizabeth-1905.

Feehan, J. C.-**Freehan & Simmons Co. , General Merchandise** 1910-1911.

Feinberg, M. L.-**Fire Dept.,** 1885.

Fenn, J. B.-**County Assessor,** 1888.

Fenwick, John-**Restaurant,** 1886.

Ferguson, C.B.-1905.

Ferguson-**Livery,** 1886.

Ferguson, S. T.-1908.

Ferry, D. H.-**Manager of Yukon Gold Co,** 1917.

Fillipelli-1905.

Fire Dept.-Lot 5, block 16, and Lot 6, block 7, 1997.

Fitzgerald **Building-**Upper Main St., 1884.

Fitzgerald, Jack-Lot 1, block 2, Main St. Helped to Lay out Murray in 1884.

Flood, Mrs. Sarah-**Prop. Murray Hotel,** 1910-1911.

Flynn, Pat-1/2 int. lot east end Main St.

Forbich, W. P.-1884.

Foster-**General Store,** 1886.

Frahling, Fran-1908.

Freed, Edward-1905.

Freeman, H. A.-Mouth of Buckskin Gulch, 1886.

Fuller-1948.

Fuller, G.-1884.

Fuller Bros.-**Meat Market,** 1902.

Fuller's Hall-Northeast corner of Main and Keeler-1885.

Fuller, M. H.-1905.

Fuller, Ronald B. & Ronald W.-Lots 10, 11, & 12, block 13, 1996.

Fuller, S.-1885, **Liquors,** 1888.

Fulton, Stewart-**Liquors & Cigars,** 1886.

Furgeson, Mrs. J. B.-**Ice Cream Saloon,** 1888.
Furs, Skins, & Hides-G. W. Goernflo.

G:

Gaetz & Baer-**Saloon,** 1886.
G.A.R. Hall-Lot 2, block 6, 1896.
Garrison, O. D.-1884.
Gatherer, Sam-1905.
Gay, Charles etal.-1884.
Gay, Evans-1884.
Gay, Lodowick-1884.
Gelineaux, Dick & Doc-**Diamond Chop House,** 1885.
Gem Saloon-First St., near rear of **Garrisons,** 1885.
General Merchandise-W. Main, 1885.
General Store-Lot 5, block 7, 1896.
George-**Furniture,** 1885.
Getter, James L.-1996.
Gibbons, Mrs. E.-**St. Nicholas Hotel, Prop.,** 1888.
Gilbert, C.M.-**Supply Store,** 1884.
Gilkey, Miss Ella-**Teacher,** 1888.
Gilpatrick, George E.-**Mgr. Murray Hotel,** 1905.
Ginn, M. J.-**Dressmaker,** 1888.
Gitten, James L.-1996.
Glick, George-**Bakery,** 1885.
Glidden, Stephen S.-1885.
Glitter, James L.-Lots 3 & 4, block 1 (Ives Addition)-1996.
Goetz, Dutch "Jake"-1884.
Golberg, D.-**Clothing,** 1884.
Golden Chest Mining Co.-1905.
Goldstein, A. K.-1884.
Granite & Allie Mining Co.-John Steen **Manager,** 1910-1911.
Grant, A.-West Main St., 1896.
Gray, Mattie and White, May-**Liquors,** 1886.
Grebil, Frank & Kimberley -Lots 1, & 2, block 4, 1997.
Grebil, Lelia-1/2 of lots 6, 7 & lots 3, 4, & 5, block 4
     1997.
Green Leaf Saloon-Next door to **Club Saloon,** 1886.
Gregory, H. S.-**Miner,** 1886.
Gribler, Joe & Co.-Part of lot corner of Main & 3rd, lot 1,
     block L 3rd, lot 8, block K.
Gribler & Winters-**Saloon,** 1886.
Griggs & Foster-**Gen. Store,** 1886.
Guse, William M.-**Saloon,** 1886.
Guthrie, T. B.-**Sheriff, Shoshone Co.,** 1884.

H:

Hackleman, J.-**Fire Dept.**, 1885, & **Saloon,** 1886.

Hall, Jesse-**Bartender, Napei & Semenza,** 1910-1911.

Hall, Bud-1905.

Hall, **Dr. J. S.**-**Physician,** 1884.

Halzman, D.-**Liquors,** 1886.

Hanks, Harold & Mary Lou-Lot 12, block 3, 1996.

Hanks, Nancy-1996.

Hanley, Thomas F.-**Sheriff,** 1885.

Harbor, Charles-1905.

Hardware Store-Lot 5, block 6, 1896.

Harkness, John C.-**Probate Judge,** 1885.

Harper, E. J.-1905.

Harrington Bros.-Placer center.

Harris-**Center Market, Prop.**, Main near 2nd, 1885.

Harris, James E.-1885.

Harris, J. H.-1884.

Harris, W. J.-**Laundry,** 1886.

Harris & Miller Meats, 1886.

Hart, William W.-**Postmaster,** 1886-1888.

Hartman, D. M.-**Boots & Shoes**, 1886.

Harvey, **Dr.** R. S.-**Phys.**, next door to **J. R. Marks & Co.** 1886.

Hawkins, W. J.-1885.

Hay & feed-Lot 5, block 1, 1886.

Haywood, Charlie-1898-1899.

Haywood, William D. (Big Bill)-IWWW-1904.

Heenly, T. F. **& Co. Saloon**-1886.

Hellman, George.

Henderson & Ferguson-**Livery,** 1886.

Henderson, George-1885.

Henderson, Mrs. W. H.-**Dressmaker**, s. 2nd St., 1886.

Henley, Martin-Lot 3, block A, Main St.

Herrick Clothes-Two doors above **Holzman's.**

Hess, Don-Lot 9 & 10, block 10, 1996.

Heyburn, W.B.-**Lawyer,** 1886.

Hight, Clarence A.-1899.

Hildebrand Bros.-S. side Main & 3rd.

Hill, Frank & Co.-Lot 2 in rear of Main St., also block 3.

Hillard, Barry N.-1899.

Hogan, T.A.-W. side Lot 2, block 2 N. Main St.

Holden, L. M.-**News Depot**-1885.

Holgman, David-**Liquors**, 1888.

Holleman-**Judge,** 1891.

Holly, Mason, Marks & Co.-**Hardware**, 1890-1891.

Holzman-**Liquors,** 1886.

Horn, Robert J.-Help lay out Murray, 1884.

Horn, S. T.-1908.

Horton, A. P.-Piety Hill.
Hospital Building.
Housley, Neil & Mary Ann -1996.
Hoyt, C. A.-**Assayer & Chemist,** s. 2nd St., 1884.
Human, W. C.-**Co. Commissioner,** 1888.
Hummell, W. W.-**Supt. of schools, Shoshone Co.,** 1888.
Hussey, Warren-**Banker, Cashier,** 1884.

I:

Ice Cream Parlor-Miss Mary Wallace, southwest corner of
   Main and 2nd St., 1886.
Ice Cream Saloon-Mr. John Coumerilh, W. Main St., 1886.
Idaho Consolidated Mining Co.-1905.
Idaho Northern R. R. Co.-John W. McCrane, **Agent,** 1910-
   1911.
Ihrig, Henry-**Sign Painter,** 1886.
Ingalls & Co.-Drays, 1886.
Ingalls, A. O.-**Supt. Schools,** 1886.
Ingland, Dave-Lot S. side Main St.
Ives, George B.-Mouth of Buckskin Gulch, 1886.
I.X.L. Clothing Store-(1885)-**Prager & Co.**

J:

Jack Waite **Mining Co.-**Paddy Burke, **Mgr.,** 1910-1911.
Jail & Sheriff Office-Lot 12, block 9, 1896.
Jameson, Theo-Lot 4, block A.
Jane, Calamity (Martha Cannary Burke)-1884.
Jenkins, Francis-**Treasurer Shoshone Co.,** 1886.
Joe Dandy **Mining Co.-**1905.
Johnson, Charles-1905.
Johnson, Frank F.-**Banker,** 1891.
Jones, W. A.-**Dist. & Co. Atty.,** 1888.
Judd, Prop.-Brunswick Restaurant, 1886.
Juelfs-1948.
Justice of the Peace-Dr. G. S. Lesher, 1902.

K:

Kanth, Fritz-**Saloon,** 1886.
Kavanaugh, Andrew-**Assessor, Shoshone Co.,** 1885.
Keeler, William-Help lay out Murray in 1884.
Keene-1948.
Kellogg, Noah S.-1884-5-**Carpenter.**
Kelly, Ada-1996.

Kelly Family Living Trust-1997.

Kennedy & Butler, block D., N. Side Main St.

Kentucky Mining Co.-Brile, **Manager,** 1886.

Kiebler, G. E.-**Mgr. Beartop Mining Co.,** 1910-1911.

Kilfeather, Mrs. M.F.-Lot 4, block A., **Mdse.**

King Mining Co.-1905.

King, William-**U.S. Commissioner,** 1885.

Kitchen, Barbara-**Postmistress,** lots 19 through 24, block 13
    1997.

Klein, Eugene-**General Merchandise and Home Furnishings**
    1885.

Kline, Joseph-**Liquor & J. P.,** one door west of **Courthouse**
    1885.

Klopinger, Mrs. & Sister-**Restaurant,** 1902.

Knights of Pythais Bldg.

Know, W. F.-1883.

Knox House-Formerly **Masonic Hall,** opposite of **P.O.,** 1885.

Knuth-**Clothes,** 1888.

Koonie, M.-Lot 6, block F., corner of 3rd & Main St.

Kosminsky, Louis-**Tailor,** 1888-opposite **P.O.**

Krewson, Fred R. & Dorothy-Lots 8, 9, 10, & 11, block 3.

L:

Lafferty, B. S.-**Restaurant,** 1886.

Lafferty Bros. & Glick-**West End Bakery,** 1885.

Lafon, Glen & Henderson, H. etal-Lots 8, 9, 10, & 11, block
    1 (Ives Addition).

Lake, Mrs. Sophia-**Laundry,** 1886.

Lambert, Matt A. & Deborah M.-Lots 13, through 16, block 12
    1996.

Landes, C. C.-**Express Office (stage), mining & real estate,**
    Post Office, 1902-1911.

Lane, M. H.-1894.

Languish, J. S.-**Saloon,** 1886.

Langrishe-**Theater**-1885.

Lansing,. J. M.-**Phys. & Coroner,** 1886.

Laughead, James-**Saloon,** 1888.

Laurient, John etal.-Lot on Gold St., rear block C., 1884.

Lavergne, Oscar-**Hay & Feed,** 1910-1911.

Law office-Lot 2, block 16, 1896.

Lawrence, William-**Bartender** with Joseph, Rasin, 1910 to
    1911.

Lesher, George S.-**Phys. & Druggist,** 1902.

Levi, A. B.-**Druggist,** 1885, & **General Store,** 1886.

Lewis, Levi-Lot 4, block 3, 1884.

Lewis, P. H.-1885.

Lindenthal, H.-**Men's clothes,** SW. corner of Main and 2nd

1886.

Linn, A.-1885.

Littlefield, **Dr**. H. R.-**Phys., Room 1, Palace Hotel**, 1885.

Livery Stable-Lots 10, 11, 12, block 7, 1896.

Livery Stable-Lots 9, 10, & 11, block 11, 1896.

Lockwood & Barnes-Hillside, 1886.

Lodahl, O. J.-Lots 5, 6, & 7, block 1, Ives Addition
   1996.

Lord, May-1905.

Loring, Frank C.-**Mining Engineer**, 1886.

Lougee, H. G**. & Co.-Assayer**, 1886.

Louisville House-Charles Manley **Mgr.**, 1902.

Luke, Mrs. Sophia-**Laundry**, 1886.

Luschessi, T.-1905.

M:

Mahew, M-**Gen. Store,** 1888.

Maher Mike-**Grocer,** 1886.

Mahew & Singleton-**Lawyers,** 1888.

Mallon, Carl- **Manufacturer of soda pop (mineral water)**
   1886-1888.

Mallon-**Coeur d'Alene Brewery**, Center Main St., 1885.

Manley, Charles-1905.

Marks, J. R.-**Hardware,** N. side of Main St. near 2nd St.
   1885.

Martin Hanley's **Hall**-Two doors from **Post Office**, 1886).

Masonic Hall-1/2 lots 6 & 7, block 4, dedicated, 1884.

Massardo, H. M. & Monteith, John-Lots 6, 7, & 8, block 10
   1996.

Mattis, J. A.-**Postmaster,** 1884.

May, F. W.-**Dentist,** 1886.

Mayer, E. B.-1891.

Mayhew, A. E.-**Lawyer,** 1886.

McCann & Dunn-**Livery Stable,** 1902.

McCorkindale, Martha-**Rooming House,** 1902-1905.

McCowen-**Restaurant,** 1885.

McCrane, John W.-**Agent, I. N. R. R.**, 1909.

McDonald & Burke-Lot on 3rd St.

McFarland, Robert E.-**Judge,** North side East Main St.
   1885.

Mcphee, Helen C.-**Postmistriss,** 1933-1959.

McGlashan, C. F.-**Publisher of the Murray Sun,** 1884.

McGowan, Harry-1906.

McGuire, Henry-1905.

McKay W. M.-**Justice of the Peace & President of the Masons**
   1885.

McKenzie, Roderick-**General Merchandise**-S. side Main St.

1885.

McKinley, E.J.-Lot 3, block A.

McLansing, L.C.-Lot cor of Gold & Keeler.

McLelland, Thomas E.-**Auditor, Clerk, & County Recorder**
1886.

McPhee, Helen C.-**Postmistress**, 1933-1959.

McWilliams, K. J.-circa., 1890.

Mears, Minnie-**Mdse.**

Meat Market-Lot 7, block 7, 1896.

Meat Market-Lot 2, block 10, 1896.

Meier & Tibbals-**Saloon**, 1886.

Melroy, Charles etal.-1905.

Merchants Hotel-Lafferty & Bracket, **Prop's.**-W. Main St.
1886.

Mertens, Robert L.-Lot 5, block 10, 1996.

Methodist Church-Lot 13, block 12, 1896.

Michieu, Pascal-1896.

Migneault-1948.

Miller-**Center Market Prop.**-Main St., near 2nd St., 1885.

Miller, Dale S. & Leanne B.-Lots 7, 8, & 9 (less 35' of N.
83'), Lot 9, block 7, 1997.

Miller, Dale & Corder, Don & Shirley-Lots 11, & 12, block
10, 1996.

Miller, J.H.-**Livery Stable**, 1910-1911.

Miller Mrs.-**Restaurant**, 1891-1892.

Millinery & Drygoods-Managed by Tena Schmidt & Mrs. Josephine Erwin
1902.

Millinery-Mrs. A. L. Scofield, E. Gold St., 1885.

Millinery-Mrs. S. W. Murphy-W. Main St.

Miner, George-**Deputy Assessor**, 1885.

Minher & Henderson-**Saloon,** 1888.

Mint Saloon-1885.

Moffitt-1885.

Mohring, Cris-**Saloon,** 1888.

Molly-B-Damn, Inc.-Lots 1, 2, 3, 4, & part of 1st St.,
block 10, also lot 4, block 8.

Moore, George-1896.

Moranti, P.-Block 10, 1997.

Morganer, **Dr.**-**Phys.**, 1885.

Moriaty, T-**Barber**, 1886.

Morphy, W. N.-**Mining,** 1886.

Mount, E.B. & Co.-**Mdse & Sawmill.**

Mullen, Thomas-2nd St.

Munhall, Arthur H.-Lot 12, block 3, 1996.

Murphy, John F.-**Supt., Cd'A. Mining Co.**, 1910-1911.

Murphy, Mrs. S.W.-**Millenery & Notions**, NW. side of Main St.
1886.

Murray Bath House-G.P. Neuns, **Prop.**-First St.

Murray Development Co.-1905.
Murray Drug Store-1905.
Murray, George-Prospector, town named in his honor, 1884.
Murray Hardware Co.-H. J. Eck., **Prop.**, 1910-1911.
Murray Hotel-George Gilpatrick **Mgr.**, 1902.
Murray Mercantile Co.-1902-1905.
Murray Cash Store-Levi, Prop.-Old **Jail Bldg.**
Murray & Wardner Tel. Line-L. Kosminski, **Pres.**, 1888.
Murray Water Co.-1890.
Music Hall-Main St. near **Bedroom Bar,** 1884.
Myers, Richard D. & Shirley M.-Lots 25, 26, 27, 28 &
    portion of lots 29 & 30.

N:

Napei, Peter-**Napei & Semenza,** 1910-1911.
Nason, C.C.-Lot on hill.
Neil, Robert Mrs.-**School teacher** and **Secretary of the**
    Masons. Lot near Alder Gulch, 1884-1885.
Nelson-1948.
Nelson, Stanley-Lots 32 & 33, block 12, 1996.
Newhall, H. H.-**Agent for Stage Line,** 1885.
News Depot-Main near 1st St., 1885.
Niedenthal & Smith-**Butcher,** 1891-1892-1896.
Northrop, Mrs. Luella-1905.
Northrop, W. P.-**Mgr. Murray Hardware,** 1902.
Nye, John-W. Main St., 1884.

O:

O'Neil C.W.-**City Lawyer,** 1886.
O'Neil, Lawrence-1905.
O'Neil, Lonza-Lot 4, s. side Gold St., 1884.
Oro Fino Mines-Paddy Burk, **Mgr.**, 1910-1911.
Orr, W.J.-1905.
Oschie, Frank-Took fatal dose of Lysol in 1911.
Otto, Albert-1908.
Otto, Mrs. Minnie-1905.

P:

Pacific Townsite Co., 1905.
Paige, N. T.-1884.
Palace Hotel-Corner 1st & Main, 1885; Calavan & Daxon
    Props., 1885**; Wood, Cusack & Co. Prop.,** 1886-also
    McCorkindale.

Palace Saloon-1884.

Pank & Lacy-**Machinery.**

Paragon Mines-L. W. Stedman, **Mgr.**, 1910-1911.

Parish, Dean & Dianne-Lots 11 & 12, block 12, 1996.

Parrish, M.-1948.

Pavilion Skating Rink.

Peck, O. E.-**Builder**

Penny, Mr.-Built first frame house in Murray.

Penny, W.L. **Dr.**-Lot on Hill.

Perry, James L.-1883.

Peters, J.-Lot 2, block B., 1886.

Pettit, W. H.-**Mining Supt.**, 1886.

Phillips, Daniel-Died Feb. 17, 1886.

Pioneer Newspaper Office-1884.

Pioneer Stables-E. Gold St., Scofield, **Prop.**, 1885.

Pollard, J. P.-1905.

Pollock, John T.-**Saloon,** 1910-1911.

Pomeroy, Richard A.-**Supt. Golden King,** 1886.

Pomeroy, P. M. W.-1885.

Porter, D.-1885.

Porter Bakery & Lodgings-1886.

Porter, W. J.-1885.

Post Office-(Across the St. from modern day **Sprague Pole Inn**) est., 1886.

Prager, Lewis-1905.

Prager, M.-1885.

Prager & Co. Clothing-1886 and 1902.

Presler, R.A.-Lot block B, N. Main.

Presley, B.-**2nd Hand Store,** S. side W. Main St., 1885.

Price, Kid.

Prichard, Mrs. A. J.-1905.

Printing Office-Lot 4, block B., 1886, portion of 1st St. 1996.

Public School-Lot 11, block 1, & lots 15, 16, 17 & 18, block 1 Ives Addition, 1896.

Purcell, J. J.-1905).

Putnam, A. A.-1884.

Pyle, Ed-**Jewelry**, 1888.

Q:

R:

Railroad Depot-Idaho Northern R.R. Train first arrived Dec., 30, 1908.

Rammelmeyer, Ernest-**Cd'A Brewery,** Center W. Main St. 1885.

Rector, Dixene J.-Lot 1, block 12, 1996.
Red Light Symposium-557 Gold St.-Molly Burdan.
Reed, S. E.-SE. Corner 2nd St., 1884.
Reeder, Frank-1883.
Reel, Edith Morgan-1996.
Renkert, Gus-Lot 4, block 7, Main St.
Restaurants-Lot 3, block 9; lot 6, block 19; lot 7, block
   8; and lot 11, block 7, 1896.
Reynalds, Wallace C. & Jo Ellen-Lots 13 through 16, block
   13 & lots 17 & 18, 1997.
Rhodes-1948.
Rice, Edwin B.-1884.
Richott, Elie-**Jeweler,** 1886.
Riordan, Dennis-Lots N. Main & W. Main St.
Roath, Lloyd & Connie-Lots 13 & 14, block 1 Ives Addition
   1997.
Roberts, J. T.-**Architect and Contractor**, 1885.
Robinson, M. H.-1905.
Robinson, Mrs. C.A.-Piety Hill.
Rockford, W.O.-1884.
Rogers-1948.
Rogers, Roy D.-Lots 19 & 20, block 1 Ives Addition, 1996.
Rokremer & Brewery-1888.
Rosalez, Rosario & Judy I.-Lots 11 & 12, block 9, 1996.
Rosin, Joseph-**Saloon**, 1910-1911.
Russell, J. N.-**Saloon**, 1888.

S:

Sales, L.-**Thompson Falls Ex.,** 1886.
Sales, Z.-Lot on 1st St. & Lot 1, block C on 1st.
Saling, Mrs. Thomas-Killed James Urquihart.
Saloon-Lot 10, block 7, 1896.
Saloon-Lot 12, block 7, 1896.
Saloon-Lot 9, block 10, 1896.
Saloon-Lot 1, block 10, 1896.
Saloon-Lot 12, block 6, 1896.
Saloon-Lot 12, block 3, 1896.
Sample Room-Joeklier-West of Courthouse.
Sargent, Myron-Alder Gulch, 1886.
Sargent-3rd St.
Savage, Frank H.-**Fruit Stand,** 1902.
Schiller, J. A.-1886.
Schmidt-1948.
Schmidt, Mrs. Fred.
Schmidt, Katherine-**Postmistress**, 1913-1932.
Schneiderjamm, Ben-**Constable**, 1902.
School District-Lots-15, 16, 17, and 18, block 1, Ives

Addition, 1997.

Schoonover, Leroy etux.-Lots 1 & 2, block 4, 1996.

Schultze, C. A.-1894.

Schweitzberger, Ralf & Shirley-Lots 23, 24, & 25, block 12 1996.

Scofield, Mrs. A. -**Milliner**, 1886.

Scofield & Son-**Pioneer Stables, prop.** E. Gold St., 1891-1892.

Second Hand Goods-B. Presley-S. Side Main St., 1885.

Sedman, Oscar-**Miner,** 1910-1911.

Selig, Charles-**Brewer**, 1886.

Sellers, Dave-1940.

Semenza, Bart-**Napei & Semenza**, 1910-1911.

Senate Saloon-1885.

Setzer, Harvey-1884.

Sherman-1948.

Sherwood, Alma E.-Lots 13, & 14, block 9, 1996.

Shimmel, F. W.-**Jeweler**, 1886.

Shametta, George-Second St., 1886.

Shipping Co., C.S.N. & T.-Charles Smith.

Shorty, Long-1908.

Shoshone County-Lots 1 through 6, block 7, 1997.

Sieger, D.-Lot 5, S. Gold St.

Sign Painting-H. Ihrig, 1886.

Silverthorn, John-1885.

Simmon, Moses S.-**Feehan & Simmons Co.**, 1905.

Simon General Merchandise.

Simpson, Charlie.

Sinclair & Lockwood-**General Merchandise**, 1885.

Singleton, Thomas T.-**Lawyer**, 1886.

Skating Rink-1884.

Skeels, C. W.

Skelton, **Prop.-Brunswick Restaurant**, 1886.

Skeman, R. H.-**Barber**, 1910-1911.

Small Bros.

Smith, Al.

Smith, Archibald.

Smith-Butler-1891-1892.

Smith, C. A.-**Secretary & Manager of Blaine & Emmett Mining Co.**, 1910-1911.

Smith, Mrs. Catherine-**Dry goods**, 1910-1911.

Smith, E. O.-**Dentist**, 1886.

Smith, Elizabeth S.-Died Oct. 1, 1885.

Smith, F.B.-**Wardner's Store.**

Smith, John W.-1884.

Smith, Peter.

Smith, Richard.

Smyth, Thomas B.-1st St.-on hillside, 1886.

Snyder, Sol-1905.
Snyder, William-**Phys.**
Sodahl, O. J.-1997.
Solam, Ola.
Solomon, Ike.
Soncek, David M.-1996.
Spalding, E. P.-**Mgr. Cd'A North Fork Mining Co.**, 1910-1911.
Spalling.
Spaulding, Sylvester-1905.
Spaulding, P. L.-1905.
Spinney, **Dr.**-**Phys.**, 1884.
Sprague Pole Inn (modern day)-Lots 9, 10, 11 & 12 (less rear 62'), block 6, 1997.
Squance, Ann-**Prop. Louisville House**, 1910-1911.
Squier, Al J.
St. Elmo Chop House-Garrison & Garrett.
St. Nicholas Hotel-Gibbons, **Mgr.**, 1888.
St. Paul & Cda. Supply Co.-1888.
Stage Line-N. Martin, **Prop.**
Stage Station-Lot 4, block 10, 1896, H.H. Newhall, **agent.**
State Bank of Murray-C. B. Craven, **Cashier,** 1910-1911.
Stagner, W. C.
Staten J. R.
Steckman, Augusta-**Bakery**, 1910-1911.
Stedman, L. W.-**Mgr. Paragon Mines,** 1910-1911.
Steen, L. E.-1908.
Stevens, J. F.-**Contractor,** 1885.
Stevenson, Frank-**First Forrest Ranger in Glacier National Park.**
Stockan, Donald C. & Lavon L.-Lots 7 & 8, block 9, 1996.
Stoll, B. F.-**Dentist.**
Stoll, W. F.-**Atty.**, 1886.
Stonery, George-Lot on block R Gold St.
Store, M.
Strasbourg, Alex-1905.
Sullivan, Con-1885.
Sun Newspaper Office-1886.
Sussi, Frank-1905.
Swain, Axel-1905.
Swain, Charles-**Postmaster,** 1891-1892.

T:

Tailor Shop-Lot 10, block 10, 1896.
Talbott, Selma Miss.-**School teacher,** 1885.
Tarbox, E. G.-**Tailor,** 1902.
Tatro, C. P.-**Abstracts,** 1886.
Teames, C. B.-**Map of Murray.**

Teems, C.R.-**Golden Chief Mine.**
Telesystem, Inc.-Lots 6 & 7, block 3, 1997.
Theriault's **Hall**-Next to **Kline's Liquor Store,** 1886.
Thibadeau, Charley-**Saloon** 1886.
Thomas, L. D.-1905.
Thomas, M. W.-1885.
Thomas, Uncle-1908.
Thompson, Ed.-**Dairy,** 1888.
Tnompson & Gelineau **Restaurant-**1886.
Thyn, John-1905-1911.
Tibbals-**Saloon,** 1886.
Tilley, M.D.-**Musical Instruments.**
Time Laundry-W.J. Harris-S. 2nd St.
Tinker, S. H.-1905.
Tobacco Shop-Lot 10, block 10, 1896.
Tocrecy, Capt. "Tonk"-1884.
Tope, Ken & Lorraine -1996.
Trask, George R.-**U. S. Mineral Surveyor,** office opposite
   Bank of Murray, 1885.
Tribedeau, Charles-**Liquors,** 1888.
Trout, J. W.-1905.
Troy Laundry & Bath-First St. near **Brewery,** 1885.

U:

Uccelli, Paul-1905.
Uncle, Levy-1885.
Union Hall #13-1886.
Urguihart, James-Killed by Mrs. Thomas Saling in 1895.

V:

Van Berg-E. Van and wife Edith-Bought old **Courthouse** in
   1947.
Vancleave, Lillian-**Postmistress,** 1932-1933.
Vaughn, William R.-1883.
Vener, Ben-**Blacksmith,** Keeler St.
Vestel, N.-Mouth Buckskin Gulch.
Vest's Saloon.
Victor Mining & Development Co. Ltd.-**Mgr.** John Thyn, 1910-
   1911.

W:

Walker. B. F.-1905.
Wall, Mrs. David-**Lady's, Clothes-Millinery,** W. Main St.

1886.

Wallace & Co.-1885.

Walleck, J. C. & Co.-**News & Notions-Stationary,** 1886.

Walling, Lila E.-1997.

Walters, Miss Nellie-**Music teacher,** 1888.

Wanie, Charles S.-**Postmaster**, 1889-1913.

Ward, A. B.-1905.

Wardner & Blossom, **General Merchandise**-1885.

Wardner, Jim-**General Merchandise**, 1885.

Watkins, Amos-**Blacksmith**, 1902.

Watkins, Mrs. Amos-**Toys**, 1888.

Watkins, Albert-**Mining**, 1910-1911.

Webber, P.-Lot 3, block D.

Wedeman, Herman-1905.

Weed & McCowan-W. Main.

Welch, D.-1948.

Wells Fargo & Co.

Wentz, F. W.-1905.

West End Bakery & Coffee House-Lafferty Bros., 1885-W. Main
St.

White Elephant Lodging House-Brown Bros. **Props.,** 1884.

White, Mary-**Liquors,** 1886.

Whittle, Frank-1905.

Wiegel, Frank-1979.

Wiege, Johnnie-1906.

Wiley & Bros.-1/2 lot 3, block A, 1884.

Wilkinson, Robert W.-**Barber Shop,** 1886, 1902-1911.

Willey Bros.-Lot 3, block E. Main St.

Williams, **Dr.** R. B.-**Phys.,** 1884.

Williams, R. R.-1884.

Wilmer, Mrs. M.-**Gem Saloon,** 1st St., Sept.22, 1885.

Wilson, A.-1884.

Wilson, B.-1908.

Wilson, Betty-1996.

Wilson, Dick-Help lay out Murray in 1884.

Wilson, John-**Blacksmith,** 1886.

Wilson, Linda L.-Lots 8 through 12, block 4, 1996.

Wilson, Ralph-1996.

Wilson, Ronald J.-Lots 8 through 12, block 4; and lots 10,
11, 12, and S. 35' of N.83' of lot 9 & portion of First
St., 1996.

Wilson & Wade-1905.

Winters Saloon-1886.

Witts, Mrs. G.F.-1905, has **restaurant,** 1891-1892.

Wolf, H.E.-1891.

Wolf-**Cosmopolitan Saloon,** near **Diamond Chop House,** 1885.

Wood, E. C.-**Saloon,** 1886.

Wood, J.-1905.

Wood, L.-**Contractor,** 1886.
Wood-**Prop. Palace Hotel,** 1886.
Wood, S.-1884.
Woods, Major-1940.
Worstel & George **Furniture-**N. side W. Main St., 1886.
Wroughton, Norvin E.-Lots 19 thru 22, block 12, 1996.
Wyant, Lon.
Wylie, Mark K.-1905.

X:
Y:
Yosemite Mining Co.-1905.
Z:
Zeigers-**Restaurant owner,** 1884.
Zimmerman, Ora-**Blacksmith,** 1910-1911.
Zuschessi, T.-1905.

UNKNOWN:

Lot 2, block G.

10

Smaller Towns

Ellensburg

Ellensburg is situated in section 12, Township 50 North, Range 5, East at the mouth of Cypress Gulch which is located one mile above the junction of Tributary fork of east Eagle Creek some nine miles above Eagle City.

The town was laid out in the spring of 1885 by James Myers, Joseph Collins, J. Huer, Rufus Dunlap, James Taylor, John Connelly, Joseph Skiffington, and Tom Skiffington. It consisted of eight blocks with lots consisting of 50-foot frontages. Main Street was named.

Ives

George B. Ives discovered gold on the West Side of the town of Murray prior to 1884 and soon the site was called Ives. It is located one-half mile west of the famous Widow claim. A store, boarding house, and a saloon were located there. Today a number of people live here and it is called the Ives Addition of Murray.

Littlefield (Butte) (Butte City)

On February 25, 1884,

Idaho State Historical Society #76,133.1
Littlefield, ca-1884

the town of Littlefield was founded by Dr. H. L. Littlefield, a physician. The famous Mother Lode and Golden Chest lode mines were located at Littlefield and proved to be very rich in gold.

Littlefield is now located under the new black-top highway to Thompson Falls, Montana, two miles above Murray at 2,890 feet elevation in Section 9, Township 49 North, Range 5 East.

At one time, over thirty building were located here as well as a Fraser and Chambers No. 44 ten-stamp mill. Originally the mine used a Spanish arrastra to crush the quartz gold ore. The mill was built in 1890. The town had a post office from September 24, 1884, to July 6, 1888, when the mail was discontinued and sent to Murray. Phil A. Markson was the first postmaster, and we remember him as a member of the original prospecting party with Andy Prichard.

In order to secure a lot in Littlefield, foundations had to be four feet high and laid in 10 days. A cabin 10 by 12 feet must be built before May 1, 1884, or $50 worth of improvements must be made. No one could buy more than two lots. One block was set aside for a school and courthouse. Lot sales boomed with the selling price listed from $50 to $500.

By 1916, the O. W. R. R. & N. Co. survey map shows fourteen buildings in the area. Lots and blocks were surveyed and laid out. Population numbers varied from zero to over 150. In 1888, only twenty three lived there, but later gold discoveries caused Littlefield to boom to 150 in 1910.

Badger State Mill Co.-Sawmill.
Baker and Tydeman-**Owners of Butte City Lodging House.**
Boland and Parker-**Owners of a saloon and restaurant**
  which was 20' X 24' and 1 1/2 stories high.
Butte City Lodging House.
Calligan, James-Lot 3, block 3.
Cameron, D. R.
Chase, Joseph E.-Lots 1 & 2, block G., Main St.
Chase and Snyder.
Demers, T.J.-Lots 3 & 4.
Littlefield, **Dr.** H.L.
Markson, Phil-**Postmaster**-Lots 5&6, block E.
Moran, James.
Nall, J.P.-House.
Parker, Miles-Lot 3, block F.
Pioneer Lumber Co.-Sawmill.
Railsback-Lot 5, block A.
Robillard, J.A.-**Postmaster**.
Roseback-Lot on Butte St.

Rositer and Bryan-Lots 2 & 3, block F., 1885-1886.
Savanagh, B.-Main St.
Sawac, B.
Seiger, Dan-House.
Shoemaker-Lot 4, block 1.
Snyder, Nash-House.
Steen, John E.-House.
Stringham, Berry-Main St.
Walls-Lot 1.
Watts-Lot 1, block 1.
Wilcox, Elgin-**Postmaster**, 1886-1888.
Unknown-Main St.
Unknown-Main St.

Osborne City

The exact date when Osborne City was founded is not known. The A. Zeese Co. map of 1884 shows it to be located on Prichard Creek about a mile above Eagle City. It was situated at the mouth of McComber Gulch on the old Bill Osborne placer claim in the southeast quarter of Section 35, Township 50 North, Range 4 East. Lots were listed on Main Street. J. S. Noble owned a saloon in town.

Burns, John.
Chandler, Mrs. M.-Wintered here.
Healy, Frank.
Jenkins, Frank.
Johnson, A. P.
Kavanaugh, Andrew.
Mills, A. F.
Nelson, A.
Noble, J.S.-**Owner, The Flag of The Union Saloon.**
Osborne, William-**Owner of a store and saloon.**
Ryan, John.
Riley, W.C.
Union Saloon.

Unknown
Lot 3 on Main St.
Lot 7 on Main St.

Paragon (Sullivan)

Stockbridge-Branard "view book"
Sullivan (Paragon) ca. 1891

Paragon was named after the Paragon mine and is sometimes called Sullivan. It is located at the base of Thompson Falls pass in section 13, Township 49 North, Range 5 East at 3,480 feet in elevation. The town was founded on May 22, 1908, and Louie W. Stedman was postmaster from May 1918 until August of 1918. Louie was also general manager and superintendent of the Paragon mine. The town was the terminus of the Idaho Northern Railroad.

Raven
(Ryerson City) (Raven City) (Bear Top)

During the Eagle City boom, anxious prospecting men and women scrambled out through canyons and into the mountains. Many of them passed by Murray and up Prichard Creek, looking for anything they could find of value. They found another wide spot in the canyon and on January 19, 1884, three days before Murray was officially founded, they began to build another town they called Raven. (Located at 3,060 feet in elevation in Sections 10 and 14, Township 49 North, Range 5 East on Prichard Creek, four miles above Murray.)

The town was named after the large number of ravens in the area and grew to a pretty good size. It had one bank, twelve cabins, eleven saloons, three stores, a number of restaurants, and a lodge. As the gold petered out, prospectors and businesses left; by 1909 Raven had only sixteen houses and one tent to her credit. The 1916 census showed only five people living in Raven. Today, nothing remains except an old washed-out bridge to the Idaho Northern Railroad track bed.

The lode mines that Raven depended upon for its existence were located on the south side of the mountains. Newly mined ore arrived at Prichard Creek via a gravity-fed wooden chute. The clean-up only averaged $10 per day, not nearly enough to support an entire town.

Byrnet, Gib-Main St.
Kellogg-Owner of the Gem Saloon.
Kennedy, D.
Lester-**Co-owner of Gem Saloon**, Main St.
Manning, Albert-Main St.
Plum, W.-**Owner of a saloon.**
Riarson.
Savage, B.
Savanagh, B.-**Furniture**-Main St.

Additional Information

11

Other Good Stuff

In doing research for this work, your authors came across a tantalizing bit of information in a 1968 correspondence between historian and author, Wendell Brainard and, perhaps the most celebrated of all north Idaho researchers and writers, Judge Richard Magnuson. These two sentences began a half-year-long search of our own.

"Dick: Here is the material we discussed. I'm sorry I wasn't able to spend more time pursuing Mrs. Goodwin's scrapbook when it was available. I don't know if shooting incident described in Rammelmeyer's diary is same one later publicized."

During our subsequent research, we found that Margaret Goodwin was named the Shoshone County Historian in 1938, and wrote a number of historical articles for the 48th anniversary edition of the Kellogg, Idaho, *Evening News*. In trying to locate her, we visited and corresponded with many historians in their own right. They are folks who know that the preservation of our history is of utmost importance.

Finally, after many months of further research, Ernest Rammelmeyer's papers were discovered in the loving care of Leo Goodwin and Nancy Graese, Margaret Goodwin's grandson and granddaughter. The irreplaceable documents had previously been faithfully kept by Margaret's son, and Leo and Nancy's father, John Leonard Goodwin, until his death May 2, 1995.

In reading through and proofing Mr. Rammelmeyer's information and speculations, we have found several errors in fact, but have presented them here in their entirety for your consideration. Keep in mind that all evidence points to the fact that he was of advanced years when Margaret Goodwin collected this material from him.

Ernest Rammelmeyer, who kept a daily diary, began his journey to the west April 30th of 1852, traveling on the Oregon Trail toward California. The portion of this journey that we found in Mrs. Goodwin's papers occurred during his forty day trek from Cedar River, Iowa, to Platte River, Nebraska. A sampling of this follows:

April 30, 1852-I took leave of my family, (wife and five boys) with the most poignant sorrow, not exceeded by the death of our first born. Went in a yawl to Buffalo, had most of my supplies for the journey on board. Was accompanied by James Buford. Had a most laborious time getting down as the wind was terrific. Came very near swamping the boat. Could not possibly have got down alone.

May 4, 1852-His writings continue, and those pages from Rammelmeyer's diary relating to his trek on the Oregon Trail have been donated to the Oregon California Trail Association (OCTA.)

Some thirty years later, in November of 1883, he arrived in the Coeur d'Alenes employed as an assayer by W. A. Clark. He was sent to Eagle at the request of (banker) W. J. Hawkins to assay gold from the different gulches which varied in value.

The Coeur d'Alene portion of his diary begins:

Passing by a drift on Trail Gulch, I saw two empty 20 gallon whiskey barrels (Old Luck Wilson's where he had left them to bleach in the sun.) They were now strapped with iron bands and a bail, to a pig tail hook, fastened to a windlass rope, hauling the pay dirt from bed rock to the sluice boxes. I ironically smiled at these buckets, which had contained so much liquid gladness in their original form to men who physically and mentally enjoy good whiskey, those who are the same before and after drinking it.

The mail came into the camps by private carriers with 25 cents carrying charge on each letter. The Postal Department felt itself impotent to inaugurate service to a quick roving spontaneous migrating people until the communities had settled down to permanency. Charges for freight hauled over the trails in the early winter of 1883 and 1884 was twenty five cents a pound. The next spring the Heron and Trout Creek Trails became impassable, then for a short time the Belknap Trail became the favorite.

There were few road houses or tents along the Heron Trail. Trout Creek had more. Both routes led over Big Baldy summit, converging at Eagle Creek four miles above Eagle City. The Belknap Trail from the summit, which was the dividing line between Montana and Idaho on the eastern trails, followed Butte Creek down to Prichard Creek about ten miles above Eagle City. The Belknap Trail was the only one that had a hostelry on the top of the dinning room, the other for sleeping quarters. This was open to the public and winter of 1883 and 1884. The snow was 25 feet deep. In the bed tent the bedding was furnished by the traveler, the bedstead the floor of the tent. It was not uncomfortable to spread ones blankets on the hard packed snow, covered with pine boughs, with a sheet iron stove going full blast. George Pease and Ed Mayer were the proprietors. They were old acquaintances of mine in Butte. While spending the day with them I noticed several scored logs. They were placed on large standing trees which were cut off at the top. I asked George if he meant to build a house on top of the sawed off trees twenty five feet from the ground, He smiles and said, "Your see I start to build from the top down. When the snow has melted 8 or 10 feet I build another story under the top one and in that manner when the snow has all melted away I have a four story house."

George went to Chile, South America, and never returned. He was born in Scranton, Pennsylvania. Mayers was born in San Jose, California. Both were fine fellows. To many men who are susceptible to mining excitement or to any irresistible frenzy for gain, the stimulation of the mind often runs away with good judgement that do not reach their goal.

Many people opined that Belknap would be the central shipping terminal into Prichard Creek, as it was an ideal town site, and Heron and Trout Creek had none. Thompson Falls was only the indifferent one. The railroad company had several side tracks and switches at Belknap to facilitate the rapid movement of their trains going east and west. The town sprung up with several substantial mercantile houses, a hotel and a daily paper. The people in Belknap believed that the road leading from their town would be the most accessible to reach the mines.

In January, 1884, the people of Eagle City were informed by a man who came from Portland, Oregon, known as Major Fred R. Reed that he would bring Chinese into Prichard Creek to assist the miners with cheap labor. This offer was rejected in an open street meeting by popular vote. The Major then suggested that he would take his coolies and build a wagon road over the Heron Trail into Prichard Creek by way of Lost Creek on the north fork of the Coeur d'Alene river about ten miles from Hummel's landing. He would be content after the completion if the road to work the celestials on the later stream in opening up placer diggin's. This proposal was also rejected by the miners. In those days the Major had a mental picture of all most all the bedrock of the creeks being heavily covered with gold dust, as did most other people in the district.

Soon after, Major Reed came to Belknap with fifty Chinese to build a wagon road over the trail into Prichard Creek. The miners informed him he could build the road on the Montana side but white labor would be used on the Idaho side. This gang under a Chinese boss began building the road from Belknap, shoveling snow, constructing corduroy over swampy places. Zigzagging ten or twelve miles from the base of the mountains to the summit it was necessary to shovel the snow from a depth of twenty five feet three or four times. Each threw the snow to the man on the level above him. It took three or four men to trench the snow to the ground twenty to twenty five feet below. They worked faithfully till the middle of April, when the pay had been promised, but it never came. They never received a cent for their work. Their rice tea and other provisions were sent pre-paid from a Chinese firm in Portland. It was piteous to see them come back from Belknap carrying their belongings oriental fashion on sticks over their shoulders.

The merchants could not sell their merchandise to the people in the mines and soon moved away leaving their houses as dead investments. By 1884 there was a deserted town. There was nothing remaining, but the train dispatcher, section crew, and two or three men. During the summer of 1884 Trout Creek, Heron and Belknap Trails were deserted it becoming clear that the Thompson Falls route was the only naturally suited grade for a wagon road into the mines from the Northern Pacific Railroad.

In January, 1884, Eagle City was at its peak of population many coming with the intention of remaining, clearing the snow off, pitching tents, others building cabins, or settling in the different surrounding gulches. Men could be seen coming and going in all directions, some with toboggans, tents, blankets and cooking utensils strapped to their backs. They came with pack trains, dog teams, sleds, and snow shoes. It was an animated picture to the observer. Despite the cosmopolitan nature of the groups, only one violent (event) occurred to mar the freedom from disturbance.

The shooting occurred at Eagle City and lasted about a minute and a half, many inhabitants were not aware of it until it was over. It was a long accepted custom, among the western territories, that a man who laid the foundations of a house of logs, properly noticed together on a lot, along a designated street for a new town, in a new mining boom, had prior rights to that ground to own, and build upon. This custom was recognized by all who built in Eagle City. Following this procedure, John Buzo, a miner from Butte, selected a lot to build upon, he moved six foot of snow from the location and lay the foundation logs. While at work two men came up and ordered him off the ground claiming they owned the lot and the improvements. Buzo was a small man, but hardy and full of dynamic action. He replied if any one wanted his lot, they'd better come well heeled. He knew they belonged to a tough gang of adventurers with headquarters at Earp brothers gambling house. The two retired to the later place procured a rifle and shotgun, and from that stronghold began shooting at Buzo. It was about 120 feet diagonally across the street between the two points. Buzo took shelter behind his building, blazing away with his six shooter in the direction of his assailants with his six shooter, thu' a high snow bank. No one was hurt. After the affray Bozo notified them he was ready to meet them again, but there was no further attack by the gangsters (Mr. Oxley witnessed this scrap from the snow bank, on the day of his arrival. I asked him if he were not frightened and he replied he didn't know what fear was...I believe him, M. G.)

No dance halls or hurdie-gurdie houses were opened in Eagle City. By the house I purchased from Mr. Woolford and opposite that of Mr. Prichard's stood the log house of Monte Verde, a woman. It had a small stage for shows the audience was seated on benches. Monte Verde and another woman and a man did stunts, sang, and danced. A flute, guitars and violins, made up the orchestra.

Monte was about 40 years old, a good looking woman, and well preserved. She had the only amusement hall in Eagle City and she ran a clean show. To say there was a dance hall run by Calamity Jane is erroneous. Monte sang in a beautifully modulated voice and gave dialogue with the other two actors. Some of the songs were of her own composing and were cleverly facetious and often satirical. In conversation she was quick with repartee. She was a colorful character of a woman, who was a survivor of the old traveling show troupe of the outpost town. Her partners were both excellent actors. Montana and Idaho in the early days, looked eagerly for the coming of these show people who traveled six or seven hundred miles in spring wagons with scenery from Salt Lake to give their entertainment. Outside of the conversant saloon, a few dances in winter Thanksgiving and Christmas, and of course Fourth of July festivals, the men had little to entertain them.

Monte Verde remained two months in Eagle. The Coeur d'Alene song with six or seven stanzas was one of her songs, composed and sung with the guitar accompaniment. It was always greatly applauded and the audience often joined her. The 160 acres referred to was a dig at the Palouse farmers who came in droves into Eagle.

> Shoulder shovel pick and pan
> Pack your blankets if you can
> Take up a homestead of a hundred sixty acre claim…
> (…and so on see History of Idaho, song complete.)

John Thaird found a nugget on Trail Gulch weighing 2 pounds and worth $400. It was 2 inches wide and 1/4 inch thick. He almost threw it away at the end of his sluice box and picked it out with a pitchfork. Biggest cleanup was in 1897 when Owen Jackson and associates took out $100,000 in gold from Trail Gulch. The biggest nugget was found in the bottom of a drift from a shaft and weighed 13 pounds.

By April, 1884, the claims on Prichard and Eagle Creek had new owners. Jumping and relocating on both creeks became an epidemic. Prichard and his associates, all farmers, not versed in federal law methods, found themselves dispossessed of all they had on both streams. There were only one or two exceptions Prichard and his associates instituted suits against those who wrongfully dislodged them first Judicial District never before had so many cases. Many men of the legal fraternity arrived before the opening of the court. The court room of Eagle City was a log structure opposite the Coy and Hess Saloon at the end of the building was a platform for the judge and clerk of the court. The jury sat opposite the judge on a bench.

The proceedings during the trials, lawyers examining the witnesses the gestures and motions were often amusing and seemingly out of order. False statements were often heard, as jurors were drawn from the defendant's sympathizers. There were none others in camp. Some of the plaintiffs had to go home to do their farm work, leaving their case in the hands of the attorneys.

It was a lamentable miscarriage of justice. Why should Prichard and the original locators have been dispossessed by outsider? They complied with the established terms and forms and with the United States Mineral code. The claims were properly staked, the discoveries on them legal and the records at the County Recorder's office, within the specified time. Everyone was aware of these facts. But no one put forth these strong reasons in favor of justice and the plaintiffs. The usual mass rule determined the outcome and it bore out the contentions of the English writer, Roscommon. The multitude is always in the real wrong.

Norman Buck had been appointed Judge of the first Judicial district court in the territory of Idaho by President Hayes. He was captain of the 7th Minnesota regiment during the war of the rebellion. After the war he
resumed his law practice and was given the appointment in Idaho. He was 5'9" tall, light complected, with an iron gray beard and he carried a walking stick from form not use. He was well preserved and affable and was kindly though reserved.

He was a much respected man and a jurist by all who came in contact with him. Often during a session of the court he would be noticeable for his enigmatical looks and manner while watching a pleading lawyer. After the verdict of several cases he recessed the court until the fall session in which few of the cases were tried.

In June 1884, after the adjournment of the court, the population of Eagle gradually declined. The *Eagle City Record* was established in February 1884, but by June it suspended publication for want of subscribers and advertised patronage. A. Bernard, the owner, moved to Murray in the forepart of June, 1884, and published the *Pioneer* there. On July 2nd Bernard killed Jack Enright who was his partner and typesetter. Enright demanded wages due for the month. They had a warm argument about the pay and in the heat of the dispute Bernard shot and killed Enright. There were two Jack Enrights in Murray and Eagle, one a printer, the other a gambler.

Eagle City had it's privileged character during the height of the boom days. Seemingly he had a peculiar right or immunity for he built a hut 8 foot by 8 foot in the middle of the street in the most frequented place, opposite the banks, stores and saloons. Nobody seemed to object. He was in the second hand business buying everything from those who returned to the railroad after a short stay. This was old man 'Shak em up.' He always could be seen in front of his hut waving a shirt, coat or pants on a stick crying, 'Shak 'em up' in an exciting mirthful way. This drew the attention of the passing populous who laughed at his idiosyncrasies.

There were those who did not have a bath or change of clothes for weeks. Parasitic creatures feeding on the skin created sensations that the old man was alluding to. He was a little old man, who was over 60 years old, and his name was Ike Trumlea   -he had been auctioneer in Salt Lake City and had a well respected family.

Rules of courtroom procedure were questionable. George McCauley, a gigantic black haired young man defiantly pulled a revolver out of his pocket menacing a lawyer who quizzed him on the witness stand. Soon thereafter McCauley was shot in an argument duel over the ownership of the Crown Point mine at the head of Milo Gulch.

Another hard fought battle in court had almost disastrous consequences. The Golden Chest mining company was made defendant in a legal action as trespassing and appropriating unlawfully, ground on an adjoining claim. Judge Claggett and Judge Heyburn were opposing attorneys in this action.

Mr. Rammelmeyer's further writings:
Mine Superintending
1905, March 5-Written for the Mining and Scientific Press by Ernest Rammelmeyer, M. E.

Much has been written about mine managing and mine superintending. This is a widely diffused field and large mines are fortunate enough to enable them to employ mine manager, mine superintendent, foreman, shift boss, assayer, surveyors, time keepers, accountants and other high-grade help. Other mines, or a large number of them, are not so fortunate as to have all these men, and I will speak here only of the mine superintendent who has charge of a mine without a large staff or who has sometimes only to rely upon his knowledge of the different departments. I do not refer at all to the manager who directs the clerical staff, keeps in touch with the owners or directors of the property or company, or who compiles the daily, weekly or monthly financial reports.

I shall dwell here only upon the duties and responsibilities of the superintendent or man in charge who has to direct and execute the work in and about a mine. His duties are multiform and his experience must be of some years standing to enable upon except their ingenuity to grapple with obstacles they were confronted with in new untried districts where their prospective mines and they were ultimately crowned with success. Skilled miners and mechanics were at a premium and not as plentiful as today. There the superintendent had to explain everything in, out of and about the mine to his subordinates to make a success of the undertaking.

These men are found in almost every mining camp in the Western States and territories and are much in evidence today. Having charge of mines throughout the mining industry to the high standard it enjoys today, recognized in the finical world as the greatest factor to any industry and second to none.

It does not matter whether a mine superintendent is a graduate of a school of mines or has worked up from the bottom of the ladder, but he must understand these essentials herein stated and be a judge of human nature. These are nowadays the requirements for a successful mine superintendent.

*   *   *

A few other colorful characters of the Coeur d'Alenes

Butch Cassidy-cached gold coins in Eagle City, 400 paces north of the Eagle Creek bridge, behind a thunder-split snag...source unknown.

Broncho Liz, (Ione Skeels)-shot her husband, Charles W. Skeels in March 1889. A competitor of Molly-B-Damn and Terrible Edith in Murray. Skeels had Ione dress like a man and work on his father's farm until he got a divorce from his wife. Liz married Skeels in Moscow, Idaho on January 2, 1888. Skeels was seeing other women, so Liz shot him to death.

Captain Tonk-was born in Missouri and was about 64 years old when he died in Murray on Friday morning, February 2, 1906. He is purported to have been Huckleberry Finn in Mark Twain's story. He is buried in Murray's Grand Army of the Republic (G. A. R.) Cemetery.

Madam Ditmar-hung out a shingle on her business place in Murray. It read "Occultist and Fortune Teller." She tried to raise the dead from

Murray's Cemetery and the local people ran her out of town. However the madam didn't mind as she had several thousands of dollars in gold dust and nuggets sewed into her dress.

Terrible Edith-Edith McCorkindale was one of two daughters of Felix Burgoine who arrived in Murray in 1884. He also owned a saloon on Main St. and the Palace Hotel and Saloon in Murray. Edith became a prostitute and her crib was on Gold Street along with Molly-B-Damn's. Jack Rostele was her boyfriend.

Wash Snyder and Jim Woods named their lead mine after Terrible Edith and were offered $60,000 cash for it by the Day brothers. They refused.
Edith died March 17, 1905, at 23 years of age and is buried in G. A. R., Murray Cemetery.

*   *   *

Earp's Coeur d'Alene mining claims in 1884
Murray and Eagle:

May 10- Consolidated Grizzly Bear lode.

Mar. 15- Enola placer.

April 2- Eagle Creek placer.

April 3- Unnamed claim placer.

April 7- McCarthy placer.

April 7- Broomfield (1/2 interest) placer.

April 15-Point of Rock (interest) placer.

April 30-Dream Gulch placer.

May 1- Golden Gate placer-

May 11-Dead Scratch placer.

May 11-Dividend placer.

May 29-Jessie Jay placer.

Earp's Associates:

J. E. Jack Enright
Alfred Holman
Daniel S. Ferguson
John Hardy

Henry White
W. T. Stoll
L. F. Butler
William Chambers
F. S. Wickersham
William Payne
Charles Habian
R. B. Graboo
W. Osborne
John Williams
John Cochrane
Charles "Red" Foley
D. T. Hayes
Charles Sweeny

Wyatt and Josie's later activities.

1884, September-October-Searched the Coeur d'Alenes in search of a cattle ranch for a friend.

1884, December 3-8-Arrive in Raton, Colfax County, N.M.

1884, Fall-Wyatt was in El Paso, Texas involved with a man named Rayner who was killed in 1885.

1885, April 14-In El Paso, Texas.

1885, May-In Aspen, Colorado, Fashion Saloon.

1885, late or early 1886-Officiated prize fight in Tijuana, N.M. between O'Neill and Nugent.

1897, Fall-Gold rush to Alaska (making several trips to S.F. between 1897 and 1902.[1]

1888-Marries Josie in Parker, AZ. (re: Earl Chafin)

1889-In Harquahia Mts. In California looking for gold. And in April was Sheriff of Boca, Nevada Co., California.

1890, October-Was a judge at a horse race at Escondido Fair in California.

1893-Attended World's Fair in Chicago.

1894-December 27-Wyatt was in Cripple Creek, Colorado. He was no doubt running a gambling hall.

1896-Referee for Sharkey-Fitzsimmons fight in San
   Francisco, California.

1897, July 15-Goes to Nome, Alaska, ran Dexter Saloon.

1900, June 29-Reported arrested in Alaska.

   July 15-Shot in Nome, but recovers from the wound.

1901, December-Wyatt and Josie leave Alaska for Los
   Angeles, Ca.

1902-Prospecting in Tonopah, Nevada. Built the Northern Saloon in Tonopah,
   Nevada in the winter.

1903-In Los Angeles, California.

1905-Goldfield, Nevada.

1906-Settled for good in Los Angeles, California.

1911-Arrested in L. A. bogus faro game.

Death comes to the Earps and their friends

1882-March 18-Morgan Earp died at the age of 31 and is buried in Hermosa
   Cemetery, Colton, California.

1887-Doc Holliday-died of TB and is buried in Glenwood Springs, Colorado.

1888-Celia Ann (Mattie) Blaylock, Earp died and is buried in Pinal, Arizona.

1893-Luke Short died at the age of 43 of dropsy (re: Miller and Snell).

1900-July-Warren Earp died at age 45-shot and killed by John Boyette, in
   the Headquarters Saloon, in Wilcox, Arizona. He is buried in the
   pioneer cemetery in Wilcox. Warren and Boyette had been arguing on
   the day of Warren's death. The coroner's inquest also noted that Warren
   was unarmed at the time he was gunned down by Boyette, but that there
   wasn't enough evidence to bring Boyette to trail for the murder.

   After the inquest, Boyette fled the area fearing reprisals by two of the
   most infamous lawmen and killers in the west. It was reported by some
   that Boyette was never heard of or seen again.

1905-October 20-Virgil Earp died of pneumonia in Goldfield, Nevada, at
   the age of 62 years, three months and two days. At the insistence of his
   daughter, he was interred on October 29th at the Riverview Cemetery in
   Portland, Oregon.[2]

1907-Nicholas Earp died at the age of 94 and is buried in the Veterans'
   Cemetery, west Los Angeles, California.

1926-January 25-James Earp died at age of eighty four and is buried at Mt.

View Cemetery, in the W. T. Edwards plot, in San Bernadino, California.

1928-Newton Earp died and is buried in Sacramento, California.

1929-January 13-Wyatt Earp died of chronic cystitis (prostate) problem, age 80 years, 9 months and 24 days At the time he lived at 4004 W. 17th, Los Angeles, California.

He died peacefully in the rented Los Angeles cottage with Josie at his side to see him through it. As she sat on the edge of his bed and watched him expire, she must have been overcome with uncontrollable grief. Josie must have thought of their times and adventures together. Here lies a man who lived for over 80 years through some of our country's most troubling times. He'd watched his friends and brothers killed around him, and yet lived through it all. His long life spanned the Civil war era and fights with marauding Indians. Through the lawlessness on the prairie; breathless, sprinting pony rides across the plains; gunfights with outlaws; and the end of the great herds of buffalo in the American West.

She must have also looked down at Wyatt's aged and sick body and thought of how this energetic, gentle man stayed by her side and how they'd laughed about life and had grown old together. Although there are those who claim that he died a man in poverty, living from the charitable goodness of others, Wyatt died in the wealth of Josie's love, which had endured for 47 years, and eternal love of our Lord. For what better life can we have in this world than to be surrounded by its beauty, with the boundless love of our life's partner, and our Creator, as well?

Two eulogies were written about Wyatt at or shortly after his death. The first was a newspaper clipping saved by Josie and noted in her book, the other, was written by Walter Noble Burns, the author of the book, Tombstone:

Here Lies a Man

So hail and farewell to the lion of Tombstone. Strong, bold, forceful, picturesque was this fighter of the old frontier. Something epic in him. Fashioned in Homeric mold. In his way, a hero. Whatever else he may have been, he was brave. Not even his enemies have sought to deny his splendid courage. The problems of his dangerous and difficult situation, he solved, whether wisely or foolishly, with largeness of soul and utter fearlessness. No halo is for this rugged, storm-beaten head. He was a hard man among hard men in a hard environment. What he did, he did. The record stands. But, weighed in the balance, he will not be found wanting. Judged by the circumstances of his career, the verdict in his case is clear   Wyatt Earp was a man.[3]

Lake Stuart, author of **Wyatt Earp Frontier Marshal**, describes his last conversation with Wyatt. Wyatt says, "The greatest consolation I have in growing old is the hope that after I'm gone they'll grant me the peaceful obscurity I haven't been able to get in life."

He was buried in the Marcus family plot in Colma, California. To honor his wish for anonymity, the location of his grave was kept secret for many years, for fear of those who might disturb his remains. Sure enough, after the location of his final resting place became known his tombstone was stolen...twice. For shame...the thieves and grave robbers who did the deed were never caught.

1941-Adelia, Earp (Edwards) died and, like her brother James, she was buried at Mt. View Cemetery in San Bernardino, California.

1944, December 19-Josie Earp joined Wyatt in death. She suffered from heart disease and senility-84 years old-lived at 1812 W. 48th, Los Angeles. They are buried next to one another in the Marcus family plot. Their bond of love for each other and for our Lord, continues on into eternity.

1947-Allie Earp dies died at age 99 and is buried at Mt. View Cemetery, San Bernardino. Her ashes were placed on top of Adelia's grave.

*   *   *

Ghost Towns of Shoshone County

Adair (Delage)
Beaver Station (Reds)
Beeler
Big Jam
Black Bear
Burbridge
Carbon
Carbonate (Carbonite)
Carson
Carter
Cougar
Coyote
Delta (Beaver City)
Duthie

Eagle (Union) Waite) Walker)
Ellensburg
Evolution
Falcon
Frisco
Gem (Davenport)
Grand Forks
Haights
Harbona
Herrick
Interstate
Jenkins
Larson
Linfor
Littlefield (Butte)
Mace
Masonia
Myrtle (Thaird)
Nelson
Pine Creek
Pottsville
Price
Prichard
Pyle
Raven (Raven City)
Shont
Silver King
Steamboat (Steamboat Creek)
Stewart
Sullivan (Paragon)
Sunset
Thurston
Union (Eagle) (Waite) Walker)
Walker (Eagle) (Union) (Waite)
Yellow Dog

(For further information on these towns, contact the publisher.)

Hunter Hot Springs photo

Hunter Hot Springs is located two miles northwest of Springdale, MT and about 20 miles east of Livingston, MT.[4]

#

3. NPRR crewman.
4. Wyatt Earp-b. 1848 d. 1929-35 years old.
5. Teddy Rosevelt-b. 1850, d-1919-55 years old.

6. Doc Holliday-b-1852 d. 1881-31 years old
7. Virgil Earp b-1843, d-1905-40 years old.
8. Liver Eating Johnson.
9. Butch Cassidy, d-1937-17 years old.
10. Sundance Kid, b-1861, d-1908-22 years old.
11. NPRR Crewman
12. Bat Masterson, b-1853, d-1921.
13. NPRR crewman.
14. NPRR crewman.
15. NPRR crewman.
16. Judge Roy Bean, b. 1825, d-1904-58 years old.
17. Ben Greenough was 13 years old.

Letter from Montana Historical Society regarding this photograph:

July 18, 1983

The Montana Historical Society has been plagued with questions regarding this wholly fabricated photo for the last ten years, when it first began to make the rounds of Western Americana publications. The Society never verified the authenticity of the photo, such is not possible as the most basic of historical research reveals the photo as a hoax. For example, in 1883, the supposed year that the photo was taken, the following is true:

Theodore Roosevelt was only 25 years old and a rising New York politician. He would not establish his Montana-Dakota ranches until 1884.
Morgan Earp had been dead for one year. He was killed in 1882.
Butch Cassidy was 16 years old.
Ben Greenough was 13 years old.
The front of the Hunters Hot Springs hotel looked nothing like the front of the building used for the backdrop in the photo. For that matter, the front of the real hotel at HHS did not get a porch until 1892.
The inaccuracies portrayed in the photo could continue. It simply is an elaborate hoax, and the hoax photo never was 'authenticated and documented' by the Montana Historical Society. It just sounds better to say that it is."

2-Wyatt Erp
3-Teddy Roosevelt
4-Doc Holiday (John Henry)
5-Morgan Erp
6-LiverEating Johnson

7-Butch Cassidy (Geo. Parker)
8-Sundance Kid (Harry Longabaugh)
10. Bat Masterson

12. Harry Britton
14-Judge Roy Bean
15-Ben Greenough

Hunters Hot Springs, Montana 1883

Candace Urton, Brady, M.T.

Hunter Hot Springs group

(What do you think? Was this photograph a hoax?)

The Fabulous Coeur d'Alenes!

Over the years, several attempts were made to resurrect the old Eldorado of the West, Eagle City, but none were successful. From her heart, though, she spawned the largest mining district on earth   what we now know as the "Silver Valley," which is located on the south fork of the Coeur d'Alene River.

Picking up where the impoverished prospectors of an earlier age had left off, large mining companies with capital were formed in or moved into the district and began to explore the depths of the Coeur d'Alenes. Industry giants such as the Hecla, Sunshine, Asarco, Coeur d'Alene and Bunker Hill Mining Companies, to name only a few. (At one time there were over a hundred active mines operating in the district.) From their mining engineer's studies has come a fabulous wealth of silver, gold and other precious and industrial metals. In 1985, a milestone, of sorts, was reached when the one billionth (1,000,000,000) ounce of newly mined silver was brought up from deep within the mines.

Over the years these giants of the mining industry have provided work for the masses and much needed tax revenue for city, state and governmental coffers. They have taken the prospector's earlier search for riches in the crevices in the rocks and gravel of stream beds, down thousands of feet into the earth to a labyrinth of shafts, drifts, and tunnels. Taking advantage of the newest technology and most efficient mining techniques, projections are that the mines will continue operating for many years into the future

The Gal Coeur d'Alene

Give the old gal a chance to step in
And she'll rob from you everything but your sin
But show her a man who can stand with her best
And she'll offer him the wealth of her breast

Calamity Jane, she knew her 'biz'
And Terrible Edith and Bronco Liz
Even Molly-B-Damn, they all sought the men
Whose pockets were filled with a million and ten

Noah Kellogg, he had a 'jack'

Who led Noah to ore, to fill his sack
The distinguished jack., his name now is down
But Noah's remembered, his name is a town

The jailhouse was known far and wide as 'Bullpen'
And it earned recognition as one Hell of a den
An item was written and sent nationwide
It told of the cruelty they couldn't abided

You can swear at her loudly
The gal Coeur d'Alene
But you'll never forget her
For she'll never be tame

Poem by Arlene C. Coulson, 1962.
The Coeur d'Alenes Company, Spokane, Washington.

Arizona Historical Society, Tucson, #27,245
Celia Mattie Earp (Blaylock)

Additional photographs

Cheney Cowles Museum/Eastern Washington StateHist. Soc. Spokane, WA.
First railway station in Spokane, NPRR, 1883

Buy a Mine or a Lot!

—— In a Country that Promises to ——

RIVAL LEADVILLE IN A FEW MONTHS.

$10 to $100 put in this new Country may make you Rich!!

We have the Original Plats of both Town and Mining Property in our Office, and are prepared to meet our Customers satisfactorily. Write to us and send your Orders. Best of References.

Butler & Wickersham,

Eagle City,   Idaho.

Coeur d'Alene mines and goldfields, 1884

BIG SKY MAGIC ENTERPRISES
Butte, Montana blasting crew

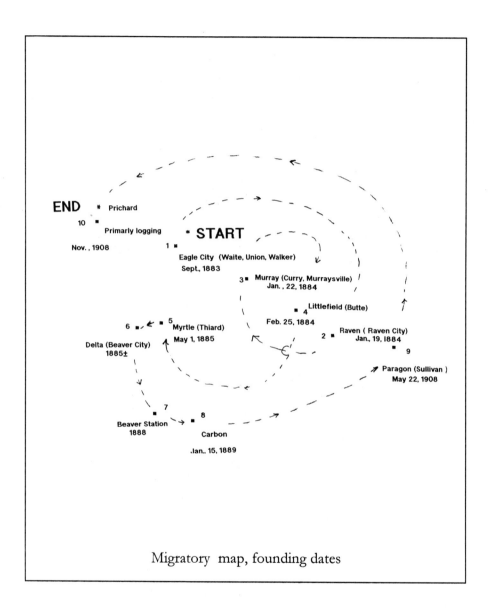

END   * Prichard

10 ■

Primarly logging

Nov. , 1908   1 ■

Eagle City (Waite, Union, Walker)

Sept., 1883

* **START**

3 ■ Murray (Curry, Murraysville)
Jan. , 22, 1884

■ Littlefield (Butte)
4
Feb. 25, 1884

6 ■ ← ■ 5
Myrtle (Thiard)

Delta (Beaver City)   May 1, 1885
1885±

2 ■ Raven (Raven City)
Jan., 19, 1884
■ 9

↗ Paragon (Sullivan)
May 22, 1908

7
■

Beaver Station   → ■ 8
1888   Carbon

Jan., 15, 1889

Migratory map, founding dates

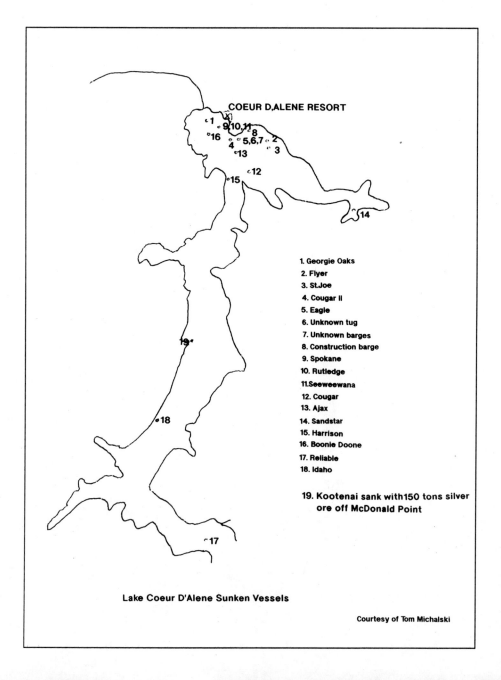

COEUR D,ALENE RESORT

1. Georgie Oaks
2. Flyer
3. St.Joe
4. Cougar II
5. Eagle
6. Unknown tug
7. Unknown barges
8. Construction barge
9. Spokane
10. Rutledge
11. Seeweewana
12. Cougar
13. Ajax
14. Sandstar
15. Harrison
16. Boonie Doone
17. Reliable
18. Idaho

19. Kootenai sank with150 tons silver
    ore off McDonald Point

Lake Coeur D'Alene Sunken Vessels

Courtesy of Tom Michalski

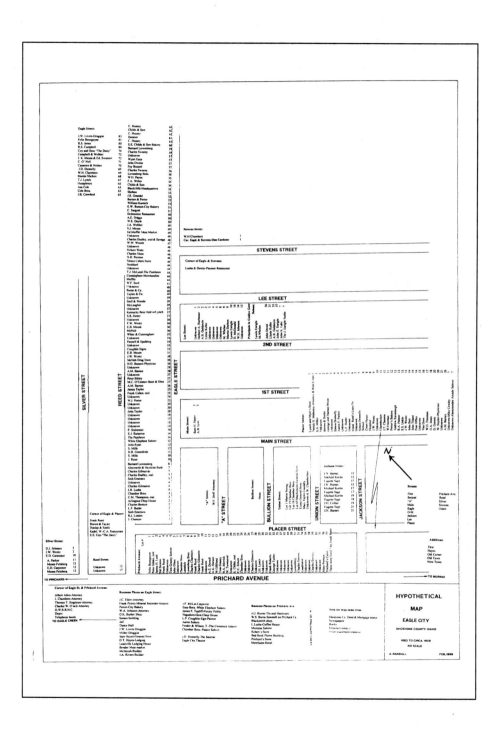

Arizona Historical Society, #76,627

Wyatt and Josie near Parker, AZ in 1920s

H-643 Columbia Wholesale

Wyatt's old home at Earp, CA.

Stuart Lake, 1931
Wyatt in his 80s, the year before his death

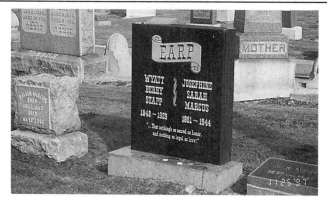

Wyatt and Josephine's graves. They rest together in
Eternal Peace.

Chris Almquist, 1992
Book sponsored in-part by Walt Almquist, Connie and Lloyd Roath,
owners of Murray's former stage stop, the Sprag Pole Inn.

Notes and Sources

Chapter 1. Geology, man and Idaho gold.

[1] Idaho public television.
[2] PBS, Lewis & Clark.
[3] Jack Nisbet, *Sources of the River.*
[4] W. Earl Greenough, *First 100 Years, Coeur d'Alene Mining Region, 1846-1946,* p.5.
[5] Randall A. Johnson, *The Ordeal of The Steptoe Command,* p.11.
[6] Rafe Gibbs, *Beckoning the Bold,* p.118.
[7] Merle Wells, *Gold Camps and Silver Cities,* p.1.

Chapter 2. The Fightin' Earps

[1] Steve Gatto, *Wyatt Earp, A Biography of a Western Lawman.*
[2] Lytle, *History of The Republic,* Vol. 2, p.33.
[3] Illinois State Historical Library.
[4] National Archives, James Earp's war records.
[5] River View Cemetery, Portland, Oregon.
[5] *Wyoming State Tribune,* July 31, 1940.
[6] Louise Barton, *One Woman's West.*
[8] Lawrence Principato, *Wild West,* June 1998.
[8] *Star Tribune* Casper, Wyoming, March 30, 1975.
[10] Frank Waters, *The Earp Brothers of Tombstone.*
[11] Ibid.
[12] Civil War Declaration for Pension, James, May 27, 1912.
[12] Wyoming State Archives, Department of Commerce.
[14] Richard Selcer, *Hell's Half Acre,* p.123.

Chapter 3. Wyatt Meets Doc Holliday

1   John Abbott, *Restoring a Badman's Good Name*, p.48.
2   Lawrence Principato, *Wild West,* June, 1998, p.115.
3   Peter Lyon, *Wild West* Magazine p.115.
4   Leon Claire Metz, *The Shooters.*
5   Richard Selcer, *Hell's Half Acre*, p.166.
6   It's interesting to note that James also had a nearly useless
    left arm, as the result of the gunshot wound he received in
    the Civil War. (In 1900 Wyatt would suffer a gunshot
    wound in Nome Alaska.)
        At the time the youngest Earp brother, Warren was in
    Colton also recuperating from the gunshot wound he'd
    gotten in a fight with rustlers on the Mexican border.
    Warren had been there since October when his older
    brothers shot it out with the cowboys at the OK Corral. When he
    heard that someone had made an attempt on Virgil's
    life, he traveled to Tombstone. Once there, he moved in
    with Virgil and Allie, and helped take care of Virgil.
7   Trinidad News, November 18, 1881.
8   The Evening News, New Albuquerque, N.M., May 13, 1882
9   Trinidad News, May 5, 1882.
10 Casey Tefertiller, The Life Behind the Legend, p.262.

Chapter 4. Oh Beautiful Josephine

1   Silverton Democrat, May 12, 1883.
2   Silverton Colorado Historical Society.
3   Editor of the Commonwealth, *Great Gunfighters of the Kansas Cowtowns.*
4   Ibid.
5   Silverton, Colorado Historical Society.
6   Paul Robert, Great Figures of The Wild West, p.52.
7   The Globe, November 13, 1883.
8   The Times, November 22, 1883.
9   The Globe, January 1, 1884.
10 The Dodge City Democrat, January 12, 1884.
11 Richard Selcer, Hell's Half Acre.
12 Luke owned one-third interest in the establishment. Then on February
    7, 1887, Luke sold his interest to Jake Johnson and the following day he
    was involved in an incident in which he gunned down Fort Worth law
    officer Jim Courtright.
13 Richard Selcer, Hell's Half Acre, p.168.
14 Andrew Morrison, The City of Fort Worth and the

State of Texas, p-28.
[15] Fort Worth Public Library.
[16] Its interesting to note here that even though Glen Boyer's book *I Married Wyatt Earp* tells of Masterson's wife giving Josephine a yellow canary named Dickie, because Josephine liked animals of all sorts, Bat wasn't married at this time. Years before, he had fallen in love with dance hall singer, Dora Hand, but in 1878 she'd been killed by an errant shot from a cowboy's gun. He later married Emma Walters, it is thought on November 21, 1891, perhaps in Kansas, but no official record of their union has ever been found. Emma was with him in New York in 1921 when he died at age 67.
[17] Wyoming State Tribune, October, 29, 1962.

Chapter 5. Stampede to Idaho Territory

[1] *An Illustrated History of North Idaho*, H. C. Davis of the Northern Pacific railroad, saw in the Coeur d'Alene mining excitement an opportunity to secure patronage for his line and also perhaps to induce permanent settlement of a region contiguous to his companies railroad, p.988.
[2] Rathdrum newspaper.
[3] *Spokane Falls Weekly Review*, July 11, 1885.
[4] *The Goldfields of the Coeur d'Alenes*, University of Idaho.
[5] *An illustrated History of North Idaho*, p.989.

Chapter 6. Awake in Eagle City

[1] L. F. Butler, *The Coeur d'Alene Mines*, 1884.
[2] *Badmen of the West*, by George Hendrix, p.137.
[3] Casey Tefertiller, *Wyatt Earp, The Life Behind the Legend.*
[4] George C. Hobson, *Gems of Thought*, p.69.
[5] When the five-some eventually reach Murray they would be "lousy" and have to delouse themselves
[6] James Montgomery, Liberated Woman, p.7.
[7] Enaville Resort collection, I-90 Exit 43 (Kingston, Idaho).
[8] Ruth Aulbach Sellers.
[9] *Spokane Evening Review*-February 13, 1885.
[10] Muriel Sibell Woole, 1958,*The Bonanza Trail*, Indiana U. Press, p.252.

1   Elliot Gay, *Yesterday and the day before*, p.9.
2   Rammelmeyer's Dairy, See *History of Idaho*, for complete song.
3   Muriel Sibell Woole, 1958, *The Bonanza Trail*, Indiana University Press, p. 252.
4   *Spokane Falls Review*, May 9, 1885.
5   *Spokane Falls Review*, April 29, 1885.
6   R. L. Wilson, *The Peacemakers, Arms and Adventure in the American West*, p.176.
7   George Hendrix, *Bad Men of The West*, p.59.
8   Letter from Richard Magnuson to John Gilchriese, December 31, 1959.
9   *Kellogg Evening News*, December 24, 1959.
10 Margaret S. Goodwin, *Rammelmeyer's dairy*
11 Spokane Falls Review, Apr. 5, 1884.
12 Richard Ripley, *The Ridgerunner, elusive loner of the wilderness*, Wally Fiscus, April 1987, p.9.
13 *History of Shoshone Co.*, p.992.
14 *An Illustrated History of North Idaho.*, p.991.
15 Ibid., p. 354.
16 Ibid., p.1060. Ives and Wolf applied for patents on their respective claims on November, 18, 1884.
17 *Half Moon Bay Review*, September 8, 1977.
18 Margaret S. Goodwin, *Rammelmeyer's diary*.
19 Elmer D. Mc Imes, *Wyatt Earp's Coeur d'Alene comrade*, Old West, Spring 1996.
20 Ibid, Vol. 32 No. 3, Spring 1996.
21 Tefertiller, Casey, *Wyatt Earp the Life Behind the Legend*, 1997, p.366.
22 John Amonson-*Wyatt Earp and the Prichard Creek Gold Rush*, p.3.
23 *An Illustrated History of North Idaho*, p.992.
24 Frank Waters, *The Earp Brothers of Tombstone*. (There is no evidence of this incident in the historical record.)
25 Letter from Richard Magnuson to H. J. Swinney of Boise, Idaho dated December 18, 1954. *City Directory*-Spokane Falls, 1885.
26 Shirley Dodson, *Historical Journal*, Dec. 1924.
27 *Spokane Evening News*, July 20, 1885.
28 Casey Tefertiller, *Wyatt Earp, The Life Behind the Legend*, p.278.
29 Chuck Hornung, *Wyatt Earp's New Mexico Adventures*.

Chapter 8. Eagle City

[1] Elliot Gay, *Mountains of Wealth.*

Chapter 9. No Notes.

City Directory

Chapter 10. No notes.

City Directory

Chapter 11. Other Good Stuff

[1] From Alaska book.
[2] Application for burial permit, River View Cemetery,
Portland, Oregon.
[3] El Paso TX Public Library, *The Truth about
Wyatt Earp*-Richard Erwin.

Bibliography

Abbott, John, n.d., *Restoring a Bad-man's Good Name.*

Alt, David and Donald W. Hyndman, 1995, *Northwest Exposures, A Geologic Story of the Northwest*, Mt. Press, 442pp.

Amonson, John, no date (n.d.), *Wyatt Earp and the Prichard Creek Gold Rush*, pamphlet, 5pp.

Anderson, Robert L., 1975, *Early Highlights and Sidelights Coeur d'Alene Mining District*, Idaho, Report, 10pp.

Anderson, Warren R., 1993, *Owning Western History*, Mountain Press Pub. Co., Missoula, Mt., 118pp.

Arlington, Leonard L. 1994, *History of Idaho,* Vol. 1 and 2, University of Idaho Press, Moscow, Idaho State Hist. Soc., 555pp.

Attebery, Louie W., 1985, *Idaho Folklife*, (ed.) by Attebery, University Utah Press, p.192-198.

Bankson, Russell A. and Lester S. Harrison, 1966, *Beneath These Mountains*, Vantage Press, p.43-80.

Bartholomew, Ed Ellsworth, 1963, *Wyatt Earp, 1848 to 1880; Untold Story*, Toyahvale, Frontier Books.

Barton, Louise, 1989, *One Woman's West*, 222pp.

Battien, Pauline, 1989, *The Gold Seekers*, Ye Galleon Press, Fairfield, Washington, p.18, 19, 21,28-36, 46, 70, 72, & 222-223.

Bell, Bob Boze, 1993, *The Illustrated Life and Times of Wyatt Earp*, 128pp

Bird, Allan G., 1990, *Silverton then & now*, p.31.

Boyer, Glenn, 1967, *The Suppressed Murder of Wyatt Earp*, The Naylor Co.

Brainard, Wendall, 1990, *Golden History Tales,* (ed.) by Ray Chapman, p.11, and 47.

Brosnan, Cornelius J., 1948, *History of the State of Idaho*, Charles Scribner's Sons, 423pp.

Burke, Martha Cannary, n.d., *Life and Adventures of Calamity Jane by herself,* Ye Galleon Press, Fairfield, Wash, 21pp.

Burns, Walter Noble, 1927, *Tombstone; An Iliad of the Southwest*, Garden City Pub.

Burrows, Jack (ed.), 1987, *John Ringo, The Gunfighter who never was,* p.28.

Butler, L. F., 1884, *Coeur d'Alene Mines, and Gold Fields*, Cushing, Thomas &

Co., Chicago, with map, 47pp..

Chafin, Earl (ed.), 1998, *She Married Wyatt Earp*, The Earl Chafin Press, Riverside, CA., 164pp., with appendix and photos.

Chaput, Don, 1994, *The Earp Papers*, affiliated Writers of America, Inc.

Chittendon, Newton H., 1884, *The Gold Fields of the Coeur d'Alene*, Circular 12, Pleasure Seekers, St. Paul, 18pp.

Churchill, Richard, E., 1997, *Doc Holliday, Bat Masterson and Wyatt Earp, their Colorado Careers*, 37pp.

Clich, Ken R., 1998, *Wyatt Earp the Missing Years*, Gaslamp Books/Museum, 139pp.

Coeur d'Alene Nugget, March and April, 1884, Eagle City Newspapers:

Coeur d'Alene Sun, 1885 and 1886, Numbers, Murray, Idaho.

Dodge, Fred, 1969, *Under Cover for Wells Fargo, the Unvarnished Recollections*, (ed.)
by Carolyn Lake, page 37 and 233.

Dodson, Shirley, 1924, *Historical Journal*.

Drazt, Joan M., 1998, *Echo of Crosscuts and Rails*, 292pp.

Dugan, Mark, 1997, *The Making of Legends*, Ohio University Swallow Press, 272pp.

Earp, Josephine Sarah Marcus, 1976, *I Married Wyatt Earp*, by (ed.) by Glenn Boyer, pages 95, note 18, 99, 100 and 102.

Elman, Robert, 1974, *Badmen of the West*, Castle Books, 256pp.

Erwin, Richard, 1992, *The Truth about Wyatt Earp*, O.K. Press.

Estes, Rev. Jim, 1971, *Tales of The Coeur d'Alenes*, Vol. 1, 79pp.

Fahey, John, 1971, *The Ballyhoo Bonanza*, University of Washington Press, Seattle and London, 288pp.

Gatto, Steve, 1997, *Wyatt Earp, A Biography of a Western Lawman*, San Simon Publishing Co., Tucson, AZ., 256pp.

Gay, Elliot, 1975, *Yesterday and the Day Before*, 227pp.

——, Mountains of Wealth.

Gibbs, Rafe, 1976, *Beckoning The Bold*, U. of Idaho Press, Moscow, 266pp.

Greenough, W. Earl, 1946, *First 100 years Coeur d'Alene Mining Region 1846-1946*. Address to A.I.M.E., 39pp.

Hart, Patricia and Ivar Nelson, 1984, *Mining Town*, University of Wash. Press, Seattle, Idaho State Historical Soc., Boise, 179pp.

Hobson, George C., 1940, *Gems of Thought and History of Shoshone County, Kellogg Evening News Press*, (ed.) by George C. Hobson, 84pp.

Hornung, Chuck, Summer, 1999, *Wyatt Earp's New Mexico Adventures*, Old

West, p.17-24.

Johnson, Randall A., 1979, *The Ordeal of the Steptoe Command*, Private Printing, 34pp.

Kingston, C. S., spring 1942, *Coeur d'Alene Gold Excitement of 1865*, reprint from the *Review* with map,
   p.1-11.

Lake, Stuart, 1931, *Wyatt Earp, Frontier Marshal*, Houghton Mifflin Co., p. 218.

Little-Livingston, D. E., 1965, *An Economic History of North Idaho 1800-1900*, Morrison Pub., 133pp.

Luke, Stella, n.d., *100 years of mining*, p. 7 & 31.

Lytle, Mark H., 1986, *History of the Republic, Vol.* 2, Prentice Hall, Inc., 712pp.

Magnuson, Richard G., 1968, *Coeur d'Alene Diary*, Binford & Mort, Portland, 319pp.

Marks, Paula Mitchell, 1989, *And Die in the West*, p. 295.

Markson, Phil, 1884, *Official Map and Hand-Book of The Coeur d'Alene Mines, Idaho Territory*, Lewis & Dryden, Portland, 31pp and a map. Ye Galleon Press, Fairfield, Wash., 46pp.

McCarty, Lea, 1957, *Wyatt Earp's Grave Robbed,* True West Magazine, p. 18-19, 35-36.

Metz, Leon Claire, 1976, *The Shooters*, Berkley Pub., 299pp.

Montgomery, James W., 1974, *Liberated Women a Life of May Arkwright Hutton*, Ye Galleon Press, Fairfield, Washington, 406pp.

Morgan, Edith, 1994, *The Northside*, Crow's Printing, Inc., a book of poems, 132pp.

Morrison, Andrew, 19(?), *The City of Fort Worth and the State of Texas.*

Nisbet, Jack, 1994, *Sources of the River*, Sasquatch Books, Seattle, 280pp.

Northern Pacific Railroad Co., 1886, *In The Gold Fields of the Coeur d'Alenes*, Rand McNally and Co., a map.

Northwest Tribune, 1883 and 1884, Newspaper Articles on Microfilm, Spokane, WA., Public Library.

O'Connor, Richard, 1957, *Bat Masterson*, Doubleday Co., 181pp.

O'Neal, Bill, 1979, *Encyclopedia of Western Gun Fighters*, University Okla. Press, 386pp.

Parry, Richard, 1996, *The Winter Wolf, Wyatt Earp in Alaska*, Tom Doherty Assoc. Books, N.Y., 381pp.

Peltier, Jerome, 1996, *Northwest History*, Ye Galleon Press, Fairfield, Wash., 164pp.

Ransome, F. L. and Frank Cathcast Calkins, 1905, *The Geology and Ore Deposits of the Coeur d'Alene District*, Idaho, U.S. Geol. Survey Prof. Paper 62, p.78-79.

Renk, Nancy F., 1997, *A History of The Shoshone County Courthouse, Murray, Idaho*, A Report for Idaho Heritage Trust & Murray Hist. Soc., 17pp.

Ripley, Richard, 1987, *The Ridgerunner, Elusive Leader of the Wilderness, Wally Fiscus.*

Roberts, Gary, Winter 1970, *The Wells Spicer Decision: 1881*, The Magazine of Western History, p. 64, note 6.

Robke, Paula B., n.d., *Oral History of McCoy*, 40 minutes, in North Idaho College.

Russell, Bert, 1984, *North Fork of the Coeur d'Alene River*, Falcon Pub., Harrison, Idaho, 440pp.

Segraves, Ann, 1994, *Soiled Doves Prostitution in the West*, Wesanne Pub., 175pp..

Selcer, Richard F., 1991, *Hells Half Acre Life and Legends of a Red-light District.*

Smalley, Eugene V., Oct, 1884, *The Coeur d'Alene Stampede*, Century Magazine, Vol. XXVILL, p.79-85.

Smith, Robert P. Wayne, 1932, *History of Placer and Quartz Gold Mining in The Coeur d'Alene District*, M.A. Theses. University of Idaho, 159pp.

Spokane Falls Review, Sept. 1883 to July 5, 1885, various newspaper articles, on microfilm, Spokane Public Library.

St. John, Harvey, Nov., 1965, *Wyatt Earp As I Knew Him*, Real West, p. 27-30.

Strong Clarence C. and Clyde S. Webb, *White Pine: King of Many Winters*, Mt. Press Publishing Co., Missoula, Mt., 212pp.

Tefertiller, Casey, 1997, *Wyatt Earp the Life Behind the Legend*, John Wiley and Sons, Inc., 403pp.

The *Northwest Tribune*, articles from the 1883 & 1884 newspapers, on microfilm, Spokane Public Library.

The Idaho Sun, Vol. 1 No. 1, July 8, 1884, Murray, Idaho, 4pp.

Turner, Alford E., 1980, *The Earps Talk*, Creative Pub., Co., p. 55.

Video, Story of Wyatt Earp. American West Series.

Walker, Paul, 1992, *Great Figures of the Wild West*, New York Facts on File.

Wallace, Idaho, Records from Shoshone County Recorder's and Assessor's Offices.

Weekly Eagle, July, 1884, Eagle City Newspaper.

Wells, Merle W., 1974, *Gold Camps and Silver Cities*, Idaho State Hist. Soc., 165pp.

Western Historical Publishing Company, 1903, *An Illustrated History of North*

Idaho, Embracing Nez Perce, Idaho, Latah, Kootenai, and Shoshone Counties, State of Idaho, 1252pp.

Wilson, R. L., 1992, *The Peacemakers, Arms and Adventure in American West.*

Withorn, Bill and Doris Whithorn, n.d., *Montana In The Good Old Days,* Vol. 1, 48pp.

——*Calamity's In Town, 1884,* 48pp.

Wolle, Muriel Sibell, 1963, *Montana Pay Dirt,* Sage Books, Denver, CO., 436pp.

Wood, John V. 1983, *Railroads Through The Coeur d'Alenes,* Caxton Printers, Ltd., Caldwell, Id., 195pp.

Index

About the Authors

Jerry Dolph traveled around the country working at a variety of jobs and in 1970, not unlike the stampeders of old, was lured to the Coeur d'Alenes by its promise of instant riches, well, a good paying job at least. Aside from all the "wealth," he was lucky enough to find his wife Jo Ann. When asked about his educational background, he said, "Give me a rock and a hammer and I know what I'm doing."

His writing career began, as it turned out, in 1988 when he was left disabled by an accident, in the depths of north Idaho's Lucky Friday Mine. He went on to write weekly columns for several newspapers and magazine articles for Rock and Gem, Gold and Treasure Hunter, International California Mining Journal, Gold Prospectors Association of America and Mining Engineering. His first non-fiction book *Fire in the Hole, the Untold Story of Hardrock Miners* was published in 1994 by Washington State University Press.

Arthur Randall lives with his wife, Sylvia, in Hayden, Idaho. He obtained degrees in geology from the Universities of Idaho and Utah. He has a strong interest in history and archaeology and has published many articles and books on western ghost town history and geology. His interests in the current book stems from the fact that Wyatt Earp lived just a few miles from his home in Hayden.